Library of
Davidson College

THE ENEMY OPPOSITE

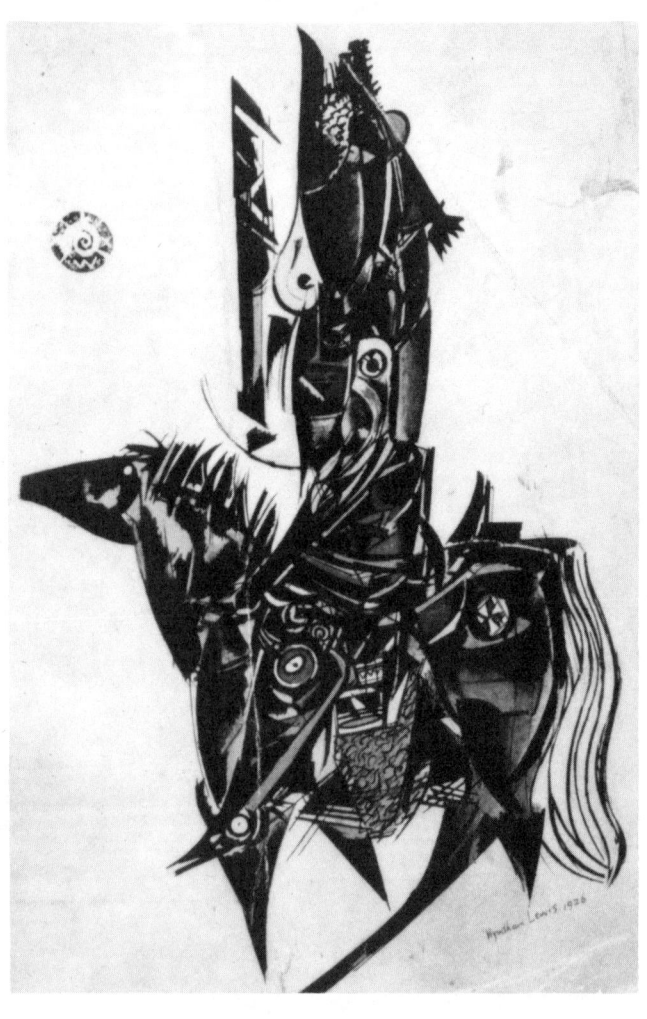

Wyndham Lewis, "Horseman," 1927.
© Copyright estate of Mrs. G.A. Wyndham Lewis. By permission.

THE ENEMY OPPOSITE

The Outlaw Criticism of Wyndham Lewis

SueEllen Campbell

Ohio University Press:
Athens

© Copyright 1988 by SueEllen Campbell
Printed in the United States of America.

All rights reserved.
Ohio University Press books are printed on acid free paper. ∞

Library of Congress Cataloging-in-Publication Data

Campbell, SueEllen.
    The enemy opposite.

    Bibliography: p.
    Includes index.
1. Lewis, Wyndham, 1882-1957—Knowledge—Literature.
2. Criticism—Great Britain—History—20th century.
3. Modernism (Literature)   I. Title.
PR6023.E97Z636   282'.91209   87-28330
ISBN 0-8214-0887-9

Designed by Laury A. Egan

*For my mother, my father, and my grandmothers,
for their example and help.*

CONTENTS

Acknowledgements	ix
Introduction	xi
List of Abbreviations	xvii

PART 1: THE ENEMY

Announcing: The Enemy Horseman	3
The Enemy Voice	5
The Enemy Stance: The Exiled Opposite	15
The Enemy Versus Ezra Pound	24
The Enemy's Audience	34

PART 2: THE ENEMY PRINCIPLES

"My Most Essential Me"	49
Personality and Mind	52
Vision and Common Sense	65
Space and Stability	75
The Berkeleyan Paradox: Influence Acknowledged	87
The Enemy Versus Henri Bergson: Influence Denied	94
The "Domestic Adversary"	117

PART 3: THE ENEMY CRITICISM

The Enemy Versus James Joyce: Literary Criticism	133
THE ARGUMENT	133
THE CRITICAL CONTEXT	147
The Enemy Versus the Zeitgeist: Cultural Criticism	165
THE ENEMY VERSUS MOSZKOWSKI	165
THE CULTURE MODEL	174
Conclusion	191
Notes	198
Index	225
A Note about the Author	233

ACKNOWLEDGEMENTS

My acknowledgements must begin with thanks to Professors Ralph Cohen and Paul Armstrong, who worked with me at the University of Virginia on the first version of this study; Professor Cohen first steered me toward Lewis, and both men helped greatly with their acute and challenging readings. More recently, Reed Way Dasenbrock gave me some very helpful criticism; I am indebted to him too.

I owe thanks to Mr. C. J. Fox and Mr. Omar Pound of the Wyndham Lewis Trust for their permission to quote from Lewis's books and to reproduce the "Horseman" drawing; and to the editors of *Twentieth Century Literature* and *The Journal of Modern Literature* for permission to use material they published a few years ago.

The Faculty Research Committee at Bowling Green State University helped support this study with a summer grant.

Finally, I want to thank several friends who have given me more than one kind of help on this project: Nancy Ward, Nancy Campbell, Jan Alberghene, Phil Terrie, Allan Emery, Peter Ryder, David Minter, and, most of all, John Calderazzo.

INTRODUCTION

> It is of inestimable value that there be men who receive things in a modality different from one's own; who correlate things one wd. not oneself have correlated. The richness of any given period depends largely upon the number and strength of such men.
> *Ezra Pound*

> What I claim is to live to the full the contradiction of my time, which may well make sarcasm the condition of truth.
> *Roland Barthes*

Among modernist critics Wyndham Lewis stands out because of the energy and drama of his "aggressive partisan pen—made to hurl epithets, or of the sort to use, in controversy, as a dangerous polemical lance."[1] With this pen Lewis created the Enemy, a flamboyant, hostile, solitary figure whose voice and stance vividly embodied the principles structuring his criticism. The frontiers of this criticism—the Enemy criticism—are best marked by the comments of his two long-time friends, T. S. Eliot and Ezra Pound. With characteristic tact Eliot said: "We have no critic of the contemporary world at once so fearless, so honest, so intelligent, and possessed of so brilliant a prose style." Pound, with equally characteristic vigor, called him "the man who was wrong about everything except the superiority of live mind to dead mind; for which basic verity God bless his holy name"; and declared, "If another man has ideas of *any* kind (not borrowed cliches) that irritate you enough to

The Enemy Opposite

make you think or take out your own ideas and look at 'em, that is all one can expect."² Always—whether he is being persuasive or obscure, entertaining or infuriating—Lewis the Enemy challenges us to think. This book, my response to that challenge, is a study of the structures of the Enemy criticism.

I use the term "Enemy criticism" in two intersecting ways. One is to delineate a body of texts. The most productive period of Lewis's career was the decade between 1924 and 1934, when he published some nineteen volumes of fiction and criticism, a "series of books devoted to the work of radical analysis of the ideas by which our society has been taught to live."³ Originally conceived as one enormous work to be called *The Man of the World,* these books illustrate the major concern of Lewis's work as a critic (and, to a considerable extent, as a novelist): the hidden connections, motives, and consequences of apparently unrelated phenomena, "the notions behind the events occurring upon the surface."⁴ These are the texts on which I focus. My central example within this group, the book I see as his best and most representative volume of criticism, is the massive *Time and Western Man,* Lewis's analysis of modern literature and philosophy (with forays into history, psychology, popular culture, theoretical physics, politics, and a score of other topics). To borrow Lewis's title for his critique of *Ulysses,* this and the other major books of this period make it possible to construct "An Analysis of the Mind of Wyndham Lewis": to study the Enemy books is to discover the ways in which Lewis thinks and argues.

I also use the term "Enemy criticism" to identify the special voice and stance Lewis created during this period. With the first issue of his one-man journal *The Enemy*—its cover drawing, its opening "Editorial," and the criticism in "The Revolutionary Simpleton" (soon to be included in *Time and Western Man*)—he introduced the Enemy, a flamboyant public personality who allowed him to advertise, focus, and

Introduction

unify his analysis of modern culture. Thanks to Lewis's considerable talents as fictionist and draughtsman, this figure is vividly and dramatically imagined. Yet it is, I believe, more than just one in a series of personae or masks.[5] Rather, the distinctive personality, voice, and stance of the Enemy embody with remarkable accuracy the structure and character of Lewis's role as a critic. This is one of my two major arguments, and the one that is responsible for my organization. Thus I look closely at the Enemy figure and what it reveals about Lewis's critical stance (in Part 1), about his principles (in Part 2), and about his practice (in Part 3). Along the way, since he is often hard to follow, and since few others have concentrated on his criticism, I also offer a certain amount of explication.[6]

Within the boundaries of my argument about the structure of the Enemy figure, my primary interest is in what I see as one of the most important but also most difficult characteristics of Lewis's work. Everywhere, and on every level, he thinks in structures of opposition. Sometimes these are obvious and straightforward; more often, though, they are confusing and apt to look—misleadingly—like self-contradiction, inconsistency, or even nonsense. This is my second major argument: that these structures of opposition are not only the natural patterns of Lewis's thinking, but also, in many crucial instances, deliberate patterns of organization and strategy.[7] These structures—and the complex and powerful mind they reveal—are for me the primary source of Lewis's fascination.

These oppositions may be divided into four groups, each with its own logic and structure. The first two are relatively easy to see; they are the oppositions Lewis advertises. The second two are more difficult because they are largely hidden beneath the surfaces of Lewis's work.

First are those that result from Lewis's dualistic habit of mind, his tendency to organize concepts in pairs of polar opposites. As the *Blast* Manifesto declared, "We start from opposite statements of a chosen world. Set up violent structure of adolescent clearness between two extremes."[8] This habit of thought is responsible for the pervasive pairs of opposites in Lewis's work—time and space, inside and outside, mind and matter, emotion and intellect. It is also responsible for some of the more complicated structures of opposites Lewis calls paradoxes: because these pairs often oversimplify, he sometimes builds complex sets of terms linked by parallelism, contradiction, and reversal. These pairs and paradoxes are everywhere in Lewis's work, and thus everywhere in mine, but I deal with them most directly in the first three sections of Part 2: "Personality and Mind," "Vision and Common Sense," and "Space and Stability."

Second are those oppositions that result from Lewis's critical stance, the stance of the Enemy opposite. Criticism, he believes, "must always retain its character of a combat between two opposite forces."[9] Many of his tactics originate in this conviction. As the Enemy, Lewis polarizes the relationships between himself and other thinkers, between his views and those he is criticizing, even between himself and his readers. This kind of opposition appears most often in Part 1, "The Enemy."

Third, at many crucial points, Lewis defines his own position and his own ideas by contrasting himself with another writer. Often he does this openly as a way of clarifying for his readers where he stands; here this group overlaps the second. But at other times he hides from his readers, and perhaps also from himself, the true nature of his relationship with these "opposites." Some of these obscured oppositions suggest the patterns Harold Bloom identifies as deriving from the "anxiety of influence"; others, I think, mark deliberate tactics especially characteristic of Lewis's Enemy criticism. I examine a variety of instances of this structure, primarily in the sections entitled "The Enemy Versus. . . ."

Introduction

Fourth, and finally, are the oppositions that mark the presence of what Lewis calls his "domestic Adversary." Beneath the surface of most of his fundamental principles and judgments lies evidence of his own "micro-cosmic opposites." In each of Lewis's major statements of belief we can also see traces of the opposite belief—in what adds up to a pervasive structure of half-hidden self-criticism, a kind of self-deconstruction. In the first half of my argument I point to these oppositions only in occasional parentheses and footnotes; then, in the section entitled "The Domestic Adversary," I bring this structure to the surface.

This aspect of Lewis's work—the centrality of these four kinds of opposition—largely resists or crumbles under traditional and especially formalist analysis, but it is substantially more accessible to contemporary criticism. This fact in itself is interesting: among other things, it marks the ways in which Lewis is as much a post-modernist critic as he is an exemplary modernist. In his work, I think, we can see the shape—the tactics, the premises—of a number of recent critical modes. His attention to textuality and his assumption that such things as popular culture, philosophy, social science, and politics can all be read as culturally revealing texts: these are post-modernist, post-structuralist characteristics. As Fredric Jameson's study demonstrates, Lewis is vulnerable to an ideological critique; but he is also himself unusually sensitive to the hidden ideologies of other thinkers and other texts. When I decipher some of his responses to the writers to whom he is indebted, I am anticipated by the Enemy's acute eye for hidden influences. Perhaps more important, beneath my own arguments are the tools of structuralist and post-structuralist analysis; these are useful largely because Lewis is also himself a structuralist and a deconstructive critic. And in the context of contemporary scepticism about impersonal objectivity, and the consequent revaluing of criticism as a creative activity, the highly personal character of the Enemy criticism, its aggressive idiosyncracy and bias, can finally be seen not as a scandal but as a strength. It is time, I think, for Lewis to reclaim his place.

And now, meet the Enemy:

LIST OF ABBREVIATIONS

ABR: *The Art of Being Ruled* (New York: Harper & Brothers, 1926).

Enemy: *The Enemy, A Review of Art and Literature*, no. 1 (London: The Arthur Press, 1927 and 1929; rpt. London: Frank Cass and Co., 1968). (All my references to *The Enemy* will be to the first issue. For "The Revolutionary Simpleton," I use the version and pages of *TWM*. Parts of Book 2 of *TWM*, most importantly the section on Spengler, were also included in the journal's version of "The Revolutionary Simpleton." No. 2 (1927) carried the first version of *Paleface*; most of no. 3 (1929) was "The Diabolical Principle.")

L&F: *The Lion and the Fox: The Rôle of the Hero in the Plays of Shakespeare* (New York: Harper & Brothers, 1927).

MWA: *Men Without Art* (London: Cassell, 1934; rpt. New York: Russell & Russell, 1964).

Paleface: *Paleface: The Philosophy of the 'Melting-Pot'* (London: Chatto & Windus, 1929; rpt. St. Clair Shores, Michigan: Scholarly Press, 1971).

RA: *Rude Assignment: A Narrative of My Career Up-to-date* (London: Hutchinson and Co., 1950).

TWM: *Time and Western Man* (London: Chatto & Windus, 1927). (The pagination in this edition—the one I have used throughout this book—is not the same as that of the American edition of 1928 [Harcourt Brace]; the 1957 Beacon Paperback edition is also different.)

PART 1:
The Enemy

Announcing: The Enemy Horseman

Flamboyant and ominous, defiant and solitary, Wyndham Lewis's Enemy "Horseman" advances into action.[1] He raises his sword and readies himself for belligerent attack and counter-attack.

The rider's upper body dwarfs his mount and dominates the drawing. From the turn of his hip to the tip of his helmet, he is as tall as his horse, from its tossed head to its tapering hoof. His torso seems massive and ponderous in its rigidity and its uprightness; the plates of armor which cover his chest do not move. Their dull brown, punctuated only by the red and white disk marking his shoulder, is cut vertically by the rider's left arm reaching down to the horse's reins. Of his right arm we see nothing except the trace of its motion, a thin curving line at the level of his waist. Out of this curve rises the blade of a sword; in a visual pun, the Enemy's arm of flesh has become an arm of steel.

Arms and bulk alone would suffice to make any warrior formidable, but what distinguishes this Enemy is his head. Resting directly on the torso, which it equals in size, this is not the head of an ordinary man but something more or less than human. Unlike the rest of his body, it seems more abstract than representative, more surreal than real. Like one of those Renaissance paintings in which fruit or vegetables combine to form a man's face, the Enemy's head, when we look at it closely, dissolves into shapes and colors little resembling human features or a soldier's headgear. Yet altogether its impact is unambiguous—outlandish, grotesque, and menacing.

Below this head and torso, the rider's leg and horse seem gaudy and mobile. Although in the upper half of the figure dull blues and browns overwhelm the few touches of color, in the lower half, brighter reds, greens, and oranges triumph. Where they are mixed with these colors, the same blues and browns look more vivid: decorated by the emblem on his horse's hip, the zigzags of his saddle blanket, and the kaleidoscopic fragments of his leg, the heavy brown of the Enemy's armor becomes the rich chestnut of his mount. Because these bright patches are smaller than those above them, they seem to weigh less, to bounce and jangle with the horse's gait. And because the horse's legs disappear into points, never really landing on the ground, its motion, too, is light.

Yet all this volatile color rests on a careful structure of force and counterforce. The forward thrust of the horse's longest leg parallels that of the Enemy's forearm and leg; the other three legs of the horse, and the lines that trace his neck and flank, point in the opposite direction. This scaffolding of crossed diagonals repeats itself in much of the detailing—the pattern of diamonds in the horse's decorative emblem, the crosshatching under its belly, the tiny zigzag of the saddle blanket. Even the horse's tail swings out, then in, then out and in again. In the bottom half of this drawing, though the parts move, the whole does not.

In the top half, traces of this grid recur, but as a controlling structure they yield to the horseman's emphatic uprightness. Just as the rider commands his mount, the solid weight of his head and torso brakes the brisk motion of his leg and his horse, and the vertical mass of the upper part of the drawing dominates the opposing vectors below. While we look at this figure, its apparent motion stops. All its energy is contained, its only outlet the slight forward tilt of the sword. Lewis's Enemy rides with a tight rein, imposing stasis on motion, compelling conflicting forces into a precarious equilibrium.

The Enemy Voice

This "Horseman" is the drawing Lewis chose to launch *The Enemy* (1927), his one-man outlaw journal. It was a particularly happy choice for the first issue's cover, not only because its bright colors and white background would catch a potential reader's eye, but also because, like a good portrait, it captures a personality. This figure shows us a good deal about Lewis's Enemy, the figure he created to dramatize his role as a critic of modern Western culture.

Most obviously, the Enemy is flamboyant—"bedizened," as Lewis later wrote (*RA* 198); of the many small figures he drew in the late 1920s, this one is almost alone in being in color rather than in black and white. At the same time, his flamboyance is controlled; beneath the color and costuming, the figure's formal skeleton has been carefully constructed. And in this underlying structure, a single decisive direction dominates a mass of conflicting opposites. Altogether, in this portrait of the Enemy, decoration is ruled by structure, lightness by solidity, kinetic by potential energy, motion by stasis.

Iconographically, the drawing is similarly suggestive. Stripped of his individual traits, the horseman is a knight—mounted, armored, helmeted, sword-bearing. Like one of King Arthur's men, he rides to protect good from evil, right from wrong. (Lewis even named his own small press—established to print *The Enemy*—The Arthur Press.[2]) Like Don Quixote he rides to preserve a past, fighting as if he did not know he must inevitably lose, against enemies he may be exaggerating, distorting, even inventing. But if the "Horseman" is both chivalric and quixotic, he is also modern and grotesque. His outlandish face tells us that Lewis the Enemy sees himself and his world not just romantically but also satirically.

As we will see, these same qualities characterize Lewis's critical stance, his critical and philosophical principles, and his practical criticism. For in addition to the "Horseman" drawing, Lewis also gives us several written descriptions of the Enemy that demonstrate that he carefully shaped this figure to embody his intentions and his perspective both vividly and accurately. From these descriptions we may discover how central to his project as a critic were the Enemy's functions and their ramifications.

Most conspicuously, the Enemy served as advertisement. The name itself, particularly as a title for a journal, would attract attention: an enemy has a great deal more dramatic potential than an ally or protector. (This name suggests other similar titles, too: Coleridge's journal *The Friend*; Ezra Pound's 1927-28 journal *The Exile*; and, perhaps most significantly, James McNeill Whistler's book *The Gentle Art of Making Enemies*, another defense of his work by an artist. Lewis refers several times to Whistler's notoriety as an enemy of the conservative art establishment.[3]) Characteristically, Lewis exploited this dramatic potential, using his special talent for exaggeration, caricature, and satire to create a figure who walks, talks, and even eats like a professional antagonist. Thus in 1932 he described "What It Feels Like to Be an Enemy":

> After breakfast, for instance (a little raw meat, a couple of blood-oranges, a stick of ginger, and a shot of Vodka—to make one see Red) I make a habit of springing up from the breakfast-table and going over in a rush to the telephone book. This I open quite at chance, and ring up the first number upon which my eye has lighted. When I am put through, I violently abuse for five minutes the man, or woman of course (there is no romantic nonsense about the sex of people

with an Enemy worth his salt), who answers the call. This gets you into the proper mood for the day.

When he walks he "swaggers," "eyeing all and sundry as if they were trespassing on the pavement," keeping a look out for a foe to attack with "a few broadsides of 'vitriol' or of 'invective.' " His only real worry (a distorted version of Quixote's difficulty) is the scarcity of worthy opponents—"*the poor quality* of his enemies."[4] As Lewis says about his character Kreisler, whose social behavior sometimes greatly resembles this Enemy's, "All his errands showed the gusto of the logic of his personality: he might indeed have been enjoying himself. He invented outrage that was natural to him, and enjoyed slightly the licence and scope of his indifference."[5]

Naturally, this Enemy speaks with a flamboyantly hostile voice—one that allowed Lewis to indulge without restraint his talent for tongue-lashing. Always casual, loosely organized, and vigorous, his prose during his Enemy years is also often very gaudy. When he wants to entertain, when he wants to attract extra attention, when he is dealing with a particularly ripe target, when he is especially outraged himself, Lewis shifts into a kind of higher gear, a tone of satiric exaggeration, the tone I am speaking of as the Enemy voice.[6] As the Enemy, speaking with this voice, Lewis delights in invective—in caricature, name-calling, exaggeration, and blatant sarcasm, in barrages of alliterative insults, blizzards of offensive images.

Caricature, for instance, appears most often and most clearly in the satiric novels of the Enemy years, *The Childermass* and *The Apes of God*, whose characters grotesquely parody the literary figures and language Lewis opposes. Not surprisingly, the most obvious caricatures are of Gertrude Stein and James Joyce, the two Enemy targets whose styles are most distinctive and so most easily mocked. Here is Stein's manner, for example, in *The*

Childermass character Satters: "Pulley has been most terribly helpful and kind there's no use excusing himself Pulley has been most terribly helpful and kind—most terribly helpful and he's been kind. He's been most terribly kind and helpful, there are two things, he's been most kind he's been terribly helpful, he's kind he can't help being—he's terribly." (Thus, through exaggeration, Lewis illustrates his argument that Stein's use of repetition—the "Stein-stutter"—makes her language sound imbecilic.) And here is Joyce as the Bailiff in the same book: "Then as for that cross-word polyglottony in the which I indulges misself for recreation bighorror, why bighorror isn't it aysy the aysiest way right out of what you might call the postoddydeucian dam dirty cul of a sack into which shure and bighorror I've bin and gone and thropped misself and all..." To this, another character responds, " 'Oh capital sir! I recognize him!' "[7] And so do we.

In the nonfiction books, caricature takes a slightly different but equally flamboyant form: damning quotations from the targeted works, followed either by a devastating table-turning parody or by pointed sarcasm. (Whistler anticipates Lewis with a relatively mild version of this tactic: his *Gentle Art of Making Enemies* is composed almost entirely of quotations—from his chief antagonist Ruskin, from other art critics, and from the popular press—accompanied by small, sarcastic marginal notes; like Lewis, Whistler lets his targets destroy themselves.) In *Paleface*, for instance, Lewis first quotes Sherwood Anderson's *Dark Laughter*: " 'Once the Indians danced there, made feasts there. They threw poems about like seeds on a wind. Names of rivers, names of towns. Ohio! Illinois! Keokuk! Chicago! Illinois! Michigan!' "[8] Then he adds his own version: " 'New York' and 'Boston,' it is true, might appear intensely romantic to a Blackfoot or a Mohican: and they may have remarked to each other, among their wigwams, sharpening their tomahawks, 'These Whites throw poems about like seeds in the wind! *Boston! Brownsville!* How beautiful!' " (213). (This technique will dominate some of Lewis's later—and lazier—books like *The Doom of Youth*, where he offers pages of numbered excerpts from newspapers followed by pages of sarcastic comments.) Or he will work from paraphrase rather than direct quotation to the same effect. In an attack on Katherine Mayo's *Mother India* (1927), he offers a mirror version of "such a mission as Miss Mayo's" that would make "an equally untruthful picture":

> The indian lady visitor or inquisitor, the 'restless analyst' from the East, could...tell the horrified Indian Public how in all the schools and universities of the United States homosexuality was rampant: then she could tell the usual stories of pregnant high-school girls—reveal whole classes carried away in one brake to the Lying-in Hospital: she could state *as a fact* that all american men were sexually impotent at thirty (hence the Broadway girl-shows), and that self-abuse was intense and universal throughout the 48 States of the Union: she could describe the death-rate per day in an american city by violent crime, quote Mencken for bits about the monstrosities of Prohibition: and she could wind up by saying that America is 'a physical menace' (cf. p. 23, *Mother India*) to the Hindu. (*Paleface*, 297-98)

After this kind of attack—a vivid and convincingly vicious negative of Mayo's book—not much is left of the victim.

In *Time and Western Man*, quotation followed by sarcasm is the Enemy's most powerful critical weapon. His remarks about Ernest Walsh and his review *This Quarter* are typical. (This criticism is aimed indirectly at Ezra Pound, who supported the journal.) He begins by reproducing some of Walsh's comments about one of his contributing authors, Robert McAlmon:

"I can't wait (howls W-sh). I can't wait *any* longer to say that Bud Macsalmon is one of the most astonishing writers since the fathers of English literature. If you care for Shakespeare, if you care for Dickens, if you care for Conrad, you will care more for Macsalmon. He is colossal without being dull. He has the deep smile and the hidden laughter of Indian women pounding maize without caring at all who is to eat it. The world eats maize. The world eats bread. Very well. Pound maize. Somebody eat by and by. Everybody got to eat sooner or later. Pound maize. Macsalmon write. He write a great deal, etc., etc." (61)

(The original passage is almost, though not quite, the same as Lewis's quoted version. Lewis edits Walsh's words without distorting his meaning, and also changes "writes" to "write" in the last sentences to emphasize Walsh's primitivism.[9]) Lewis's eye for the ridiculous is good enough that he wouldn't *need* to add any commentary, but as the Enemy he cannot resist:

[Walsh] goes on to say of Bud and his friends that they are "the school that writes by instinct." And he illustrates this by quoting their spelling—they spell *tries* as *trys*, he exultantly points out. They are *true primitives*. All these primitives have had, like children, the same difficulty: they have not been able to spell! And yet how expressive their little faults of orthography can be! What a nice archaic feeling it gives one to see *tries* spelt *trys!* (61)

And a page later he continues,

You get the full flavour of the breathless hurried confidential lisp of the little baby girl, rushing to its mother's knee and pouring out coyly its winsome chatter, do you not, with our Mr. W-sh?... "Told oo all that me have, oo naughty mammie oo" is at all events the type of his main line of writing. "Belly well. Pound maize. Somebody eat by and by," is a side track. (63)

Such passages combine the tactics of the mimic, the caricaturist, and the astute literary critic—with the satiric rudeness of the Enemy. (And indeed, many times in his criticism, Lewis drops the Enemy's satiric tone but retains this procedure—damning quotation followed by pointed comments—almost always to equally good effect. Lewis knows a good self-caricature when he sees one.)

We "get the full flavour" of the Enemy voice most clearly, though, in another tactic—in unrestrained, exuberant name-calling, in extended, insulting, metaphoric epithets, in piles of tongue-rolling adjectives. This tactic reminds us that Lewis first met the public as a Blaster: the Enemy inherits the rhetoric of the Vorticists—and their models, Marinetti and the Futurists. It is in this tactic, too, that we most clearly recognize Lewis's affinity with the traditional figure of the railer, the satirist/malcontent whose main weapon is invective. (His continuing interest in this figure is clear: in his early *Timon of Athens* drawings, in the approving discussions of Timon, Apemantus, and Thersites in *The Lion and the Fox*, and in scattered references elsewhere.[10]) The Enemy voice combines the Vorticist's sharp-tongued iconoclasm with the railer's mastery of the curse—and, much of the time, with a rough and exuberant sense of humor that is distinctively Lewis's own. Sometimes this slapstick vituperation saturates the Enemy criticism, sometimes it just punctuates; sometimes—depending largely on the reader's own opinions—it delights, sometimes it offends.

For instance, the criticism of Gertrude Stein in *Time and Western Man*. The Enemy's insults can be witty and apt: Stein "may be described as the reverse of Patience sitting on a monument—she appears, that is, as a Monument sitting upon patience" (78). They can also be heavy-handed: she writes "like a child—like a confused, stammering, rather 'soft' (bloated, acromegalic, squinting and spectacled, one can figure it as) child" (65). But Lewis's gaudy rhetoric is always polemical; however extravagant and offensive, his metaphors always make his arguments. Here are two descriptions of Stein's style:

> Gertrude Stein's prose-song is a cold, black suet-pudding. We can represent it as a cold suet-roll of fabulously reptilian length. Cut it at any point, it is the same thing; the same heavy, sticky, opaque mass all through, and all along. It is weighted, projected, with a sibylline urge. It is mournful and monstrous, composed of dead and inanimate material. It is all fat, without nerve. Or the evident vitality that informs it is vegetable rather than animal. Its life is a low-grade, if tenacious, one; of the sausage, by-the-yard, variety. (77)

> ...this capable, colossal authoress relapses into the rôle and mental habits of childhood. Fact is thrown to the winds; the irresponsible, light-hearted madness of ignorance is wooed, and the full-fledged *Child* emerges. This child (often an idiot-child as it happens, but none the less sweet to itself for that) throws big, heavy words up and catches them; or letting them slip through its fingers, they break in pieces; and down it squats with a grunt, and begins sticking them together again. Else this far-too-intellectual infant chases the chosen word, like a moth, through many pages, worrying the delicate life out of it. The larynx and tongue of the reader meantime suffer acutely. Every word uttered threatens to obsess and stick to his tongue. (78)

These comments are characteristic: the Enemy uses metaphors to decorate, to entertain, to shock—and to argue.

One more example: here, again, is an attack on Stein, this time embedded in the analysis of Hemingway in *Men Without Art*:

The Enemy Voice

> The sort of First-person-singular that Hemingway invariably invokes is a dull-witted, bovine, monosyllabic simpleton. This lethargic and stuttering dummy he conducts, or pushes from behind, through all the scenes that interest him. This burlesque First-person-singular behaves in them like a moronesque version of his brilliant author. He *Steins* up and down the world, with the big lustreless ruminatory orbs of a Picasso doll-woman (of the semi-classic type Picasso patented, with enormous hands and feet). It is, in short, the very dummy that is required for the literary mannerism of Miss Stein! It is the incarnation of the Stein-stutter—the male incarnation, it is understood.
>
> But this constipated, baffled 'frustrated'—yes, deeply and Freudianly 'frustrated'—this wooden-headed, leaden-witted, heavy-footed, loutish and oafish marionette—peering dully out into the surrounding universe like a great big bloated five-year-old—pointing at this and pointing at that—uttering simply "CAT!"—"HAT!"—"FOOD!"—"SWEETIE!"—is, as a companion, infectious. His author has perhaps not been quite immune. Seen for ever through his nursery spectacles, the values of life accommodate themselves, even in the mind of his author, to the limitations and peculiar requirements of this highly idiosyncratic puppet. (29)

And so Stein's influence has distorted Hemingway's characters, especially his first-person narrators; worse, it has distorted his values in the direction of imbecilic passivity. All this invective makes the argument—in a voice unmistakably the Enemy's.

This is the voice that Lewis's critics have called strident and hysterical. Certainly it is a far cry from the cool, careful prose of contemporary critics like T. S. Eliot and I. A. Richards. Lewis slings mud at his targets; he mimics them and jeers at them. As the Enemy—critic, satirist, railer, showman—he speaks with a voice anything but measured, detached, impartial. Vivid and virulent, this personality guaranteed—at the very least—that Lewis's criticism would be conspicuous.

The Enemy Stance:
The Exiled Opposite

Like the "Horseman," the Enemy is more than just a flamboyant surface. All the Enemy's swagger and blustering reflects the structure of Lewis's critical stance—his position in relation to the ideas and people he writes about.

How he defined and understood his own role is relatively easy to discover: we need only look at the two essays in which he announces his reasons for calling himself an Enemy, the "Editorial" of the first issue of *The Enemy* and the "Preface to Book I" of the first edition of *Time and Western Man*. But the more closely we look at these announcements, the more we see that there are also complications and ambiguities underlying what seems a dramatically obvious stance.

Lewis begins both of these pieces with a classical analogy to his own role as social critic. For the journal's epigraph, he uses a passage from Plutarch's *Moralia*:

> "A man of understanding is to benefit by his enemies.... He that knoweth that he hath an enemy will look circumspectly about him to all matters, ordering his life and behaviour in better sort...forasmuch as amity and friendship nowadays speaketh with a small and low voice, and is very audible and full of words in flattery, what remaineth but that we should hear the truth from the mouth of our enemies? Thine enemy, as thou knowest well enough, watcheth continually, spying and prying into all thine actions." (iv)

The Enemy Opposite

As an Enemy, Lewis can say things no friend could or would say. Enemies need not—indeed must not—flatter, nor need they concern themselves with making or keeping friends. Expected to offend, to slander, to libel, an Enemy may speak the truth because he is free from the restraints of civility. In short, this Enemy is "the unfriendly truth-teller."

To Plutarch's portrait, Lewis adds a description of the Cynics. This second analogy, he explains, is "against himself" and should not be taken too literally. He quotes from Caird's *The Evolution of Theology in the Greek Philosophers*:

> "When some aspect of thought or life has been for a long time unduly subordinated, or has not yet been admitted to its rightful place, it not seldom finds expression in a representative individuality, who embodies it in his person and works it out in its most exclusive and one-sided form, with an almost fanatical disregard of all other considerations—compensating for the general neglect of it by treating it as the one thing needful. Such individuals produce their effect by the very disgust they create among the ordinary respectable members of the community.... Their criticism of the society to which they belong, and of all its institutions and modes of action and thought, attracts attention by the very violence and extravagance of the form in which they present it. And the neglected truth, or half-truth, which they thrust into exclusive prominence, gradually begins by their means to gain a hold of the minds of others, forces them to reconsider their cherished prejudices, and so leads to a real advance of thought." (*TWM* 4, Lewis's ellipses)

The Enemy's outlandish behavior attracts attention not only to Lewis but also to the ideas he wishes to spread. When one's ideas are unpopular or unfamiliar, they require some kind of advertisement; and for publicity, notoriety

The Enemy Stance: The Exiled Opposite

serves as well as fame. Like the Cynic, the Enemy may goad his society into thinking differently. By throwing all of his weight onto one side of the scales, Lewis hopes to restore a proper balance. This Enemy is a "gadfly," an "unpleasant, neglected-/half-truth teller."

What is clearest in these two essays, though, is Lewis's insistence that the Enemy be recognized as "a solitary outlaw" whose attitude is "vigilant" and "hostile." In the first two paragraphs of the *Enemy* "Editorial" alone, Lewis refers to himself (either directly or by metaphor) as "a solitary antagonist," "a solitary outlaw," an outsider, an exile, and one in "solitary schism." And he repeats similar self-descriptions in book after book.

To these descriptions we must add at least one more. As other critics have noticed, the Enemy stance is much like that of the romantic artist/genius, standing aloof from his society because of his greater insight. (Of course Lewis would not have admitted this similarity in the Enemy years; but even he would agree that he began his career in the pattern of such late-romantic figures as Wilde and Whistler: remember his black hats and capes.) Here Nietzsche—who often sounds exactly like the Enemy—provides a telling analogy: "More and more it seems to me that the philosopher, being *of necessity* a man of tomorrow and the day after tomorrow, has always found himself, and *had* to find himself, in contradiction to his today: his enemy was ever the ideal of today." Or here: "He shall be greatest who can be loneliest, the most concealed, the most deviant."[11] The Enemy, we might say, stands at the intersection of two traditions: the romantic and the satiric.

Enemy, artist; satirist, romantic genius; "unfriendly truth-teller," "unpleasant, neglected-/half-truth teller"; "outlaw," Cynic, railer, gadfly. Alone, each of these roles is clear enough; together, their unstable value points us to an underlying ambiguity. The Plutarchian Enemy stands fairly clearly for good against evil; the Cynical Enemy may do good, but he does it at the cost of part of his own humanity. The gadfly's exile is a strategic choice and the romantic's exile proves his genius; but the outlaw and the misanthrope stand outside society because their differences and resentments have distorted them. All of these figures have in common a stance of solitary opposition, but underlying the simplicity of this stance are complexities of motive and self-image. And Lewis's extreme choice of opponents adds to the complexity of his role. With the Enemy he announced his opposition to the most comprehensive of foes: not only Nietzsche's "herd" or Arnold's "philistines" but also his own friends, his own society, his own culture, in short, his own "Time." The Enemy of Everything, the Absolute Opposite—this is a risky stance. Negative or positive, self-destructive or liberating, futile or constructive: as Lewis clearly knew, the Enemy must walk a fine line, keep a difficult balance.

One danger is the fate of the Cynic: unfocused, unproductive misanthropy. As he warns in *The Art of Being Ruled*, "*Hatred of stupidity* is a most dangerous thing to encourage in yourself or others. It must have as a policy, or widely-indulged-in practice, the most diabolical results" (94). Although he does not intend to describe himself here (in this book he *says* he simply accepts the "stupidity of the masses" as a neutral fact), the potential for self-criticism is evident enough. He moves closer to acknowledging the dangers to his own soul in his novels, where he sometimes creates characters whose ideas clearly resemble his own but whose behavior demonstrates the dangers of these ideas.

Both of the main characters in *Tarr* illustrate this relationship (remember that Lewis revised this novel at the same time he was writing the Enemy books). He identifies Kreisler as an Enemy-like figure in a number of ways: in the passage I've already cited describing how he invents outrage that is natural to him; in Bertha's direct identification of him as "the enemy . . . a bandit, a house-breaker, after all a

The Enemy Stance: The Exiled Opposite

dangerous violent person."[12] But this character is distorted and controlled by his anger, his feeling that he is an outsider, his resentment at the way the world treats him. His outrageous conduct is at first amusing but then turns bad: the violence in him explodes, he rapes Bertha, challenges an enemy to a duel and murders him, and then kills himself in despair. Tarr, too, is like the Enemy. Consider this description: "His sardonic dream of life got him, as a sort of quixotic dreamer of inverse illusions, blows from the swift arms of windmills and attacks from indignant and perplexed mankind. But he—unlike Quixote—instead of having conceived the world as more chivalrous and marvellous than it was, had conceived it as emptied of all dignity, sense and generosity. *The drovers and publicans were angry at not being mistaken for a legendary chivalry, for knights and ladies!* The very windmills resented not being taken for giants!"[13] This Tarr resembles the satiric/quixotic Horseman, the dramatic figure whose main problem Lewis identifies as "*the poor quality* of his enemies." But just a page earlier Lewis also warns: "[Tarr's] contempt for everybody else in the end must degrade him: for if nothing in other men was worth honouring, finally his own self-neglect must result, like the Cynic's dishonourable condition."[14] And Tarr, like Kreisler, finally accomplishes nothing. Even if Lewis says that his analogy between his role and the Cynic's is not to be taken too literally, such passages show that he recognizes this danger as one he faces himself. And in the late *Self-Condemned*, as many readers have recognized, René Harding—unquestionably a semiautobiographical character, self-exiled from his country and culture—destroys himself (and his wife) with the intransigence and ultimate nihilism of his critical opposition to the world.

A second, less private danger in the Enemy stance derives directly from one of its major effects, to isolate Lewis from his contemporaries by exaggerating the differences rather than the similarities between himself and others. Differences, for Lewis, become oppositions. But this exaggeration—dramatized and reinforced by the sometimes seductive outlandishness of the Enemy—can also lead Lewis into an extreme sense of opposition: his choice to oppose everyone else sometimes flips over into a sense that everyone else is against him. Thus he says often that he has been rejected by the rest of his society: explaining the analogy between himself and the Cynic, for instance, he writes, "I 'create disgust,' that I have proved, 'among the ordinary respectable members of the community'" (*TWM* 5). And in the *Enemy* "Editorial," he argues that if he were attacking persons (and not their works), "it would be certain that the number of words we expended against them in public would be immeasurably out-numbered by those flung against us in private." Similarly, in *Paleface* he says, "Do not let us fear to hurt people's feelings by our laughter, since we may depend on it they will not spare ours" (271).

The sense of mutual enmity demonstrated by such remarks functions, for Lewis, both destructively and constructively. It is destructive insofar as it resembles paranoia; and as Lewis's career progressed, his conviction that he was the victim of persecution became more and more pronounced. One characteristic of paranoia—at least in its twentieth-century literary form—is that to fear persecution is also to invite it. In Lewis's case, not surprisingly, his virulent attacks on important literary figures did eventually contribute to his difficulties in finding financial backing and publishers; the fictional dimension of the Enemy role did not protect him from making real enemies, or giving real offense. (Nietzsche warns: "How *personal* does a long fear make one, a long watching of enemies, of possible enemies!"[15]) We can see both his paranoia and his awareness of its two faces in a poem Lewis published in 1933, "If So the Man You Are," where the "outlaw" has become an "outcast." The Enemy speaks:

The Enemy Stance: The Exiled Opposite

> And still and all, we know the invisible prison Where
> men are jailed off—men of *dangerous* vision—
> In impalpable dark cages of neglect,
> Invisible walls by self-protective sect
> Or cabal against the Individual built,
> (At best with honorifics and lip-service killed).—
> Well understanding tactics such as these,
> Conversant with historic instances,
> You can hardly blame an "Enemy" who forestalls
> Such treatment and puts up his own high walls.[16]

This Enemy builds his own walls in anticipation of the walls he fears others will build: in either case he loses his liberty.

Yet if Lewis anticipates rejection, he also exploits it—in what I see as the most pervasive and characteristic version of the Enemy stance. Knowing—or fearing—that his hostility will have social ramifications, he offers that consequence to his readers as an advantage of his position. "There will be nobody with whom I shall be dining tomorrow night (of those who come within the scope of my criticism) whose susceptibilities, or whose wife's, I have to consider," he explains in *The Enemy*, and so his "observations will contain no social impurities whatever" (ix). His exclusion from his society certifies the honesty of his criticism. "If the public is not aware of the advantages it derives from such circumstances as these," Lewis writes, "it is time it awoke to its true interest. Why does it not exact of its chosen servants some such social or unsociable, guarantee?—on the principle of the treatment of the Chinese painters of the great period, who, when their talent became noticeable, were at once exiled to a beautiful wilderness, more suitable than the city to the confinement, or rather the delicate metaplasis, expected of them" (*Enemy* ix). As the exile of the Chinese artists signified their greatness, the

Enemy's exile will prove his worth. Clearly Lewis sees himself most often as a sort of gadfly/scapegoat, whose role, though it may involve personal sacrifice, is essential to the survival and progress of civilization. "Some of us," he writes in *Men Without Art*, "possess such humility as to enable us to sacrifice ourselves to what we regard as the public good—well knowing that our advocacy of unpopular beliefs must destroy us economically, and raise up every sort of obstacle in our path" (194). If the whole truth is to be spoken, someone—an Enemy outlaw if necessary—must take on this difficult role.[17]

But at the same time Lewis also offers us a quite different—and wholly positive—way to understand his role as exiled opposite. In the *Enemy* "Editorial," with what his reader comes to recognize as a characteristic pattern, he completes his sketch of the Enemy with a rhetorical twist that expands his idiosyncrasy into universality. On the one hand, he stands alone against his time; on the other hand, he is "by no means alone." "No individual to-day is our enemy," he explains, "but rather our time that of each of us severally, in our capacity of individual—in some cases of energy" (x). He opposes himself to other individual people less than he feels himself—as an energetic individual—opposed by his "time"; he sees the "Zeitgeist" as threatening the very principle of individuality and consequently each individual person.[18] Or, as he says in *Paleface* after claiming that he, like all natural leaders, is an outlaw, "We are in a world in which we are all in some sense outlaws, at the moment, for our traditions have all been too sharply struck at and broken and no new tradition is yet born" (87–88).

Years later, describing his Enemy stance, Lewis commented again on this paradox:

> The particular note of solitary defiance...is not to be traced, oddly enough, to love of the ego, but to a

The Enemy Stance: The Exiled Opposite

sense of *typicalness*: to a type out of place. I have never felt in the least alone.... Certainly there were not many people who thought as I did about anything. I did not look upon myself as 'a rare type,' however. I could not understand why most of my acquaintances looked at most things as they did, and as I did not.... I would like to lay stress on what is the essence of this paradox: namely the originality in question did not seem peculiar to me as an *individual*. (RA 197, Lewis's emphasis)

If only because he is an individual, he is necessarily solitary. But there is nothing to stop others from recognizing that they, too, must stand alone.

In his society, Lewis believes, antagonists like himself are rare—far more rare than they ever should be. For we are mistaken if we behave "as though to be a 'critic' at all were not to be an 'enemy'; or as though it were possible, or would even occur to anybody, in any time, to *criticise*, if he did not wish to *change*" (*Enemy* x). Characterizing himself as a "solitary outlaw," Lewis the Enemy at the same time insists that all other critics—which is to say all thinking persons—should share his exile.

The Enemy Versus Ezra Pound

One of the most obvious things about outlaws and exiles is that they are defined as opposites. As Lewis asks, "How can we evade our destiny of being 'an opposite,' except by becoming some grey mixture, that is in reality just nothing at all?" (*TWM* 6). Depending for their identity upon the society they oppose, opposites exist less as positive than as negative forces. Enmity does not define an independent position; it defines a relationship between at least two positions. On the whole Lewis keeps this aspect of his role in front of his readers and exploits its potential for advertisement. He is happy to announce that he has designed his position to negate what he sees as the dominant trends of the Zeitgeist, and he reminds us often that his main purpose is to oppose the time-cult, rather than to detail a positive alternative. If we look closely, though, we find that Lewis is not always equally frank. Sometimes his boisterousness distracts us from noticing how he also defines himself as an opposite in more subtle—and more fundamental—ways.

Lewis launched his outlaw criticism in "The Revolutionary Simpleton," the bulk of the first issue of *The Enemy* and the first book of *Time and Western Man*, with hostile analyses of Gertrude Stein, James Joyce, and Ezra Pound, three writers he acknowledges as "strongly established leaders, of mature talent." Of these analyses, despite the greater length and notoriety of the Joyce section, the two short chapters devoted to Pound best epitomize the voice, the stance, and the critical tactics of the Enemy. They do so in two major ways. On the surface Lewis criticizes Pound for capitulating to the cult of time and, as with his other targets, focuses only on those aspects of the poet's work that most clearly reveal the time-cult's weaknesses. In its energetic rhetorical excess, its strong polemical bias, and its blatantly one-sided judgments, this attack is quintessential Lewis. At the same time, a closer look reveals several features that suggest that something more is at stake here than a simple demonstration of Pound's failings. Beneath the surface these brief chapters serve a second special function: the attack on Pound, Lewis's lifelong friend, dramatically embodies the Enemy's role of opposition.

Lewis structures his criticism of Pound around two extended metaphorical insults.[19] Pound, first, is a "revolutionary simpleton," a propagandist and "impresario." All too readily he lends his support to any artist or artistic endeavor claiming to be "revolutionary." Some of these, like the avant-garde musician Antheil, seem to Lewis to be "really aiming at something *new*." But others are humbug—and, Lewis charges, Pound doesn't know the difference. Lewis's primary example is the journal *This Quarter*, supported by "Ezra Pound, as patron saint." By demolishing the "revolutionary" pretensions of this journal, Lewis indirectly attacks Pound as an enthusiastic "simpleton," incapable of independent critical judgment. "Ezra is a crowd; a little crowd," Lewis says; "his mind [moves] in grooves that have been made for it by his social milieu." The Enemy's second metaphor—one that refers more directly to Pound's own poetry—is that Pound is a "parasite," albeit a "great intellectual" one, and a " 'big bug' in his class." One effect of this epithet is to devalue the previous collaborations between the two men, by characterizing Pound as a parasite on Lewis's originality: Pound "is the *consumer*...It is *we* who produce; we are the creators; Ezra battens upon us. And he is the most gentlemanly, discriminating parasite I have ever had, personally..." As we will see, this effect is one of the major functions of the Enemy's attack on this poet.[20]

More directly, both of these metaphors embody Lewis's serious criticism of Pound—while tempering that criticism with praise for his formidable talent for interpreting the past: "*By himself* he would seem to have neither any convictions nor eyes in his head. There is nothing that he intuits well, certainly never originally. Yet when he can get into the skin of somebody else, of power and renown, a Propertius or an Arnaut Daniel, he becomes a lion or a lynx on the spot. This sort of parasitism is with him phenomenal." Pound's strength, Lewis argues, is his ability to imagine himself as another person, especially a dead one; his weakness is that at the same time he cannot deal directly with his own immediate world. In both of these metaphors, Lewis implies that Pound operates too much through other people and too little on his own—that he is "that curious thing, a person without a trace of originality of any sort." He explains,

> The particular stimulation that Pound requires for what he does all comes from without; he is terribly dependent upon people and upon "atmosphere"; and, with a sensationalist of his type, in the nature of things little development is possible, his inspiration is of a precarious order, attached as it is to what he regards as his ròle, handed him by a shadow to whose authority he is extremely susceptible, a Public he despises, is afraid of, and serves. So he is easily isolated, his native resources nil.

The Enemy attacks Pound as a man who sees through other eyes better than through his own, a man who fails to live in the present because he is "in love with the past": "He has never loved anything living as he has loved the dead."

To illustrate these accusations, of course, Lewis offers concrete evidence, not only from Pound's current enthusiasms, but also from his current poetry, the early Cantos. Individually, many of Lewis's exhibits are convincing, and so his criticism seems to some extent justified. In his descriptions of Pound's poetry, moreover, Lewis is in reasonable agreement—his rhetoric aside—with other contemporary critics, both hostile and friendly, who also find Pound to be at his best in dealing with the past, not the present.[21] But in contrast with these other critics, there are a couple of significant omissions from Lewis's remarks. Unlike a friendly critic such as Eliot, Lewis does not concern himself with Pound's sophisticated prosody. He does comment on some specifically formal features of the poems, but only to illustrate his arguments about the quality of Pound's mind and personality; he cares less here about the poetry as poetry than about what it reveals of the poet. On the other hand, Lewis conspicuously differs from most of Pound's detractors in that he never complains about the obscurity of his work—surely an obvious target for an attack on this poet. And, of course, there is also the significant addition of the Enemy's rhetoric. Lewis's virulence, I think, disguises the gap between his particular pieces of evidence and his major argument about Pound's lack of originality. If he is persuasive in detail, he is surely unjustified on the whole; his view is too extreme to seem reasonable.

But the attitude toward Pound in "The Revolutionary Simpleton" is also inconsistent with Lewis's other remarks about his friend's work. Both before and after this attack, Lewis's published criticism is largely positive, emphasizing his respect for Pound's genius and his feeling that the two artists want many of the same things in the arts. In a defense of "Homage to Propertius" in 1920, for instance, Lewis vigorously attacked a hostile critic: "It is a part of the same blind conservatism, hatred of a living thing, that men of letters, 'true and honest' ones, painters and musicians, of this community have to bear with when attempting to break through the hybrid social intellectual ring to something that is a matter purely of the imagination or intelligence, and not mixed with officialdom or social attitudes."²² Here he allies himself with his friend—who loved the past no less in 1920 than he did seven years later—as artists dealing with the "living thing," operating with "pure" imagination and intelligence. Similarly, in remarks published not long after "The Revolutionary Simpleton," Lewis praised Pound and explicitly revoked part of his earlier criticism. In *Blasting and Bombardiering* he wrote, "I still regard him as one of the best... poets," and, "Once, in a moment of impatience, I used the word 'simpleton': and—in addition to everything else—I am again impatient. Of course he is not that. But he demands *perfection* in action, as well as in art." Even more strikingly, he describes Pound's creativity both as an impresario and as a poet: "...the dynamic rôle of his critical sympathy: in every fact a *creative* sympathy.... I have never known a person less troubled with personal feelings. This probably it is that has helped to make Pound that odd figure—the great poet and the great impresario at one and the same time. Also, he is the born teacher; and by his influence, direct and indirect, he has brought about profound changes in our literary techniques and criticism: changes, in both cases, for the better."²³ These remarks—not those in "The Revolutionary Simpleton"—typify Lewis's lifelong attitude toward Pound and his work.

All these inconsistencies suggest that Lewis intends the attack in *The Enemy* and *Time and Western Man* to serve some special purpose, but they do not reveal what that purpose might be. We come closer to understanding it when we notice further that in several instances Lewis attacks Pound for doing something that he does himself. For example, he accuses Pound of seeing people "only as types": "There is the 'museum official,' the 'norman cocotte,' and so on," he says. But in the same pages Lewis himself writes of the "time-child" and the "revolutionary simpleton." Again, Pound is censured for his current role as "impresario" and his love of drama: "It is *disturbance* that Pound requires; that is the form his parasitism takes." Yet of course these remarks appear in the journal announcing the Enemy, who is clearly also an impresario of sorts, and who is undeniably dramatic. Similarly, Lewis argues that Pound's only important contribution to *Blast* had been the skill and energy of his "fire-eating propagandist utterances." Such an accusation blatantly ignores the fact that a large part of Lewis's own contribution—and, indeed, of Vorticism itself—was just as much propaganda and fireworks. When Lewis remarks, "From the start, the histrionics of the milanese prefascist [Marinetti] were secretly much to [Pound's] sensation-loving taste," he is criticizing in his friend something he might equally well criticize in himself.

Now Lewis does not acknowledge these resemblances. If he did he could defend himself against the charge of deceit by arguing that he sees the seemingly fine distinctions between the two artists as reflections of important matters of principle. Pound's character types are conventional; Lewis's are new. Pound seems to present these clichés unselfconsciously; Lewis displays his as critical weapons and deliberately satirical simplifications. At issue, he might say, is the difference between originality and parasitism—often, certainly, a subtle difference, but a crucial one nevertheless. Separating Pound's propagandizing from the Enemy's is an even clearer line: Pound puts his energies into advertising for others while Lewis advertises only himself. Pound's readiness to spend his time on other, less talented artists rather than on his own work seems to Lewis a serious mistake—one that leads directly to Pound's inability to create by himself. The personality that Pound's propagandizing reveals is "considerable and very charming," but it is also characterized by "the habit of unquestioning obedience and self-effacement." The Enemy's dramatics, in contrast, are self-aggrandizing, dogmatically individualistic, defiantly idiosyncratic. The difference again is that between the parasite and the true artist; in this case what matters is the use to which one puts one's energies.

But, of course, Lewis does not make this defense or point out the principles that are at issue. To do so would also be to reveal the similarities between himself and Pound. As it is, only if we remember who is writing this analysis do we recognize Lewis's sleight-of-hand. Juxtaposed with the noisiness of the Enemy's insults, this silence tells us that these chapters function in two ways: on the surface they criticize Pound's capitulation to the cult of time; beneath the surface they embody Lewis's role of opposition. Without making his intentions explicit, Lewis defines the Enemy stance by treating the many similarities between his friend and himself as absolute oppositions. To prove that he stands alone against his time, he must exaggerate his differences from this figure who might seem to resemble him too closely. Early in his discussion, Lewis suggests as much: "Pound's name and mine," he writes, "have certain associations in people's minds. For the full success of my new enterprise it is necessary to dispel this impression."

Pound's support of *This Quarter*, then, serves as an illustration of the folly of group activity. All too often, Lewis implies, groups function mainly to disguise the creative dullness of their individual members. Certainly in this journal Lewis found an easy target; as we have seen, the passages he quotes and his sarcastic comments successfully expose its absurdity and pretentiousness. Pound loses credibility by association; regardless of how good one's own poetry might be, one should also have the critical acumen to recognize and repudiate "humbug." Furthermore, we gather, no one who could thus "innocently" endorse such humbug could have the intelligence Lewis would expect in a first-rate artist. By damning Pound through *This Quarter*, Lewis demonstrates that his own self-exile has been wise—even necessary.

Pound further serves Lewis as a symbol of his past—or at least that part of his past that could undermine the credibility of the Enemy's stance. "I will start," Lewis writes, "by giving the briefest possible account of how, in the past, we came to work together." But what follows is a transparently biased version in which Lewis minimizes Pound's role and implicitly appropriates for himself the credit for the creative achievement of Vorticism. Pound, he explains, had nothing to do with the real artistic innovations of the *Blast* group except to supply "the Chinese Crackers, and a trayful of mild jokes, for our paper; also much ingenious support in the english and american press; and, of course, some nice quiet little poems—at least calculated to vex Signor Marinetti with their fine passéiste flavour." Pound's literary efforts, according to Lewis, were not especially experimental, unlike the works of the painters who dominated the group; "His poetry, to the mind of the more fanatical of the group, was a series of pastiches of old french or old italian poetry, and could lay no claim to participate in the new burst of art in progress." Although he attributes these opinions to his other collaborators, Lewis clearly offers them as his own assessment of Pound's role; and indeed, this is a judgment Lewis continued to repeat in later years.[24] Now many—though not all—of Pound's *Blast* poems *were* "antiquarian and romantic," at least in contrast with the Vorticist graphics or Lewis's play, "Enemy of the Stars," and a large part of his role in the venture *was* his energetic propaganda. But if this description seems on the whole accurate, it is hardly fair. For one thing it ignores the revolutionary nature of Pound's early poems (the *Blast* pieces aside), especially his experiments with Imagism (though Lewis might well not have thought these experiments particularly interesting). More important, it ignores the fact that much of Vorticism's importance *was* the publicity it engendered. And, as I have said, it ignores Lewis's own considerable propagandizing and fireworks. The effect of all of this is to characterize what might be seen as a balanced collaboration of two innovators as a parasitic relationship in which Lewis provided all the important creative energy.

Thus Lewis disassociates himself from his rabble-rousing activities by condemning Pound's and distances himself from his own past membership in a group of revolutionary artists by reminding us about *Blast* in a way that minimizes the importance of its other contributors. Furthermore, he explains, his *Blast* period is over: "Its object has been achieved." In the twelve years that have passed, the artistic circumstances have changed radically, and what the young Lewis had good reason to do would no longer serve any purpose. Now, as he says in the *Enemy* "Preface," he has left the "nearest big revolutionary settlement" behind to act alone, as the new situation demands. By reminding his readers of his Vorticist years (when he was in the middle of the "revolution") at the same time that he defines his new situation (which, he tells us, follows a "long period of seclusion and work"), Lewis makes it clear that his isolation is self-imposed, that he has chosen to reject the alternative of group activities deliberately.[25] The contrast with Pound, again, dramatizes how important it is that Lewis's Enemy be a *solitary* outlaw.

It is for the same reason, it seems to me, that Lewis begins his analysis of Pound with an account of their association—an account that, moreover, by mentioning the help Pound had given him, suggests Lewis's personal indebtedness. He refers to the "personal regard" in which he holds Pound and explains, "Once towards the end of my long period of seclusion and work, hard-pressed, I turned to him for help, and found the same generous and graceful person there that I had always known; for a kinder heart never lurked beneath a portentous exterior than is to be found in Ezra Pound." Even in these friendly remarks, though, the Enemy's tongue is barbed. Again coloring what could be a neutral statement, he continues, "For some time it has been patent to me that I could not reconcile the creative principles I have been developing" not simply "with Pound," but "with this sensationalist half-impresario, half-poet." Below, similarly, he remarks, "It is a question if his support is at any time more damaging or useful."[26] Lewis tells us first of his personal regard for Pound, and then begins his series of metaphorical insults. Precisely because he is Lewis's real friend, Pound serves the Enemy as a symbol of all friendship.

So Lewis chose to criticize Pound in "The Revolutionary Simpleton" not in spite of their long personal friendship but because of it. As he announced in the epigraph to *The Enemy*, he wished to set himself against friendship, to defy its obligations, to assert both his isolation and his freedom to tell the truth. His attack on Pound advertised the seriousness of his new role as a critic: an Enemy who will publicly criticize even an old and valued friend will not easily be daunted by lesser social pressures. But in this attack we can also see the sleight-of-hand that sometimes underlies the Enemy's flamboyant truth-telling. To convince his readers of the honesty of his criticism, Lewis—in the stance of the Enemy opposite—chose to conceal part of the truth about his and Pound's long association.

The Enemy's Audience

One of the practical problems that sometimes results from Lewis's stance of belligerent opposition is a troubled relationship with his audience. To whom does the Enemy speak? For whose benefit are his sarcasm and ridicule? Like a politician he has only a few possible audiences. He may address his foes—those who have rejected and scapegoated him. He may address his allies—the others of his own "type" who have remained silent. Or he may address the undecided—those who have so far shirked their responsibility to declare their allegiances. These are the choices a politician would have, and like a politician, Lewis must adapt his rhetorical strategy to fit each audience's attitude.

But the Enemy's personality, of course, is anything but politic. His flamboyant hostility and emphatic solitude exacerbate the difficulties about audience any writer would have to face. Lewis's problem here has two aspects: on the one hand, he must try to keep his readers' interest and engage their sympathy; on the other hand, he must maintain his position as an enemy to everyone and everything. The virulence of his attacks on his opponents may widen the gap between them; the Enemy's forays are less likely to command the attention of his foes (as his comparison to the Cynic assumes) than to alienate them permanently. At the same time, that virulence is essential to his dramatic personality. An Enemy does not court his foes with flattery. Similarly, his lack of restraint may offend those who might otherwise agree with him; his violent sarcasm may overwhelm the ideas it is intended to decorate. And when he speaks to his silent allies, he implicitly contradicts his fundamental insistence that he is a *solitary* antagonist. The Enemy's relations with his third possible audience suffer from similar difficulties. As Lewis makes clear in *The Art of Being Ruled*, he has nothing but contempt for those he sees as the unthinking masses; consequently, when he addresses the audience of the undecided, he is likely to alienate them as he does his declared opponents. As with the audience of allies, the Enemy's advertised isolation inhibits communication with the undecided: to gain support, as to recognize it, would be to destroy his role as a lone outlaw.

In some of the Enemy books, these problems are kept largely under control. But even where there are no blatant difficulties, we can see the underlying structural complications and the potential for worse trouble. Here is a sober passage from the hostile analysis of Spengler's *Decline of the West* from *Time and Western Man*:

> I do not know if it will appear to every reader worth while detecting and exposing the almost insane inconsistencies of such a writer as Spengler: but I think that it is so because this kind of sham does take in a great many people, and it does have a far-reaching and extremely poisonous effect. The swallowing of such inconsistencies means that *people are being taught not to reason, to cease to think*. So it has appeared to me worth while to expose it at some length. (303)

On the whole, Lewis suggests, he addresses his essay on Spengler to those who "are being taught not to reason," those who have been taken in by Spengler's "insane inconsistencies"; but here he speaks to those who must agree with him, since presumably no single reader would acknowledge his or her own failure to think.

When Lewis's tone is serious, the conjunction of these attitudes—his appeal to some readers and his attack on others—is not especially disturbing. He even offers an explanation of the apparent contradiction:

> I am not here superciliously underrating the intelligence of the majority of readers. Most non-professional readers of such a semi-popular book as Spengler's (which proved actually the greatest highbrow best-seller of the last ten or twenty years) have very little leisure for reading. They never read such a book as Spengler's unless it is thrust under their nose. Most of the things it treats of, even commonplaces of philosophy or criticism, appear to them as marvellous and arresting discoveries—for it is the first time that they have made acquaintance with them. If educated people, as students they were far too busy enjoying themselves or cramming for an exam to attend to such austerities or luxuries of the intellect. So they are totally unprepared for such a reading, and certainly unqualified to arrive at an informed opinion. This is not a question of intelligence or of aptitude so much as one of training. (263–64)

Yet even in this explanation, where his attitude should be clearest, there is an underlying problem—partly a structural one, partly one of tone. Despite its evident intention, this passage is full of casual insults to Lewis's own readers. For Spengler's audience is actually much the same as Lewis's—the "general educated person." In patronizing Spengler's readers, consequently, he also patronizes his own. To be told that one does not lack intelligence or aptitude is not unflattering, but one may well dislike being classed with those who must be forced to read and who, because of frivolity or laziness, are wholly ignorant of even the commonplaces of informed opinion (indeed, no one who has to be forced to read is likely to make it this far into Lewis's long book). The readers about whom Lewis speaks in this passage are the uncommitted or easily swayed, and the implication of his explanation is that he writes to educate that third audience. But the explanation itself seems to be addressed to a different audience—one that already shares Lewis's own perspective.

What we see here is a relatively subtle instance of the strategy that works best for Lewis: to play one of his audiences against another, to alternate between addressing a reader who must be persuaded and one who has already joined him. At its best this strategy effectively forces, or wins, the reader's agreement. We are won when Lewis associates our opinion with his own; we are forced when he associates our opinion with his target's. This is what occurs in this passage from his attack on the "historical relativism" of Bergson, Croce, and Carr:

> You are supposed to burst into rapturous song at the mere thought that you are *co-operating*, in one 'great' (very great) communal work (of art), with a toiling, joyous crowd of forbears and descendants. (You know that in cold fact you have nothing much yourself to be joyous about; you are aware that the generations behind you, could you visit them, would scarcely be found so romantically situated as in this Santa Claus dream for good little 'proletarians.' But no matter. Do not let us spoil the picture.) It is *tremendously exciting* to think that we are actually *making history with our own hands*—and—just think of it! 'History' is *all there is!* So *we* are all there is, too!... We look round, and there is Julius Caesar, with a cheery smile, in blue overalls and sandals, come to give us a hand! It is all so glorious and splendid, when you come to think of it, that it makes one happy to be alive, and at the same time quite ready to die.... (*TWM* 236–37)

Inside the parentheses Lewis addresses the reader sensible enough to join with him in seeing the implications of these philosophers' views. Outside the parentheses he vigorously ridicules the reader foolish enough to agree with them. If only on this one issue, and regardless of our general view of Bergson or Croce, the Enemy's rhetorical strategy leaves us little choice but to ally ourselves with Lewis.

Yet the same strategy can also misfire. Consider this section from his attack on Sherwood Anderson's *Dark Laughter:*

'Ah, the good kind Nigger! Would that those hard unsympathetic White Men were as good to "kids" as that! Give me a Nigger every time—if you're a little innocent kid (as I am for the moment, in misty-eyed memory) breaking the hard, cruel, White law, which forbids you to run away from home, and which imposes its disgusting White *discipline* upon you. Ah, if the White Mommer and Pop could only understand! As the Nigger understands! The Child is a thing that requires understanding! He is a wild, rousseauesque thing, a fragment of wild Nature. He hates discipline! He wants to run wild! The Nigger is nearer to Nature: he understands the Child. *Up, the Nigger! Down the White Mamma!* And especially, *Down the White Papa!*'....

That is the andersonian message: and when we have wiped our eyes and put our handkerchiefs away (still sniffling a little, and still red around the eyes)—if we *ever* do that at all, of course!—let us open our little peepers and see what has been happening to us all. We've been having such a hell of a good time, such a lovely luscious cry, and so much luxurious sob-stuff has been our bath for so long...that to be a little inflexible, and on the cold side, will be a change, at least. Suppose we begin to do what—in such a radiant, free and highly emotional world—we should never never do at all: I mean, fall into that beastly condition, so abhorrent to all emancipated, freedom-loving Children of Nature, to all Behaviourists, to all Bergsonians... and Emergent Evolutionists—that condition we call (as it were in mockery of our 'reflexes') 'reflection.' How would that new state of mind affect our view...? (*Paleface* 225–26)

Here again Lewis addresses both audiences with his unrestrained Enemy voice; and here again he intends to use ridicule to coerce our agreement. But in this passage, I think, the danger of this voice is evident. The same rhetoric that can amuse—even when it may shock us with its excesses—can also offend. When Lewis exceeds his reader's tolerance, then his flamboyance will sound like tastelessness—or, in this case, bigotry—and he will succeed only in alienating us. The difference between the successful Enemy rhetoric and the offensive is not so much in Lewis's language, though, as it is in the reader's willingness to participate. One reader will enjoy the same passage another will hate; one will keep reading—perhaps chuckling with an illicit kind of amusement, perhaps nodding in agreement—while another will slam the book shut. An argument we might listen to if it were made in more measured language may become offensive much more rapidly in the Enemy's voice; flamboyant language may exacerbate the reader's difficulty. And when Lewis is making an argument his reader would never agree to, his dramatic offensiveness will only anger. The Enemy argues by rhetoric, not logic (though there is always some logic behind the rhetoric). When the rhetoric appeals to us, we don't notice the absence of logic; but when it appalls us, we do.

If the acuteness of this danger depends on the reader, though, Lewis's relationship with his audience also suffers from an internal problem: his own sense of his readership is never quite secure. In book after book he tries to describe this audience. But beyond a fairly consistent appeal to "the general educated person," these descriptions—and the attitudes they imply—reveal a fundamental uncertainty. Does he write for the average reader? For the intelligentsia? For a very few especially intelligent readers? For other artists/writers/satirists/etc. only? And how does he feel about these readers? Consider a few of these descriptions:

> ...if it is my good fortune to be read by a variety of readers, of unusual intelligence, but to whom the few books required are not easily accessible, and who are in any case repelled by what is called history, then my brief, unvarnished collection of notes may be welcome. (*L&F* 12)

> Most books have their *patients*, rather than their *readers*, no doubt. But some degree of health is postulated in the reader of this book. (*ABR* xi)

> My main object in *Paleface* has been to place in the hands of the readers of imaginative literature, and also of that very considerable literature directed to popularizing scientific and philosophic notions, in language as clear and direct as possible, a sort of key.... It is a system that will enable any fairly intelligent man, once he opens his mind to it, and seizes its main principles, to read under an entirely new light...(109)

And this suggestion about the readers of *War and Peace*:

> It should only be placed in the hands of those who are in a position to understand it. The people who read such books, after all, should be the rulers. (*ABR* 123)

So far, Lewis is at least complimentary to his audience: we are fairly, and perhaps unusually intelligent; we are (mentally) healthy; and—possibly—we should be the rulers.[27] But here is a description that shifts into mild insult:

> [This book] is destined for the ignorant, or inattentive, rather than the intolerant. It may provide a few people,

The Enemy's Audience

in positions of some influence, with a background of common-sense. (*The Jews, Are They Human?* 8)

Nor is this shift entirely a question of different audiences for different books. In almost every book we could find a passage suggesting more than one image of the reader at the same time.

Consider the wavering evident in this section from *Men Without Art*:

> But in fact beyond a clearly defined, and quickly overtaken limit, you must be prepared to work a little bit, to look an abstract idea in the face and mildly cudgel your brains, if you are going to understand much about books and other products of the artistic intelligence. By this means, at all events, namely that of progressing by easy stages from the particular to the general, it has been my object to lead on the general reader—the 'plain reader' perhaps is better—to an understanding of the absolute necessity of looking behind the work of art for something which is not evident to the casual eye...

So far, fine: I—a general reader, a plain reader—am fairly bright, and I am not too lazy to think. (Incidentally, several other books, *Time and Western Man* and *The Doom of Youth*, for instance, offer similar explanations for beginning with the concrete and popular and moving into the more difficult questions. In all cases, I think, there is a hint that Lewis is being patronizing, but on the whole the logic of the explanation dominates.[28]) But the next few pages add confusion to this fairly straightforward description. First, Lewis offers a dramatic rendering of this "Plain Reader," who says things like " 'I like a nice novel—I am a youngish Plain Man and I don't mind a spot of love, but I prefer *mystery*: give me a good gory murder all the time!' " Then, recognizing that his tone has slipped, that he is now parodying the reader he has just described as his own, he regains con-

The Enemy Opposite

trol with a version of the strategy we have seen, playing one reader against another: "If you are not so Plain a Reader as all that I apologize for this 'Rugger Blue' interlude... but it is just as well to be prepared for the worst!" But who is this "not-so-plain reader"? The next explanation shifts again: "My present essay is not even for the 'Plain Reader,' so much as for the 'Plain Writer'; and not *too* 'plain,' even at that, I may as well add." And the final touch is the remark that he thinks this book might interest "the lay reader" (*MWA* 7-11). From the reader willing to work, to the general reader, to the Plain Reader, to the not-so-plain reader, to the Plain Writer, to the not-too-Plain Writer, to the Lay reader: even if we escape the ridicule of the murder-mystery lover, we are never going to understand clearly whether we are the readers Lewis intends to address. As Lewis himself protests (in another context), "Heaven knows to what public it is addressed."[29]

A more serious problem occurs when this kind of confusion veers into clearer insults. What often happens is that Lewis confuses a third-person attack on a hypothetically stupid or ignorant or inattentive reader [Bad Reader] with a second-person address to his own hypothetically intelligent one [Good Reader]. Consider these examples:

> There is, of course, some exaggeration in this analysis: but it is only by over-stressing the significance of such material that the true meaning of all such writing can be laid bare for the inattentive [Bad] reader. The [Bad] reader must be induced somehow to contract the habit of reading between the lines. That is really the way to read such stuff, if you [Good? Bad?] must read it (and masses of [Bad] people do), the way I have just been reading it for you [Good]. (*Paleface* 229)

> And it is in very militant reaction against this tendency, artist that I am, that I have taken up these critical

weapons, and loudly call upon you [Good Reader] to take up yours as well—as far as that is possible, and as far as it is consonant with your [Bad Reader] duties as a good Marxist boy or girl, or a good little Camelot du Roi, or good little rationalization-robot, that is perfectly understood! (*MWA* 156)

The insult in this last example is particularly blatant; but it is not really exceptional.

A similar effect occurs when Lewis insults another author's readership, without recognizing that his is probably almost the same audience. (In fact, it would seem a premise of his *criticism* that the readers should be the same: why bother attacking a writer for someone who hasn't read his or her books?) We've seen him do this in a mild way with Spengler's readers. Similarly, in a book consisting largely of cuttings from popular magazines and newspapers, he cautions, "There is one thing that must always be borne in mind: namely that such competitions as that announced by *The Evening News* and all such 'Youth' articles are strictly for the consumption of *crétins*.... That is the majority of the newspaper public, it is true" (*The Doom of Youth* 82). But wouldn't his own readers also read newspapers? If not, why warn them about the ideology of these "youth articles"? And in an even more obvious insult, Lewis slams the "almost unbelievably stupid audience" of Matthew Arnold's *Celtic Literature* (*L&F* 320). The context of this remark cannot adequately explain why the readers of one book of Arnold's should differ from the readers of his other books—or from the readers of Lewis's own books about literature, books that often quote Arnold with clear approval and agreement. This kind of difficulty, logically enough, occurs most often in the books whose main purpose is to analyze the way those in power manipulate everyone else.

All of these different problems marking Lewis's relationship with his audience—problems with the Enemy voice, with the Enemy's structure of perpetual opposition, with Lewis's uncertain and problematic sense of who will read his words—reveal one basic tension. Lewis's stance of solitary opposition and his habitual contempt for the public are always precariously balanced against his (paradoxical) sense of universality and the respect for others this sense would imply. There is always the danger that the Cynic's contempt for his fellow man will spill over into contempt for his audience,[30] that the Enemy's self-exile will turn into imprisonment, that Lewis's delight in the dramatic energy of the Enemy voice will blind him to the risk of going too far.

These structural dangers do not, of course, wholly account for the many and complex kinds of audience trouble Lewis suffered during his long career.[31] There are certainly other factors internal to the way he wrote his books: the difficulty in understanding his argument without reading more than one long work; the demands he makes on his reader to follow him through an often Byzantine analysis of all kinds of matters—social, cultural, economic, scientific, political; even the trouble he made for himself and his publishers with his sometimes inadvisable intemperance of language. And a fuller explanation would also have to consider the intertwined effects of such external factors as his early notoriety as a rabble-rouser, trouble-maker, and (artistic) revolutionary; the real enmity caused by his satirical attacks on powerful literary figures; the unpopularity—especially in literary circles—of many of his political sentiments both then and now; the conspicuous (with hindsight) and serious mistakes in judgment of his political analyses in the 1930s. By no means did all his troubles result from the Enemy voice or dramatic stance: in several of the most problematic books of the thirties, *Hitler* for instance, Lewis used very few of the Enemy's rhetorical tactics. The Enemy's relationship with his audience reveals the structure

The Enemy's Audience

and causes of only part of what could go wrong for Lewis.

Lewis was unquestionably aware of all of these problems; in one place or another, he comments on each of them. Two of these passages are particularly illuminating, showing us some of the crucial tensions in his choice of the Enemy personality, voice, and stance to dramatically embody his role as artist/critic. Both, typically, are remarks about another writer's audience; but both quite clearly function also as self-analyses. In the first, from *Men Without Art*, Lewis contrasts the artist's current situation with that of the "classical artist," who shared his values with his patrons, his society, and his audience, and consequently supported those values: "Now, no artist today recognizes this duty, for the very good reason that it is extremely difficult for him to share the values of his audience, if he is a good artist, and he probably feels that he will be accomplishing a better work by imposing a few of his own values upon *them*, rather than by translating into a delectable artform their pernicious and unsatisfactory principles of conduct. That is why artists like Tolstoy, or our own Mr. Lawrence, turn themselves into preachers, and become insufferable moralists into the bargain" (193). Such a description can only remind us of Lewis's self-portrait as the Plutarchian Enemy and the Cynic: his own purpose puts him at odds with his society in exactly this way, and he shares this risk.

The second passage (actually two), from *The Art of Being Ruled*, offers, I think, as acute an analysis of Lewis's position as any:

> A book of this description is not written for an audience already there, prepared to receive it, and whose minds it will fit like a glove. There must be a good deal of stretching of the receptacle, it is to be expected. It must of necessity make its own audience; for it aims at

> no audience already there with which I am acquainted. I do not invent... a class of *esprits libres*, or 'good Europeans,' as Nietzsche did. I know none. (xii)

But significantly, later in the same book he returns to the topic of Nietzsche's audience:

> Many great writers (and Nietzsche was of course a very great one) address audiences who do not exist. Nietzsche was always addressing people who did not exist. To address passionately and sometimes with very great wisdom *people who do not exist* has this disadvantage... that there will always be a group of people who, seeing a man shouting apparently at somebody or other, and seeing nobody else in sight, will think that it is they who are being addressed. (123–24)

Surely this also illuminates Lewis's own situation. Like Nietzsche, the Enemy stands alone against his culture; like Nietzsche, Lewis exposes himself to misunderstanding—indeed, courts it—by the passionate intransigence of his opposition.

PART 2:
THE ENEMY PRINCIPLES

"My Most Essential Me"

In one of the more remarkable passages in *Time and Western Man*, Lewis tells us how he makes decisions. In fulfilling "our destiny of being 'an opposite,' " he explains, we must take care that our "fixation" be "upon something fundamental, quite underneath the flux."

> Yet how are you going about this fixation, you may ask; how will you tell offhand what is essential and what is not, for the composing of your definite pattern; and, even among essential things, how do you propose to avoid the contradictory factors of empirical life; since every one includes, below the possibility of change, dispositions that war with one another? Well, the way I have gone about it is generally as follows. I have allowed these contradictory things to struggle together, and the group that has proved the most powerful I have fixed upon as my most essential ME. This decision has not, naturally, suppressed or banished the contrary faction, almost equal in strength, indeed, and even sometimes in the ascendant. And I am by no means above spending some of my time with this domestic Adversary. All I have said to myself is that always, when it comes to the pinch, I will side and identify myself with the powerfullest Me, and in its interests I will work. And luckily in my case the two sides, or micro-cosmic 'opposites,' are so well matched, that the dominant one is never idle or without criticism. It has had to struggle for supremacy first with critical principles within, and so it has practised itself for its external encounters. This natural matching of

opposites within saves a person so constituted from dogmatism and conceit. If I may venture to say so, it places him at the centre of the balance. (6–7)

Several things suggested by this passage are central to my view of Lewis. Like the "Horseman" drawing, for instance, this description reveals the two structures of opposition and dominance. There, they underlie the gaudiness of horse and rider; here, they characterize the kind of thinking that underlies the Enemy's flamboyance. We have seen how this private drama of conflict and dominance parallels the structure of Lewis's public critical activity: these mental disputes are like those the Enemy forces on us by being our opposite. As we continue we will see further evidence of these patterns in Lewis's opinions—and some of the consequences of their sometimes uneasy juxtaposition.

What particularly interests me now is how this passage itself indicates the center of a balance. The language here combines an apparently sincere tone—not the Enemy's satiric voice—with the Enemy's typically combative vocabulary. Speaking *as* the Enemy, Lewis regards ideas as warring factions; speaking *about* the Enemy, at the same time, he recognizes the strength of other opinions than his own. Moreover, as we have seen, Lewis thought of his critical position as paradoxically both idiosyncratic and universal. As the Enemy he emphasizes his isolation while only hinting at his sense of community. But here, again, speaking about the Enemy, he characterizes the core of his idiosyncrasy— his "most essential ME"—in terms that point to a kind of detached, non-personal universality. Lewis suggests that by collapsing the "contradictory factors" that cause disagreement into the terms of his own private argument, he avoids the danger of solipsism; the "critical principles within" allow him to balance his uniqueness with his common humanity.

In our search for these balancing principles, we are

helped by Lewis's own awareness of his responsibility to announce his premises to his readers. As he wrote in his autobiographical *Rude Assignment*, "Indeed, all people who set themselves up as critics should be obliged, before they begin, to provide a statement of first principles, to which their criticism can be referred: just as in politics one is generally aware of the specific theory of the State favoured by the writer" (*RA* 55). In the books of the Enemy period, Lewis presents these first principles through two pairs of terms—pairs whose paradoxical structure echoes that of the Enemy himself. On one side of his internal scales, Lewis urges a criticism that is highly personal, even idiosyncratic; on the other side, as his explanations of this "personality" indicate, he believes that criticism must also be based on the universality of a non-personal intellect or "mind." Similarly, on the one hand, naming his ideas a "philosophy of the eye," Lewis proposed a criticism based on "vision"—particularly the painter's special vision; on the other hand, he argues that we can and must avoid solipsism only by staying in touch with what he calls "common sense"—the "ordinary" experience of reality he believes we all share. These two pairs of principles—personality and mind, vision and common sense—shape his criticism and underlie his allegiance to the "space philosophy" that he outlines in the central work of the period, *Time and Western Man*.

Personality and Mind

Among the reasons Lewis gives for naming his journal *The Enemy* is that no one expects an enemy to attempt a judicious objectivity. "So named," he explains, "it publicly repudiates any of those treacherous or unreal claims to 'impartiality,' the scientific-impersonal, or all that suggestion of detached omniscience, absence of *parti-pris*, which is such a feature of our time (in which every activity, even the least amenable to exact method, apes positive science) that it has become, indeed, the stock-in-trade of any fairly knowing critic" (*Enemy* ix-x). Such claims are "treacherous" and "unreal" because impartiality is impossible. Criticism is a human, not a mechanical, activity, and none of us, no matter how hard we try, can free ourselves from our most basic prejudices and preferences. "None of us," he says, "can lay claim to the possession of this perfect instrument of truth—we are all only dealing in different degrees of falsity" (*MWA* 71). Inevitably, our judgments result from our special experiences and circumstances. For Lewis, the limits set by personality are not a prison but the ground of all the intellectual integrity and freedom we can have.

Few would argue that a critic can wholly avoid bias. The question is whether or not we should try to minimize our prejudices. T. S. Eliot—who in this respect can be considered a spokesman for the dominant kind of modern criticism—argues that we must try to approach an ideal impartiality: "The critic, one would suppose, if he is to justify his existence, should endeavour to discipline his personal prejudices and cranks—tares to which we are all subject—and compose his differences with as many of his fellows as possible, in the common pursuit of true judgment." For Eliot, moreover, critics who do not attempt objectivity also abandon all principles: "Those who obey the inner voice ... will not be interested in the attempt to find any common principles for the pursuit of criticism. Why have principles," he asks sarcastically, "when one has the inner voice? If I like a thing, that is all I want; and if enough of us, shouting all together, like it, that should be all that *you* (who don't like it) ought to want."[1]

Lewis disagrees. For him, Eliot's kind of impartiality is both impossible and undesirable. As the exaggeration that characterizes the Enemy illustrates, for Lewis all principles begin from personality. In an essay in *Men Without Art*, Lewis expands on his differences with Eliot by calling him the figure who "stands for the maximum of *depersonalization*": "The personality is not, I think, quite the pariah it becomes in the pages of Mr. Eliot: I do not believe in the anonymous, 'impersonal,' catalytic, for the very good reason that I am sure the personality is in that as much as in the other part of this double-headed oddity, however thoroughly disguised, and is more apt to be a corrupting influence in that arrangement than in the more usual one, where the artist is identified with his beliefs" (72, 91).[2] In Lewis's eyes "true judgment" cannot result from disguise, however well meant.

Lewis rejects impersonality on ethical grounds: for him, both honesty and liberty depend on partiality. Because we have no choice but to write as individuals, he argues, we can judge honestly only when we publicize not only our conclusions but also their bases in our own interests. When we pretend to be objective, we lie not only to others but also to ourselves. This particular pretense seems to Lewis especially dangerous: "This delusion of impersonality could be best defined as that mistake by virtue of which persons are enabled to masquerade as *things*. A simple belief in the 'detachment' and 'objectivity' of science, the anxiety of a disillusioned person to escape from his self and merge his personality in *things*; verging often on the worship of *things*... of such experiences and tendencies is this delusion composed" (*ABR* 27). Because it masks our errors and uncertainties, the objective approach to criticism—as to science—allows us to evade our responsibilities.

At the same time, it robs us of our intellectual freedom—the kind of freedom Lewis cares about most. "*Persona* for the Roman, meant a *free* person only; a slave was not a *person*, but a *res* or *thing*," he explains; "We shall not deny that human freedom is also, in our opinion, bound up with this personality" (*TWM* 317–18). To be persons rather than things, we must judge as openly independent individuals. Making a virtue of necessity, then, Lewis asserts that intelligent and ethical criticism actually *depends* on our partiality. "For the whole virtue of accurate observation," he writes, "is that it is a *person* observing" (*RA* 70).[3]

This conviction informs Lewis's criticism in several ways. Most spectacularly, of course, it underlies the Enemy's personality. In that role the critic is not only free to speak flamboyantly, he is compelled to do so, to advertise the individuality of his opinions. The very outrageousness of the Enemy's pronouncements proclaims his independence. Indeed, when he speaks most offensively, when he insults and calls names, he is most "personal." By exaggerating, he forces us to realize that both he and his targets must take responsibility for their statements. "The ideas discussed are held by people after all," Lewis reminds us; "the works under review have names attached to them" (*Enemy* xiv). On the other hand, by exaggerating he simultaneously underlines the freedom his principles allow. A *person*, the Enemy shows us, can do or say *anything*. Further, by overemphasizing the differences between the critic and everyone else, the Enemy dramatizes the essential uniqueness of personality. If our quirks help distinguish us from others, then even our quirks are essential to our originality and intelligence.

Personality and Mind

Again his essay on Eliot clarifies Lewis's position—and the relationship between the Enemy's flamboyant exaggerations and Wyndham Lewis's real ideas. "If there is to be an 'insincerity,' " he announces, "I prefer it should occur in the opposite sense—namely that 'the man, the personality' should exaggerate, a little artificially perhaps, his beliefs—rather than leave a meaningless shell behind him, and go to hide in a volatilized hypostasization of his personal feelings.... the man is thus 'most himself' (even if a little too much himself to be quite the perfect self, on occasion)" (*MWA* 91). And, as he argues in a 1934 essay called ' "Detachment' and the Fictionist," such exaggerations paradoxically lead to an increased detachment and decreased subjectivity:

> As a fiction writer, and in handling the contemporary scene... In order to get the maximum of drama out of it you must 'in the destructive element immerse'; allow it to bring into play your personality... You must not be afraid to say, 'In this, I am a partisan!'... Further, you will find that the more you use your personality in this deliberate fashion, the less notice you will take of it—the less it will interfere with you.... You will find you will achieve more true 'detachment' that way than by playing at Mr. Fair-Play...

As the Enemy, speaking with the Enemy's voice, Lewis artificially exaggerates his real biases—in the interests of honesty. "You play at being yourself," he concludes, "and so you *are* yourself."[4]

But the Enemy is only the most dramatic illustration of Lewis's principle of personality. That principle also requires that his style be casual and colloquial. Lewis consistently writes in the first and second persons, reminding us always that we are people reading the words of another person. Nearly every page is thickly sprinkled with you's and I's, I believe's and to my mind's. This feature of his style became

The Enemy Opposite

more pronounced as the Enemy personality and principles developed: *The Art of Being Ruled* and *The Lion and the Fox*, the first two books of this period to be published, are much more personal in style than an ordinary book about politics or Shakespeare would be, but they are impersonal compared to the later *Time and Western Man*, *Paleface*, and *Men Without Art*. *The Enemy* and its "Editorial" mark a clarification of the connection between principle and style.[5] Thus we find such passages as these, telling us what Lewis has been doing, what he will do next, and how he feels about what he is doing:

Next after the Russian Ballet I propose to range, for analysis, an old associate of mine, Ezra Pound. There are some obvious objections to this, chief among them the personal regard in which I hold him. Since the War I have seen little of Pound. Once towards the end of my long period of seclusion and work, hard-pressed, I turned to him for help, and found the same generous and graceful person there that I had always known...(*TWM* 54)

Unable to ignore in my analysis of what underlies the literary and pictorial expression of the present time, the political factors so busily at work, I find myself with some surprise writing about human skins. And under more normal conditions I should probably be ranged upon the other side of the argument. I am really driven into the position of the Devil's Advocate to some extent...(*Paleface* 19–20)

In the five foregoing chapters I have been road-making—a Roman occupation! And I have been driving my causeway across what is in fact an inconvenient and insanitary bog. More and more Roman!—But I could scarcely claim that my objective has been an imperial one. It has been even in part private and personal. But the public spirit, the Roman spirit, has been present as well. It has been my intention in short that *other* people, whose business takes them in this direction, should make use of the road I have been constructing with such care. (*MWA* 172)

> Against this moralist exploitation of a highly immoral situation some voice has to be raised. My voice will have to serve for the present [since] there is no other (...although its accents have an unmistakably personal sound, since I am an artist first, and a critic afterwards) until such time as a more respectable advocate can be found. There is no time to be lost, gentlemen of the jury! That is my excuse for appearing before you, with all my sinful infractions of the moral law upon my head, in a case that is, in fact, it is common knowledge, my own, and in the interest—can I deny it?—of my many books. But at least there is this to be said—we all know where we are! I lay no claim to being a disinterested party or to being a pure servant of the Law. I am a partisan.... And what we must assume it is your desire to hear is...the truth and nothing but the truth. That, *foi de gentilhomme*, you shall hear from my lips, or at least that portion of the truth that is all that any individual can lay claim to. *That* you shall receive pure and unadulterated. More I cannot say, and he who lays claim to more is misleading you, whether he is conscious of doing so or not. (*MWA* 130)

To a reader accustomed to an impersonal critical style, or to a writer accustomed to minimizing personal references, this prose is surprisingly loose. But it is a deliberate looseness. It denies the illusion of objectivity, forcing us to read as if we were in conversation with Lewis rather than as receivers of facts he has merely organized.

As my last example shows, this colloquial style further allows Lewis to fill the most important requirement of a personal criticism—to keep one's reader aware of one's premises. Rather than try to hide or underplay them, Lewis tries to keep his biases on the surface of his analyses. Thus in all these books, he clearly states his position and his motives for writing (except in *The Art of Being Ruled*, he does this in the first page or two), and he returns often to explain how the issues he criticizes matter to his work as an artist and a writer. So he tells us in *Time and Western Man* that because his deepest beliefs—aesthetic, ethical, political—are contradicted by those he calls the "time-philosophy," and are threatened by the "time-cult's" ascendancy, he feels it his responsibility to try to destroy his adversaries' credibility and to offer an alternate philosophy. Furthermore, Lewis insists, it is *our* responsibility to recognize and act upon our own deepest beliefs, just as he has done. In this sense his criticism is as much example as argument: he offers us his ideas—both his premises and his conclusions—as an example of independent thinking. To convince us of his view of Shakespeare or convert us to his "space-philosophy" is only half of his project; equally, he wants to show us how to think for ourselves by making us see that we must know and accept our own motives and principles.

Certainly Lewis does not believe that such self-knowledge comes easily. We hide our biases and desires from ourselves as often as from others. And those desires are almost never simple; our interests usually contradict and qualify each other. Lewis does not underestimate the confusion and conflicts we face: he believes that the contradictions in our minds should teach us to think more clearly and argue more vigorously. Still, he insists, we must decide which things matter the *most*, and keep those things before us as we judge. Just as in the "Horseman" drawing the conflicting vectors of the horse are dominated by the single vertical of the rider, so we too must subordinate the warring particulars to our essential patterns.

Moreover, in Lewis's eyes compromise and mediation—like the pretense of objectivity—confuse intellectual and ethical issues by allowing us to evade our responsibilities. If seeing both sides of every question is natural to an active mind, we can neither criticize nor act effectively until we choose which side we will support. As he argues in ' "Detachment' and the Fictionist," "The only important thing is to be on the side to which you belong, if you understand me. There is no right side or wrong side. That is nonsense. *Sub specie aeternitatis* both sides are equally right. But what *is* unalterable is that there is a right and a wrong side *for you*." [6] And in *Time and Western Man* he writes, "What is suggested here is that, in such a crisis, all the weight of our intelligence should be thrown into the scales representing our deepest instincts" (187). We must fix "upon something fundamental, quite underneath the flux."

Yet as the language of these statements suggests, Lewis does not intend that we should base our decisions on our emotions. Personality, for him, does not imply emotional distortion. In their dislike for unreasoned and unreasonable criticism—"If I like a thing, that is all I want"—he and Eliot agree. But while Eliot sees personality as irresponsible and emotional, Lewis means by this word something essentially rational. His personality is individual, certainly, rather than communal, but it is also external, public, and sharable, not internal and private. As he explains in *Men Without Art*, the ' "self' or 'personality'... is merely a living adequately at any given moment" (74). The Enemy exaggerates Lewis's understanding of this "self": "Of course I am not using a 'personality' in the *Ballyhoo* sense—I do not mean an individualist abortion, bellowing that it wants at all costs to 'express' itself, and feverishly answering the advertisement of the quack who promises to develop such things overnight. I mean only a constancy and consistency in being, as concretely as possible, *one thing*—at peace with itself, if not with the outer world, though that is likely to follow after an interval of struggle" (75). If the Enemy—who surely represents this "interval of struggle"— does occasionally slip over this dividing line, bellowing like "an individualist abortion," it is clear that Lewis does not intend this effect: he wishes this exaggerated figure and voice to embody, not to distort, his principles.

Lewis sees his principle of personality, I think, as a balancing term between objectivity and subjectivity; his stance is both more subjective than a modern critic's scientific objectivity, and less subjective than, say, stream-of-consciousness. He is concerned to distinguish his personality from subjectivity—the kind of personal involvement he admires from the kind he hates—but it is a difficult distinction both to make and to maintain. For his readers the difficulty is increased because in this matter (as in many others), he does not use his terms consistently. In one place he will use a word in a special way—often, his main terms reverse ordinary usage or connotation—while elsewhere he will revert to the common use of the word. Sometimes, these apparent contradictions can be easily resolved in context; for instance, when he says criticism is "objective," he is attacking, but when he says the material world is "objective" he is praising. But contextual fluctuations do not account for all of the difficulty with these terms. Underlying Lewis's argument, I think, is a paradoxical definition of personality as an individualized, even idiosyncratic, intellectual force, simultaneously private and public.

In an essay of 1925, "Physics of the Not-Self," Lewis tries to define a "principle of the not-self," which closely resembles his principle of personality. This is among his most ambiguous pieces—distinguishing his serious from his ironic statements is almost impossible in places, his logic is obscured by loose references and pronouns, and he shifts

Personality and Mind

the terms of his argument without any clear directions to the reader—but it does spotlight the paradox underlying his terminology. Explaining that he intends "to show the human mind in its traditional rôle of the enemy of life," Lewis works through a series of terms joined by association and equivalence: the not-self (is) the philosopher's (uncertain) "truth" (is) mind (is) intellect (is) altruism (is) ultrahuman (is) inhuman. This concept, he suggests (again indirectly, by juxtaposition), is somehow like the ancient philosophical concepts of Socrates, Plato, and Hindu metaphysics: Socrates' two levels of goodness, the higher one associated with knowledge and the philosopher; Plato's two levels of knowledge, the higher one that of essences; and the Vedic identification between the atman and the brahman, the individual soul and the power sustaining the cosmos, the self and the not-self.[7]

Like these ancient concepts, Lewis's "not-self" is structured paradoxically: "established in the centre of the intellect," it is also simultaneously "an enemy principle," and so, we know, a principle of personality. Remember how he defines the Enemy to be at once idiosyncratic and universal, and read this description of the "not-self":

> The man who has formed the habit of consulting and adhering to the principle of the *not-self* participates, it is true, in the life of others outside himself far more than does the contrary type of man, he who *refrains* from making any use at all of this speculative organ. But he is not, for that reason, *more like* other people. He is *less like* them. For is he not one in a great many thousand? And to be like other people he certainly should be less them and more himself. Hence his altruism only results in differentiating him, and in leaving him without as it were a 'class,' even without a 'kind.'[8]

So the *personality*—the hallmark of the Enemy—marks the

same principle as the "inhuman" *not-self*: public, altruistic, and intellectual, but still essentially individual.

Lewis's "not-self" is the intellectual core of the "self." Because thought distinguishes persons from animals and things, the "not-self" is consequently the essence of personality, and personality the essence of intelligence. Insofar as we transcend emotion through reason, then, judgments may be simultaneously *personal* and *disinterested*. Many years later Lewis offered a simpler—and much clearer—explanation that abandons some of his special terms: "Let me agree, then, to the word 'detached', in the limited sense of habitually reserving judgement, and not expressing oneself by action, and, in perhaps the most important things, holding to the deliverances of reason.—Impersonal detachment is another matter" (*RA* 70).[9] A political candidate, for example, must stand as an individual with his own reasons for wanting office, his own opinions about his opponents, and his own political principles; but that kind of frank individuality does not require that he replace reason with emotion.[10]

In *Time and Western Man*, where he focuses most directly on such philosophical issues, Lewis calls the other side of personal idiosyncrasy the "mind." Like the "not-self," "mind" is the underlying structure of the self, the non-emotional part of our personality that makes us individuals capable of independent thought. The importance Lewis assigns to this term—like that he gives to personality—shows very clearly in his language. Frequently, as we saw, he punctuates his comments with reminders of his presence; one of the most common of these phrases is "to my mind." More important, two of his main classifying terms are "time-mind" and "space-mind"; he characterizes writers and artists as having one or the other. And when he speaks of other people, he consistently and casually refers to the type or quality of their mind. "Miss [Jane] Harrison's mind," for instance, "is a perfect *time-mind*" (240, Lewis's emphasis);

Pound's "mind can be best arrived at, perhaps, by thinking of what would happen if you could mix in exactly equal proportions Bergson-Marinetti-Mr. Hueffer (with a few preraphaelite 'christian names' thrown in), Edward Fitzgerald and Buffalo Bill" (54). Many of these references—especially those occurring in his more flamboyant attacks—seem to be uncalculated, but frequently Lewis obviously intends to direct our attention to an artist's mind as the central factor in his or her creativity. In Stein's *Composition as Explanation*, for example, "We have, I believe, one of the clues to this writer's mind. It tells us that her mind is a sham, to some extent" (66). Similarly, Lewis calls his long essay on Joyce—the most important chapter of "The Revolutionary Simpleton"—"An Analysis of the Mind of James Joyce."

The other Enemy books are marked by the same emphasis. *The Art of Being Ruled*, for instance, is "a sort of ark, or dwelling for the mind" (16); there, as in most of the books of this period, Lewis argues against what he sees as a broad cultural movement against the intellect and towards sensation (cf. 252). And *Paleface* points out how D. H. Lawrence's primitivism (like Sherwood Anderson's) always insists "upon *mindlessness* as an essential quality of what is admirable" (176)—unlike Lewis, who says, "I would rather have the least man that *thinks*, than the average man that squats and drums and drums, with 'sightless,' 'soulless' eyes: I would rather have an ounce of human 'consciousness' than a universe full of 'abdominal' afflatus and hot, unconscious, 'soulless,' mystical throbbing" (196). Whenever mind or intellect are on one side of an opposition, that is Lewis's side, the Enemy's side.

As passages like these suggest, quality of mind is for Lewis an entirely proper basis for judgment.[11] From it comes all our personal power; it alone enables us to transform chaotic impulses into controlled and useful energy—and to transform our isolation into community. This essential energy is simultaneously creative and intellectual. Thus *Time and Western Man*, Lewis says, "is among other things the assertion of a belief in the finest type of mind, which lifts the creative impulse into an absolute region free of... 'history' or politics" (18). And the "supreme instrument of research" is, as it has always been, "the independent critical mind" (11). Hence Pound's epitaph: "Wyndham Lewis, the man who was wrong about everything except the superiority of live mind to dead mind; for which basic verity God bless his holy name." Just as the gaudy surfaces of the "Horseman" and the Enemy reveal their rigorous underlying structures, we find that Lewis's principle of personality is supported and balanced by his conservative emphasis on intellect.

Vision and Common Sense

"Whatever I, for my part, say," Lewis explains, "can be traced back to an organ; but in my case it is *the eye*. It is in the service of the things of vision that my ideas are mobilized" (*TWM* 7-8). So, he says, in *Time and Western Man*—again, because of its focus on philosophy, the central text for the development of the Enemy's principles—he offers us a "philosophy of the eye" (418). In statements like these, I think, he uses "vision" and "eye" metaphorically to bridge the gap—again—between the isolation of his "powerfullest Me" and the intersubjective universality that he believes is grounded in "common sense."

When we describe our biases, we indirectly describe our community. As we might expect, by identifying himself as a painter criticizing literature, politics, science, and philosophy, Lewis emphasizes how he differs from other critics. His activity is "partisan" and "specialist," and its slant toward vision is personal. "I am an artist," he says in *The Art of Being Ruled*, "and, through my eye, must confess to a tremendous bias.... my eye is always my compass" (403). "My occupation," he writes, "is not one that I have received by accident or mechanically inherited, but is one that I chose as responding to an *exceptional* instinct or bias" (*TWM* 7, my emphasis). He explains further: "No doubt what made me, to begin with, a painter, was some propensity for the exactly-defined and also, fanatically it may be, the physical or the concrete" (*TWM* 129). For him, painting is a calling, not a job; his visual work, he argues, has shaped his critical perspective.

By emphasizing his experience as a visual artist, though, Lewis also implicitly claims community with a larger group. His responses, he says, are an artist's, and would be shared by many others. "The definiteness of those instincts, those of a plastic or graphic artist, make his responses to the philosophic tendencies around him more pointed than if he were a scholar mainly, or if he approached them from some political position, or as a professional of philosophic thought" (*TWM* 7). Every now and then, he refers casually—and usually cryptically—to the relationship between his profession and the purpose of his criticism. But while he does seem to think he speaks for artists as a group, he never really develops that aspect of his criticism, and sometimes he even denies his similarity with other painters. "There are artists and artists," he reminds us, "and it is certainly true that many would take opposite views to those of the present writer" (*TWM* 7). (D. H. Lawrence, for instance, when "he took to the brush instead of the pen ...turned out to be incompetent Gauguin!" [MWA 128]; Lawrence's literary values, which Lewis sees as opposite to his own, produce an equally opposite, and equally lamentable, visual art.) Rather than emphasize the middle ground of his community with other artists, the Enemy chooses instead to stress his isolation at one extreme and his universality at the other.

Most often, when he describes the larger community he wishes to speak for, Lewis draws his boundaries on other grounds than occupation. Like all philosophies, he says, his "could perhaps more exactly be described as the expression of the instincts of a particular kind of man, rather than an artist among men of other occupations" (*TWM* 7). Of course this qualification undercuts his remarks about the artist's special sensibility; he loses the precision of his identity as a painter to a more vaguely-defined category and a potentially larger group of people.[12] But this definition, I believe, corresponds much more accurately to Lewis's real position and real concerns.

What matters most to Lewis about artists is not their

Vision and Common Sense

ability to draw or paint, but their inevitable intimacy with vision. As he remarks in an essay of 1922, "The Credentials of the Painter," "The fundamental claim of the painter or sculptor, his fundamental and trump credential, is evidently this: that he alone gives you the visual fact of our existence. All attachment to reality by means of the sense of sight is his province or preserve."[13] Thus one of his main purposes for proposing his "philosophy of the eye," for writing *Time and Western Man*, is to convince his readers that they too are creatures of vision; he speaks for and to those who value sight as their most important sense. This community is one that he would like to make as large as possible. Vision, he believes, should be recognized as a supreme universal value.

This belief had obvious immediate consequences both for Lewis's fiction and for his criticism. One was this famous proclamation: "Dogmatically...I am for the Great Without, for the method of *external* approach—for the wisdom of the eye, rather than that of the ear" (*MWA* 128). Another was the method of *The Apes of God*, where "*the eye* has been the organ in the ascendant"; as Lewis proudly claimed, "No book has ever been written that has paid more attention to the *outside* of people" (*MWA* 118). Such assertions punctuate all of Lewis's Enemy works; they are a battle-cry, a deliberate overstatement (as *The Apes of God* was, I think, a deliberate working-out of the consequences of this position). Such "dogmatism," such one-sidedness, derives from Lewis's feeling that the time-cult's interest in "insides" is unfairly dominant; the Enemy's role is to redress the balance.

Lewis's championing of the eye also structures his criticism of other Modernist writers. Lawrence's interest in "mindlessness" is matched by an interest in the "sightless" and the "visionless," adding up to an interest in " 'the consciousness in the abdomen,' " the Unconscious, which "takes the privilege of leadership away from the hated 'mind' or 'intellect,' established up above in the head" (*Paleface* 177). Henry James, who "had an excellent eye in his head, when he consented to use it," did not leave the "abstract" landscape of North America soon enough, and so "his activities were all turned *inwards* instead of *outwards*" (*MWA* 149–53). And Virginia Woolf's world is "a very dim Venusberg indeed," populated by "a myopic humanity" whose "Venus has become an introverted matriarch, brooding over a subterraneous 'stream of consciousness' " (*MWA* 168). Like his belief in the mind, Lewis's emphasis on vision permeates his critical judgments.

As he did with his definition of the critic as an enemy—and with his paradoxical identification of the personality and the mind—Lewis uses his references to "the eye" both to define his own position as exclusively as he can and to claim that his personal biases are in some basic way universal. "The Credentials of the Painter" offers a familiar explanation: "The painter participates more in life itself in one way than any other artist; but in another sense he is the most removed from it."[14] And late in the argument of *Time and Western Man*, when he thinks it necessary to qualify his terms, he clarifies the connection he has assumed between the artist and other people:

> If by 'philosophy of the eye' is meant that we wish to repose, and materially to repose, in the crowning human sense, the visual sense; and if it meant that we *refuse* (closing ourselves in with our images and sensa) to retire into the abstraction and darkness of an aural and tactile world, then it is true that our philosophy attaches itself to the concrete and radiant reality of the optic sense. That sensation of overwhelming *reality* which vision alone gives is the reality of 'commonsense,' as it is the reality we inherit from pagan antiquity. And it is indeed on that 'reality' that I am basing all I say. (418)

Lewis thinks his painting makes him especially able to recognize the nature of things, yet at the same time he firmly believes that the reality he thus discovers is not idiosyncratic. He consistently refers for his authority to what he believes are shared principles and sentiments—shared, he presumes, by all intelligent and sensible persons. By basing his judgments on vision, he makes his intensely personal criticism simultaneously private and public when he assumes a visually-based "common sense."

Lewis uses the phrase "common sense" to mean several different things at the same time. The passage I have just quoted suggests the first of these: our common sense is sight. These two key terms—common sense and the eye—intersect when Lewis wishes to remind us that we share an ability to *see* things; that if only because our eyes and our brains are physiologically similar to others', we see similarly; and that our notion of the world derives largely from what we see and perceive of it. He emphatically does not mean that we know through our retinal impressions alone; he cautions us to remember that our perceptions depend on the interaction of all our senses—*and* our minds. He opposes the "isolation" of the eye, particularly from the sense of touch (*TWM* 418–19), and he distinguishes our "sensations" from our "perceptions":

> The traditional belief of common-sense, embodied in the 'naïf' view of the physical world, is really a *picture*. We believe that we *see* a certain objective reality. This contains stable and substantial objects. When we look at these objects we believe that what we are perceiving is what we are *seeing*. In reality, of course, we are conscious of much more than we immediately *see*. For in looking at an orange lying before us on the table, we are more or less conscious of its contents, we apprehend it as though we could see all round it, since from experience we know it is round, of the same colour

and texture, from whatever position it is examined, and so forth. (*TWM* 408)

When Lewis refers to our visual sense, he means not pure visual sensations but those sensations after they have been screened and categorized by our minds, "For we are not conscious of this inrush, but only of its accommodation to the waiting forms of cognition" (*TWM* 414).[15] Or as his character Tarr—who is a painter—more concretely explains, " 'I meant only that everything we *see*—you understand, this universe of distinct images—must be reinterpreted to tally with all the senses and beyond that with our minds: so that was my meaning, the eye alone sees nothing at all but conventional phantoms.' "[16] Lewis also does not mean that we all see identical things; because our minds and our memories work *with* our senses, our perceptions differ. The similarities in vision that make common sense are the ground from which our individual creativity—our individual vision—grows.

Yet despite these qualifications, Lewis does mean that sight is our most important sense. In this context we can understand more clearly his claim for an artist's special privilege: painters, by inclination and by training, are more aware of the primacy of the eye. An artist, or anyone with an artist's instincts, sees more self-consciously—and therefore more vividly, more directly, and more accurately—than others can.

The second meaning of Lewis's "common sense" is our *ordinary* sense of the world—those experiences of reality on which we base our everyday lives. For Lewis, we must base our judgments—both critical and philosophical—on these direct experiences. Generally, he believes, by relying on the ordinary we discover truths that are immediate and concrete; we avoid constructing sophisticated but abstract theories that completely lose touch with the physical world we live in. Lewis is well aware that this common sense can change. Indeed, his whole project in *Time and Western*

Man could be called an attempt to halt such a change. He writes, for instance,

> The material world continues to be dealt with in a masterly fashion on the assumption of the 'material' postulates of 'common-sense,' and that is the end of it. This would be ignoring, however, the fact that these conceptions of the external world are intended to supersede those of the classical intelligence and of the picture of the plain-man: that it is proposed to teach Relativity-physics and the relativist world-view everywhere in our schools: and that vast propaganda is carried on by popular treatises and articles to impose this picture upon the plain-man and the simple common-sense intelligence. In other words, the 'common-sense' of to-morrow, it is proposed—the one general *sense* of things that we all hold in *common*—is to be transformed.... And, of course, there is nothing at all that once people are familiarized with it and taught to take it as a matter of course, does not seem natural, and that would not therefore assume the authority of a 'common-sense.' (432–33)

So his appeals to our common sense are to the traditional or classical sense—that of the "plain-man." And he wishes always to persuade us that this traditional world-view is more to our advantage than the artificial, mental world that twentieth-century scientists and philosophers construct. As he explains: "By this proposed transfer from the beautiful *objective, material* world of common-sense, over to the 'organic' world of chronological mentalism, you lose not only the clearness of outline, the static beauty, of the things you commonly apprehend; you lose also the clearness of outline of your own individuality which apprehends them" (175). As his language shows, he conceives of this common sense in visual terms; what we know of the physical world through sensory evidence is more important than anything we could deduce about what might lie beneath its surfaces.

In Lewis's eyes "common sense" is finally, and most importantly, our *shared* sense of things, the source of intersubjectivity. Only because we share certain perceptions do we escape solipsism; only his faith that he and his readers have the same basic experiences in living permits him to maintain his individuality and still understand and be understood by others. Each of us, he argues, lives in "the physical world that we all share *in common*...our common world in which we all meet and communicate" (*TWM* 191). Or as he says in his argument for the classical against the romantic, "All compact of common sense, built squarely upon Aristotelian premises that make for permanence—something of such a public nature that all eyes may see it equally—something of such a universal nature, that to all times it would appear equal and the same—such is what the word *classic* conjures up" (*MWA* 188). Some, whose minds have been "debauched with learning," may have already lost touch with this public, physical, visible world; Lewis would remind these people of what they have forgotten.[17] In the light of this view of "common sense," we can see one kind of audience Lewis imagines for his books, at least those having to do with the arts or with philosophy. Those who know that they share a "common world" are the readers he addresses as allies; those who have lost that awareness are the readers he wishes to convert.

At bottom, the three meanings for the central phrase "common sense" merge. To Lewis, the world we share is identical to the everyday world and to the world we know through vision. Because it is, our deepest personal interests will not be idiosyncratic but communal, not private but sharable. The world in which we can live by recognizing these relationships, Lewis wishes to convince us, is the best world. He promises: "This concrete and 'material' world—which is all that is *common* to us, and which is therefore justly named the 'world of common-sense,' as opposed to the 'mental' world—is a truly fantastic paradise" (*TWM* 186). If, on Lewis's example, we are faithful to our own principles, if we stay in touch with the vivid reality embodied in personality and the visible world, we can share the artist's vision.

These, then, are Lewis's Enemy principles: personality and mind, vision and common sense, two pairs of terms that paradoxically unite the idiosyncratic and the shared. We can see them all come together in a passage near the end of *Time and Western Man*, where Lewis writes:

> The sense of personality, of being a person, is, according to us, the most vivid and fundamental sense that we possess: sharper and more complete than sight, built up like sight with reminiscence, though belonging to an infinite rather than a finite memory, so much so indeed that some philosophers have thought that this sense was memory only: and it is also essentially one of *separation*. In our approaches to God, in consequence, we do not need to 'magnify' a human body, but only to intensify that consciousness of a separated and transcendent life. So God becomes the supreme symbol of our separation and of our limited transcendence.... It is, then, because the sense of personality is posited as our greatest 'real,' that we require a 'God,' a something that is nothing but a *person*, secure in its absolute egoism, to be the rationale of this sense. (463)

We imagine our "God" as a "person" because our sense of personality is our "greatest 'real.' " With this, I think, we can understand the meaning of an earlier passage: "In these difficult new adjustments that I am here proposing to you," he has explained, "our *definition* must be sought in the rigidity of the principle at the base of all our arguments; a rigour as though there, at the base of the necessary dialectical instability, there were planted a God" (*TWM* 257). Personality and mind, vision and common sense, memory, separation: these terms here mark the greatest 'real.' These are the terms of Lewis's "most essential ME," the principles controlling "the necessary dialectical instability," the strong vertical dominating the warring diagonals in the Enemy's self-portrait.

Space and Stability

Lewis never pretends to be what he is not—a trained, professional philosopher. On the contrary, with a characteristic swagger, he defines himself in part as opposing that position. "I do not feel at all impelled to explain myself when I am examining a mere philosopher," he says confidently; "he speaks my language, usually with less skill, but otherwise much the same as I do" (*TWM* 10). Instead, he writes as an individual who sees no reason "why a person should refuse himself the right to use his wits" just because he is not a specialist (11). For Lewis, "a philosophy is always a thing that helps a man to live and to enhance his powers" (364).

Time and Western Man (the source of all quotations in this section except where I've noted otherwise) provides us most clearly with the evidence we need to reconstruct Lewis's personal philosophy, since his own beliefs play an essential role as the ground from which he criticizes the "time-philosophy." Insisting that he intends primarily to attack the time-cult, rather than to offer an independent philosophical treatise, Lewis constructs this critique of modern thought upon one central opposition: the "time-mind" and "time-philosophy" versus the "space-mind" and "space-philosophy." These are "the poles of the human intelligence" (103). Always, they are "confronted, eternally hostile to each other, or at least eternally different" (102). Although he uses this structure of opposition mainly to expose the weaknesses of various modern philosophers, inevitably—just as the Enemy, though he is defined by difference, still has his own distinct personality—Lewis's own beliefs and values emerge as a philosophical and practical alternative. The main terms of his space-philosophy follow directly from his critical principles: beneath his allegiances to personality, mind, vision, and common sense, we find him asserting the primacy of space over time, living mind over dead matter, and stability over flux.

The first thing to establish is Lewis's working definition of "space." For the most part, I find, it is accurately described by a statement made by Samuel Alexander, one of Lewis's main targets among the time-philosophers: "We then formulate the two conceptions, one of a Time which flows uniformly on and the other that of a Space immoveable: what are commonly known as Absolute Time and Absolute Space, and, so far as I can judge, the ordinary or 'common-sense' notions of Time and Space."[18] Thus Lewis says that "*Time*...is merely change or movement" (167); and "the exterior world is where 'Space' is" (435). Yet these statements tell only part of the story, for in *Time and Western Man*, Lewis very often uses these terms metaphorically, much as we have seen him use "vision" and "common sense." To him, "Space seems...by far the greater reality of the two, and Time meaningless without it" (445), not because one concept is philosophically "better" than the other, but because of the more practical consequences with which he associates them.

For Lewis the painter, the first practical advantage of space is its association with vision. The "philosophy of the eye" is a space-philosophy because of our intuitive, common sense agreement that space is accessible to vision while time is not. Like his attitudes toward personality and mind, this view of the kinship between vision and space shows in Lewis's language, which is consistently permeated by spatial and visual metaphors. The time-mind manifests itself on the *parallel* social and philosophical *planes* and there are time- and space-*views*; personalities and thought-systems are *patterned*; we must *look below the surface* of ideas to dis*cover* what is at the *bottom*. In part, of course, this usage results simply from the prevalence of such naturalized metaphors in our language. Still, Lewis might well argue, the prevalence of spatial images in English would itself affirm the primacy of space in our common sense world.

Lewis's particular affirmation of the spatial, though, is equally unmistakable in his more studied images. What we see in the world of common sense, he says, is a "picture" the time-philosophers would replace with a "moving picture" (408); his task is to "prop people's eyes open for half a minute, and my point would be perfectly clear to them: for the landscape I am describing lies all round them: or rather, the main feature of it, to which I am drawing attention, it is impossible to escape from: it is as ubiquitous as Fujiyama in a japanese print" (239). Occasionally, with the kind of backhanded flourish that characterizes the Enemy, he even spatializes time. We've seen this already in the extended metaphor describing his activity in *Men Without Art* as road-making: those "Roman" roads are crossing the "bog," the "waterlogged stretch of territory" that is "the post-war decade-and-a-half" (173). Or, in a more pointed example from *Time and Western Man*, he writes: "The world in which Advertisement dwells is a one-day world. It is necessarily a plane universe, without depth. Upon this Time lays down discontinuous entities, side by side; each day, each temporal entity, complete in itself, with no perspectives, no fundamental exterior reference at all" (28). All of these metaphors function as reminders to his readers that in our ordinary, shared picture of reality, we are surrounded by visible space.

Similarly, Lewis insists, space is intimately linked with mind. This association, too, shows in his metaphors. Thus in one particularly suggestive—and characteristic—image, he describes the mind as a "picture-gallery": "We were introduced to that extraordinary Aladdin's Cave, that paradise...*our minds:*...the magnificent private picture-gallery of its stretched-out imagery was thrown open, and we were allowed to wander in it in any direction, and to any private ends we pleased" (401). The time-philosopher complains that the "intellect 'spatialized' things" (168); Lewis the space-philosopher agrees and rejoices. For him, when we stop "spatializing" things, when we stop seeing theoretical issues visually, we also stop thinking about them. Again, Lewis does not mean by his emphasis on vision to isolate the senses from the mind; rather, he insists, mind and sense always act together in our perception of the world. And that perception—both visual and mental—is timeless: "We have overridden time to the extent of bestowing upon objects a certain timelessness. We and they have existed in a, to some extent, timeless world, in which we possessed these objects, in our fastness of memory, like gods" (412). And so the mind, too, is timeless (444). Again, a remark of Alexander's clarifies Lewis's meaning: discussing universals, he explains that they are "not timeless or eternal as being out of time, but as being free from limitation to a particular time."[19] For Lewis, thought as much as vision operates in a spatial world.

One of the most important characteristics of this spatial world—with its ties to the visual, the common sense, the mind, and thus the personality—is that in it, Lewis believes, we can maintain a clear distinction, a clear opposition, between a dead material world and the living mind. In one way or another, he argues, the time-philosophers have sought to dissolve this distinction and destroy the autonomy of both matter and mind. On the one hand, the simple but vivid perceptual object of common sense disappears, dissolved by time into a series of slightly different objects. The "disintegration of the world-picture of 'commonsense,' " he explains, has been "effected by the introduction of private and subjective time-systems, by the breaking up of the composite space of the assembled senses into an independent space of touch, a space of sight, a visceral space, and so forth: the conversion of 'the thing' into a series of discrete apparitions" (426). To Lewis the painter, far more is lost than gained by this conceptual change. He prefers an external world of dead, relatively changeless matter—"the ordered picture of the classic world, and equally the instinctive picture we inherit from untold generations of men" (426).

On the other hand, Lewis argues, the "*conscious* life of will and intellect" disappears, replaced by "some sort of *unconscious* life" (318). In a metaphor that reminds us of his Enemy role (but without the Enemy's invective), he explains what has happened:

> A long time ago a battle was engaged between the *Unconscious* and the *Conscious*: and we have been witnessing the ultimate triumph of the *Unconscious* of recent years. The *Individual* and that part of him that is *not* individual, also joined issue: for the civil war was taken up, in the interior economy of the personality, sympathetically, at once. Inside us also the crowds were pitted against the Individual, the Unconscious against the Conscious, the 'emotional' against the 'intellectual,' the Many against the One. So it is that *the Subject* is not gently reasoned out of, but violently hounded from, every cell of the organism. (320)

Here again is the model of the warring opposites within, the conflicting diagonals of the Horseman drawing—in terms that make it clear how Lewis recognizes his "most essential ME": the One, the Individual, the single self, the Conscious. In insisting that change is the primary characteristic of reality, the time–philosophers substitute for the single (conscious) self a series of "distinct, intermittent *selves*" (364), "a multiplicity of chronologic selves" (*MWA* 97), controlled, moreover, by unconscious forces. Of course Lewis deplores this kind of fragmentation. In the world of the time-cult, both object and subject are dissolved into fragments, mind and matter merge into each other, and our power as thinkers is abandoned. In his space world, he claims, matter stays dead and we retain our primacy.

Behind all of Lewis's convictions about the advantages of space over time lies one more central belief. Just as time means change, space means stability; and, Lewis insists, we have much more to gain by emphasizing stability than we do by emphasizing change. In this insistence he again stands in clear opposition to the time-philosophers, who hold that "space-time *possesses no quality at all, except motion*" (441, Lewis's emphasis); "For all practical purposes, 'time' and 'motion' are identical, as we find them applied in the philosophies under consideration" (213). For them, reality is flux. Our world constantly changes, they say; if we think things are ever stable, we are deceiving ourselves. But, Lewis challenges, "As a *realist*, in the most sensible acceptance of the word, and as of course we all are, whatever we are merely called, what is the strongest impression you receive from the external world, or nature?" The answer should be obvious: "Certainly stability, I, as a realist, should say: decidedly not one of change. For change you have to look, to wait for, you have to detect it" (211). (Notice here his use of first- and second-person pronouns and their implicit appeal to common sense.) We don't expect our surroundings to remain identical, but we are rarely conscious of gradual changes and often notice sudden differences with surprise; we know that we are getting older, but ordinarily we are not aware of our pulse-beat or the slow changes in our bodies.

To represent the time-cult's view, Lewis offers the example of Bertrand Russell, who argues that the fading of our wallpaper proves that every day the paper itself is *essentially* different: "'The assumption,'" Russell writes, "'that there is a constant entity, the wall-paper, which "has" these various colours at various times, is a piece of gratuitous metaphysics'" (427). But for Lewis, on the contrary, that "assumption" is entirely appropriate, while the notion that we

Space and Stability

are ordinarily conscious of an all-encompassing flux is "gratuitous metaphysics." In holding that our wall is covered with the *same* paper in January as in December, Lewis reminds us, we are not denying that change occurs: "Every one knows that the wall-paper on their wall will fade... It has just as much 'permanence' ascribed to it by commonsense as indeed it is likely to have. There it is, after all, day after day... It *is* 'permanent' in the sense in which we metaphysicians of the mere world of 'common-sense' mean permanent" (428). This common sense permanence is the same as continuity: in Lewis's space-world, continuity and stability can be taken for granted.

The same is true of our sense of ourselves. As he explains in *The Art of Being Ruled*, the time-cult emphasizes the discontinuity between different temporal versions of the self, while he values the continuity: "The more highly developed an individual is, or the more civilized a race, this *discontinuity* tends to disappear. The 'personality' is born. Continuity, in the individual as in the race, is the diagnostic of a civilized condition. If you can break this personal continuity in an individual, you can break *him*. For *he* is that continuity" (*ABR* 229). We all know that we change, but, he insists, we still primarily think of ourselves as continuous, as single entities. Lewis requires personality, and ' "personality," as we use that term, is nothing but stability" (*TWM* 365).

When he opposes stability to flux, then, Lewis does not posit an absolute permanence; he argues that stability is more important than change. Traditionally, he points out, the question has been whether "there was anything *besides*, behind, or over and above the Flux, or whether, on the other hand, there was nothing but that" (247). The difference between Lewis's view and the time-cult's is one of emphasis: just as we can call a glass half-full or half-empty, we can value either stability or change. Where the time-philosopher holds that change negates permanence, Lewis sees permanence—or continuity—as enclosing and dominating change. Any mind aware of its own direct experience, he believes, must admit the priority of its perception of stability.

More is at issue in this question of stability, though. In Lewis's eyes a world-view that embraces the stable rather than the changing—a space-world rather than a time-world—is ethically superior, both on the level of the individual and on the level of society. He asks, "In a man's way of regarding himself, it is socially of capital importance that he should regard himself as *one person*. Is it not? That is surely beyond any possible question. It is only in that way that you can hope to ground in him a responsibility towards all 'his' acts" (364). Just as the critical stance of impersonal objectivity encourages irresponsibility, so too, he believes, by emphasizing changes we undermine our sense of direct responsibility for our ideas and actions. If I am encouraged to see myself as a "different person" every day, I might not feel it necessary to behave today as if I will be held accountable tomorrow for what I have done.

Lewis identifies this effect in his criticism of T. S. Eliot's "pseudoism": the "disintegration into a multiplicity of chronologic selves" that Eliot claims allows him to avoid "providing an authoritative answer to the no doubt more and more puzzled questions of the crowd of ardent followers... on the grounds that he is no longer the *same* Mr. Eliot, but another, so cannot possibly know what *The Waste Land* Tom planned and intended." Even worse, according to the Enemy, "if you marched up to him five minutes after he had 'released' some 'outburst of words' in this manner, and exclaimed, 'Ha ha! Got you this time my fine fellow! What did you mean when you wrote *that*—and *that*!' he would be quite capable of replying with the utmost detachment: '*Who* wrote *what*? I am sorry, I am entirely unable to answer you. I have not the least idea!'"

(*MWA* 97). What is here literary irresponsibility marks a dangerous pattern, a pattern Lewis sees in many other places. As he argues in *The Art of Being Ruled*, "The popular upshot of the Relativity theory [with its emphasis on 'the great god flux']...is to shake people's confidence everywhere in their own opinion, [and] it enables them to circumvent other people's" (401). The time-philosophers' emphasis on flux encourages ethical disorder, Lewis believes, while his valuing of stability promotes a sense of individual ethical responsibility.[20]

On the level of society, stability is a crucial value for Lewis for somewhat different reasons: first, that only in a stable world can artists create and thinkers think; second, that only with stability—with order—will we have peace instead of war. After the Great War, these two convictions surface often in Lewis's books, sometimes alone, sometimes intertwined; they are a major source of continuity in his long and various career. Consider these remarks:

> I would remind you that all that I have written in the course of my career betrays an almost morbid love of order.[21]

> All any true scientist or true artist asks is to be given the opportunity, without interference, indifferent to glory, to *work*. (*ABR* 121)

> You need go no further than the very practical and unsentimental fact, or facts, of the most vital interests of an artist being ruined by orgies of violence and 'action,' to understand my attitude, if you look for personal motive in it. It takes a long time without interruption to do anything worth doing in an art or science, and that...the accursed philosophy we are discussing denies us. You could not describe such opinions as 'selfish,' seeing that the interests represented are identical

> with everybody else's in this respect, except those of such as make money or acquire power by means of war of all sorts. (*Paleface* 248)

> How then is bloodshed or violence to be regarded? Essentially as an excess, nothing more.... As measure is the principle of all true art, and as art is an enemy of all excess, so it is along aesthetic lines that the solution of this problem [of violence] should be sought rather than along moral (or police) lines, or humanitarian ones. The soberness, measure, and order that reigns in all the greatest productions of art is the thing on which it is most useful to fix the mind in considering this problem. (*ABR* 66)

And finally, one of the clearest expressions of Lewis's own sense of the genesis of his beliefs, from *Hitler*:

> I do not write this book *from choice*, for instance: I would far rather, if it rested with me, be engaged in scientific research, or in artistic creation. Ever since in the War, where I served on the Western Front with the Artillery, I was first under fire, there are certain questions I have asked of life which it would never have occurred to me to ask before. The War, as you are aware, went on and on, and these questions in the end *asked themselves* as it were, with a more obstinate urgency every day....
>
> A state of emergency came to appear for me, as for most soldiers, a permanent thing. Unlike, I daresay, most of my companions, I realized that something in this 'storm of steel' required explaining...And since that time it is naturally easier to convince me of the imminence of such a condition or of its being a condition inherent in the very nature of our life....I, figuratively, have never smiled again. At all events, I have never grinned to order....

Space and Stability

So, under the compulsion of such emergency conditions, values change, and we are forced to admit arguments which, in other circumstances, we might regard as unsound. In brief, we are compelled, I think, to lay more stress upon what is pragmatical and *useful*, and less upon what is perhaps eternally true. It is a case of *force majeure*.[22]

When we remember Lewis's initial premise that "a philosophy is always a thing that helps a man to live and to enhance his powers" (*TWM* 364), the line of reasoning that connects a space-philosophy with ethical and social order and thus with peace (in opposition to the time-philosophy, disorder, and war) seems somewhat less extraordinary than it might otherwise. And when we remember the experience of many British soldiers in World War I and the wide-spread pacifism it engendered, we can more easily understand the line of reasoning that begins with the personal "I found myself in the blood-bath of the Great War, and in that situation reflected on the vanity of violence" (*ABR* 136) and ends with a philosophy valuing stability.

Space, for Lewis, implies vision, mind, personality, stability, responsibility, order, and peace. A philosophy based on space is a practical philosophy, an aesthetic philosophy, a philosophy an artist or a thinker can live by. So, he writes,

> Regarding mind as Timeless, it is more at home, we find, with Space. And as stability is the manifest goal of all organic life, and the thing from which we all of us have most to gain, we see no use, in the first place, and in the second see no theoretic advantage, in this fusion [of space and time]. For the objective world most useful to us, and what may be the same thing, most 'beautiful,' and therefore with most *meaning*, and that is further to say in a word with most *reality*, we require a Space distinct from Time. (444)

The Enemy Opposite

And just a paragraph later he concludes, "Space seems to us by far the greater reality of the two, and Time meaningless without it. Time as change was the 'Nothing' of the Greek, and it is ours" (445). Space—its final important value—saves us from nothingness.

The Berkeleyan Paradox: Influence Acknowledged

In *Paleface,* noting that "it has a good deal of bearing on what I everywhere have to say," Lewis explains how he sees himself in the context of the history of philosophy:

> Extreme concreteness and extreme definition is for me a necessity.... Against the mysticism of the mathematician I find myself with Bishop Berkeley (though, of course, he is claimed by the enemies of the concrete, strangely enough): I am on the side of commonsense, as against abstraction, as was Berkeley....
>
> To *solidify, to make concrete, to give definition to*— that is my profession: to 'despise the fluid'... and 'to postulate permanence'... to crystallize that which (otherwise) flows away, to concentrate the diffuse, to turn to ice that which is liquid and mercurial—that certainly describes my occupation, and the tendency of all that I think. (253–54)

We have seen how he develops the terms of his position; now we must see how he understands this relationship with Bishop Berkeley, one of the few thinkers whose influence Lewis ever directly embraces.[23]

At the base of Lewis's philosophical dispute with the time-cult, he tells us in *Time and Western Man,* is a paradoxical contrast between the abstractness of the "realist" time-philosophers and the concreteness of "such an 'idealism' as that of Berkeley, Bradley or Bosanquet." He explains, "If I added, as is indeed the case, that such an extreme idealist doctrine as that of Berkeley...stood even fanatically for the *concrete*...the reader who had not given much attention to philosophy would be completely mystified, no doubt, as indeed Berkeley foresaw would be the case when he first launched his doctrine. But that is a paradox that it is extremely important to lay hold of at the outset" (*TWM* 169). Although Berkeley's world, Lewis says, "is too dim in its mentalism, and dark, definitely, sometimes—and the disproportion of his theologic bias is a great obstacle ultimately," still it is "one of the best of all possible philosophic worlds" (480). Lewis claims a place in the tradition of Bishop Berkeley's absolute idealism: in Berkeley's *Principles of Human Knowledge,* he finds several of his own central terms and one of his own characteristic structures of thought, a complex set of oppositions joined by paradox.

For Berkeley, nothing exists without the mind: "All those bodies which compose the mighty frame of the world, have not any subsistence without a mind...their being is to be perceived or known; that consequently so long as they are not actually perceived by me, or do not exist in my mind, or that of any other created spirit, they must either have no existence at all, or else subsist in the mind of some Eternal Spirit."[24] In this he is an idealist. Yet he insists that such idealism implies a vivid, concrete, and particularized world—the world we are directly given by our senses. "Whatever we see, feel, hear, or any wise conceive or understand, remains as secure as ever, and is as real as ever," he explains. "We are not for having any man turn *sceptic,* and disbelieve his senses; on the contrary, we give them all the stress and assurance imaginable." The world Berkeley sees is not an imaginary one, in spite of its dependence on mind: "The ideas of sense are more strong, lively, and *distinct* than those of the imagination; they have likewise a steadiness, order, and coherence, and are not excited at random, as those which are the effects of human wills often are." So in this, Berkeley's idealism is concrete. The two aspects of this argument may look contradictory to some—as they did, for example, to Samuel Johnson—but to Berkeley they go hand in hand. "Some truths," he says, "there are so near and obvious to the mind that a man need only open his eyes to see them."[25]

Quoting this last remark, Lewis suggests how he has adopted Berkeley's vision: Berkeley "clings, and I think successfully, to his paradox: thus 'a man need only *open his eyes* to see' that there is nothing there except what his mind puts there; and so forth. This last scrap of quotation will serve to show the reader, I think, how berkeleyan idealism is by no means incompatible with the kind of vivid realism that is being advocated in these pages" (*TWM* 474). Lewis sees Berkeley as a model for preserving what Lewis once calls a "purer duality" (209)—not simply the distinction between mind and matter, but that between live, causative mind and dead, unthinking matter. For both, mind only is alive and creative and real. And for both, matter is by contrast unreal. Lewis alters Berkeley's emphasis slightly when he speaks of the unreality of matter: for Lewis, matter is unreal because it is unthinking, not because it is unthought or unperceived. He explains that he shares the view of Berkeley and of traditional science that matter is "a collection of 'unthinking things.'" But, he asks, "What is so *unreal* as a collection of 'unthinking things,' of dead, inanimate matter?" (473). "In this sense it is argued here that the entire physical world is strictly unreal"; the "deadness" of a thing "is the guarantee, as it were, of its *unreality;* nothing so thoroughly as that secures the ascendancy of 'the mind'" (184).

Like Berkeley, in these beliefs Lewis is an idealist. And at the same time, like Berkeley, he sees his idealism as concrete—as paradoxically describing a solid, vivid, sensual world. In his comment on Berkeley's paradox, Lewis continues: "For he implores you merely to 'open your eyes' and to *see* that the world is not real in the sense you had thought: the wider you open them the more you will perceive that this is the case. And yet in another sense for that very reason the more real it will be" (474–75). In the unreality of the material world lies its own kind of reality. Again, Lewis juxtaposes the two terms: "If there is one thing more than another that is essential to provide a 'sense of reality'—our sheer sensation that there is something *real* there before us—it is the deadness, the stolid thickness and deadness, of nature.... What is most sensationally 'real' (as ultimately it is, perhaps more than anything else, demonstrably unreal) is the *deadness* of nature, once more" (*TWM* 212). It is this conviction that provides a context for understanding Lewis when he says such things as that "we have lost our sense of reality," that "what we have in the place of our lost sense" is "our 'subjectivity' " (*Paleface* 100): to merge mind and matter is to destroy them both, to replace a real world with an unreal, subjective one. Only by regarding mind as live and matter as dead—mind as real and matter as unreal—can we maintain both the creative supremacy of our intelligence and the vivid concreteness of the perceptual world. In contrast with the fluctuating, evolving worlds of the modern abstract realists, a conceptual world like Berkeley's is stable and intelligible. Only an idealist philosophy seems to Lewis to allow the "vivid realism" of the classical vision.

Lewis's endorsement of Berkeley is not only—or even most importantly—a philosophical conviction. It is also an aesthetic choice—a preference for a world view that most persuasively expresses his *vision* of life. As he suggests in *Men Without Art,* "To return to the robustest artist: the intellect athletically enjoys itself in the midst of matter, and is not afraid of objective things because it has the power to model them and compose a world of its own out of objective substances" (231). Some of his most direct statements of his own beliefs show us in their uncharacteristically poetic language how Lewis's idealism coincides with his artistic sense of our place in the world. He writes, for example:

> To make things *endure* (to make something *solid,* relatively indestructible, like a pyramid) is of course, as well, a sort of magic, and a more difficult one, than to make things *vanish,* change and disintegrate (though that is very remarkable too). Of these opposite functions of magic we daily perform one, in our sense-perception activity, better than magic could. This function we justly call 'creativeness'.... The objects of our perception, with their mystifying independence and air of self-sufficiency... are far more uncanny than the unity we experience in our subjective experience. These strange *things,* that stand out against a background of mystery, with their air of being *eternal,* and which really appear to be 'caused' by nothing that we can hold and fix, and from which we can see them being actually produced, are far stranger than we are, or more brutally and startlingly strange.... But these 'objects' are the finished product of our perceptive faculty, they are the result, as we are accustomed to explain it, of the organizing activity of our minds. (*TWM* 372–73)

Like an artist, each of us creates our own world, shaping the dead matter around us into amazing images.

Here, I think, we see one of Lewis's fundamental decisions about which of two warring opposites represents his "most essential ME"—and, to my mind, one of the things that makes him such a powerful exemplar of the transition into the modern world. *"The illusion must... be our 'real,'"* he insists (*TWM* 403, my emphasis). For "we are surface-creatures only, and by nature are meant to be only that, if there is any meaning in nature." Through perception and imagination, we create the surface of the things around us, and those surfaces are more significant to our lives than

The Enemy Opposite

anything we did not create could be. "We are surface-creatures," he reminds us, "and the 'truths' from beneath the surface contradict our values. It is among the flowers and leaves that our lot is cast, and the roots, however 'interesting,' are not so ultimate for us" (*TWM* 402).

Curiously, his reference here is to Nietzsche, as we can see from a revealing passage in *The Art of Being Ruled*: "What [Nietzsche] said instead was:—

> Oh, those Greeks! They knew how to *live;* for that purpose it is necessary to keep bravely to the surface, the fold and the skin, to worship appearance, to believe in forms, tones, and words, in the whole Olympus of Appearance! And are we not coming back precisely to this point, we daredevils of the spirit, who have scaled the highest and most dangerous peak of contemporary thought and have looked around us from it, have *looked down* from it!

Had Nietzsche from the first followed these instructions himself, should we ever have heard of him? Yet his advice was not wholly perfidious. For it was not unlike a miner arriving at the surface from a very deep and uncomfortable pit, and saying, 'Ah! how pleasant the sun is! Give me the good old surface of this rotten earth. Never you go down *there!*' " (126–27). And some time later Lewis draws the point even more explicitly: "That these things *on the surface* are different to what they are in the depths or the interior, and that we are *surface creatures,* is the truth that Nietzsche insisted on so wisely. All the meaning of life is of a superficial sort, of course: there is no meaning except on the surface" (*ABR* 268). Modern science and realist philosophy may be right in their way—our chairs and tables may indeed be made of invisible, constantly moving particles, and our images of them may indeed change at every instant—but the less exact vision of everyday perception is still our *native* vision. Berkeley's "gimcrack world of

The Berkeleyan Paradox: Influence Acknowledged

facades" is "an extremist philosophy for *surface-creatures*" (*TWM* 480)—and so it is an appropriate philosophy for us.

This kind of statement makes it clear once again how much Lewis sees a philosophy as something to live by rather than as an attempt to describe reality accurately. "So," he says, "with bridle and bit we ride the phantoms of sense, as though to the manner born. Or rather it would be more descriptive of our actual experience to say that, camped somnolently, in a relative repose of a god-like sort, upon the surface of this nihilism, we regard ourselves as at rest, with our droves of objects—trees, houses, hills—grouped round us" (*TWM* 473). Over the nihilism explored by the time-philosophers—"the 'truths' from beneath the surface"—Lewis chooses for his "real" the "illusion" of the surface.

The Enemy Versus Henri Bergson:
Influence Denied

Lewis makes it clear that he regards Bergson as central to the time-cult. As he explains, "Bergson's doctrine of Time is the creative source of the time-philosophy. It is he more than any other single figure that is responsible for the main intellectual characteristics of the world we live in, and the implicit debt of almost all contemporary philosophy to him is immense" (*TWM* 166). Yet despite such statements, Lewis maintains a curious distance from this philosopher. He rarely turns his formidable critical attention directly upon Bergson; most of the time, he deals instead with other artists and thinkers—George Bernard Shaw and George Sorel in *The Art of Being Ruled;* D. H. Lawrence and the behavioral psychologist Louis Berman in *Paleface;* Oswald Spengler, Bertrand Russell, Samuel Alexander, and Alfred North Whitehead in *Time and Western Man*—who, Lewis believes, owe to Bergson their central concepts. Rather than explain Bergson's views himself, Lewis is likely to reproduce the comments of one of these "disciples"—and allow the quotation both to present Bergson's idea and to suggest his own opposing idea. Thus he quotes Alexander: " 'We are, as it were, *to think ourselves into Time. I call this taking Time seriously.* Our guides of the seventeenth century desert us here. Besides the infinite, two things entranced their intellects. One was Space or extension; the other was Mind. But, entranced by mind or thought, they neglected Time. *Perhaps it is Professor Bergson in our day who has been the first philosopher to take Time seriously*' " (*TWM*

The Enemy Versus Henri Bergson: Influence Denied

222; first emphasis Alexander's, second Lewis's).[26] Such a statement illustrates Lewis's argument that the problem of time and the influence of Bergson are basic to modern philosophy; and it neatly endorses his opposition between time on the one hand and space and mind on the other. But this kind of quotation functions only very indirectly as part of a critique of Bergson himself.

Where Lewis usually quotes abundantly from the works he criticizes, moreover, he quotes Bergson himself only a handful of times. He devotes a very short chapter to him in *The Art of Being Ruled,* where he mentions the *Introduction to Metaphysics* and the *Essai sur les données immediates de la conscience* (translated as *Time and Free Will*), but this chapter—"The Great God Flux"—is remarkably evasive, offering only a few quotations with minimal commentary and this summary: "Briefly, the root impulse in Bergson's philosophy was a rendering back to LIFE, magiscular abstraction of a feverish chaos, all that the mind had taken from her to build into forms and concepts" (401). He does assert here that "Bergson is indeed the arch enemy of every impulse having its seat in the apparatus of vision, and requiring a concrete world. Bergson is the enemy of the Eye...I can hardly imagine any way in which he is not against every form of intelligent life" (403); but he does not clearly explain how this is so (and, too, this book appeared before he had announced or defined his own position as philosopher of the eye).

Even in *Time and Western Man,* a book that could be defined as an extended critique of Bergson's influence on modern culture, where Lewis's primary task is to examine the time-philosophy itself, he devotes only one brief section, "Space and Time," to explaining in very general terms what Bergson understands by space and duration. (Again, all of my quotations in this section come from *Time and Western Man,* except where I note otherwise.) This section is unremarkable insofar as it follows the pattern of most of

The Enemy Opposite

the Enemy criticism, mixing often accurate, reasonable analyses with a strong and often unreasonable polemical bias. What *is* unusual in this summary is that Lewis fails to identify his source. Here as elsewhere in this book, his main exhibits come from Bergson's *Creative Evolution;* but Lewis never tells us so. (Indeed, that title appears in *Time and Western Man* only once and then merely to gloss a remark made by William James.) If we pull on the loose thread of this odd omission, we will see the text unravel—to reveal a central instance of one of the basic structures of the Enemy criticism: Lewis defining himself through hidden opposition.

One effect of this omitted title is to separate Lewis from Bergson. When we look further, we discover him doing this even more explicitly. "The influence of Bergson," he explains,

> went down beneath the wave of formal enthusiasm that immediately preceded the War. In the arts that movement brought imagination back once more, banishing the naturalist dogmas that had obtained for fifty or sixty years. Impressionism was driven out and the great ideals of structure and of formal significance were restored, to painting and sculpture, at all events.... There was a very powerful reaction in France against all that Bergson represented. But the War and einsteinian physics have turned the scales once more. There is naturally no question of reinstating Bergson; there are plenty of others of the same sort, but with a more up-to-date equipment, without having recourse to him. (156)

Here Lewis reminds us that he is a painter, and that as one of the leaders of this formal reaction away from impressionism and toward imagination, he judges with authority. In the context of the arts, Bergson becomes a figure from the past, a dead figure who is "naturally" not to be brought back to life. But even as a philosopher, Lewis tells us a few pages later, Bergson is dead: "By students of philosophy Bergson is still read, but by no one else. Even by these he is read as little as possible, I should imagine. Until I began my scrutiny of the contemporary time-philosophy I knew him very little" (167). This statement—which introduces a discussion of Bergson's influence on Whitehead and others—is even more personal than the last. Lewis unambiguously labels Bergson as a writer who is of limited and purely historical interest.

But if with these remarks Lewis dismisses Bergson as insignificant, at the same time he assails him with invective at every opportunity. In his analyses of other philosophers, Lewis's tone is generally serious, moving only occasionally into mild sarcasm. When he refers to Bergson, though, we hear the unrestrained voice of the Enemy. Bergson, he says, "is the perfect philosophic ruffian, of the darkest and most forbidding description: and he pulls every emotional lever on which he can lay his hands" (174). "He discovered nothing; he interpreted science; and he gave it an extremely biassed interpretation, to say the least" (161); his metaphysic is "pretentious" (27) and insincerely optimistic (344). Bergson and Nietzsche were "popular purveyors to the enlightened Everyman" (309). "Until the coming of Bergson, [the vulgar mercantile class] could not have found a philosophical intelligence sufficiently degraded to take their money and do, philosophically, their dirty work. The unique distinction of that personage is that he was the first servant of the great industrial caste-mind arriving on the golden crest of the wave of scientific progress" (214). And this is just a sample. Whenever Lewis's analysis draws near to Bergson or the "sickly ecstasies of *élan vital*" (216), the Enemy emerges to kick what Lewis has told us is a dead horse.

Now we can only wonder what it is about Bergson that has provoked such behavior. Of all the important philosophers he criticizes, Bergson is the only one whose seriousness, sincerity, and occasional virtues Lewis refuses to recognize. We find a clue to what is going on, I think, in a remark I have already quoted, where Lewis says, "Until I began my scrutiny of the contemporary time-philosophy I knew him very little." For this is certainly untrue. Early in those prewar years when Bergson's influence was giving way to a new spirit of formalism, Lewis lived in Paris and attended his lectures. In a letter written over twenty years after *Time and Western Man,* Lewis describes this period: "Paris, where I went soon after Rugby, was my University. There I followed Bergson's lectures at the College de France, and shared the philosophical studies of friends of mine then at the Ecole Normale.... Bergson was an excellent lecturer, dry and impersonal. I began by embracing his evolutionary system. From that I passed to Renouvier and thus to Kant. When one is young *on fait des bêtises, quoi!*"[27] Lewis wrote this letter to explain his qualifications to teach a philosophy course based on *Time and Western Man;* as he recognizes, such first-hand experience does increase his authority as a critic of philosophy. But in *Time and Western Man* itself, as we have seen, Lewis makes no such claim. Nor does he acknowledge here his unquestionable acquaintance with Bergson's ideas through the early enthusiasm of T. E. Hulme, who had explicated and translated Bergson in 1911 and 1912, not long before the years of his and Lewis's close association.[28]

It has long been recognized that Lewis's theory of satire comes directly out of Bergson's work on comedy. But it has only recently been noticed that Bergson's influence on Lewis goes still further.[29] And no one has yet demonstrated quite how much—and in what ways—his space-philosophy owes to this "perfect philosophic ruffian."[30] When we look at Bergson with Lewis in mind, *Creative Evolution* emerges as a hidden model—a model Lewis mirrors, inverts, and conceals throughout the philosophical arguments of *Time and Western Man*.

As I have said, aside from the summary in "Space and Time," Lewis spends little time directly scrutinizing Bergson, but he does do so in three significant passages: three places where Lewis allows us to pass through his argument into Bergson's and thus begin to see the relationship between the two. He handles each one differently; the less he has to hide from us, the more openly he engages his opponent. Though each seems at first glance simply to be an apt illustration for Lewis's point, these passages turn out on closer examination to be traces of a hidden influence. They show us where the two texts touch, where the model breaks through the surface of the Enemy's apparently autonomous antagonism, and Bergson is revealed as the opposite against whom Lewis has defined himself as a philosopher.

The first of these passages (first in order of complexity, though last in the book) has to do with the nature of art. Lewis is analyzing the aesthetics of the time-cult through the example of Henri Brémond's *La Poésie Pure*. Brémond quotes Bergson as his authority, so Lewis reproduces for us two of the passages Brémond uses. These come from *Time and Free Will*, not *Creative Evolution*, and their source is identified, so that although Lewis does distance himself from Bergson by working through Brémond, he also confronts him openly. Lewis dissects these two passages in exactly the same way as he does his specimens from other time-minds. Here is the first passage: " 'The word which is sharply outlined, the brutal word, which is the receptacle of all that is *stable,* all that is *common, and consequently impersonal,* in human experience, crushes or at all events covers over the more delicate and fugitive impressions of our individual conscience' " (190, Lewis's emphasis). And the second: " '(The object of art) is to send to sleep the active or rather the recalcitrant forces of our personality, and thereby to induce in us a condition of perfect docility, in which we realize the idea suggested to us, in which we sympathize with the sentiment expressed. In the methods employed by the artist you will discover, in an attenuated form, refined and in some way spiritualized, the methods by which in a general way the hypnotic trance is induced' " (191).[31] For Bergson, Lewis points out, the clearly defined word is brutal, "and whether you are a man or a word, to be called 'brutal' is not the nicest thing that can happen to you; and it is quite certain that Bergson is aware of that, and that he uses it to prejudice us against the word he is attacking" (191).

Moreover, Lewis objects that Bergson contradicts himself on the role of personality: in the first passage he seems to wish to rescue the personality from the brutal, stable word; in the second passage he wants to put that personality to sleep in the interests of more intense experience. Lewis assumes that the "more delicate and fugitive impressions of our individual conscience" can only be the same as "the recalcitrant forces of our personality," for surely, he says, the "essence of a personality, or of an 'individual consciousness,' is that it should be *stable*" (192). And in any case, Lewis argues, to send that stable force to sleep can hardly enhance our "individuality": "If it is reduced to 'a condition of perfect docility,' in which anything that is 'suggested' to it it accommodates, in which it sympathizes ecstatically with its dear hypnotist—that may or may not be very agreeable for it; but we certainly cannot claim, except with our tongue in our cheek, that, if we are the hypnotist, we are liberating it from oppression, or that we are enhancing its 'individuality' " (192). These passages, Lewis concludes, have enabled him to give us "a sidelight on the particular system of intellectual fraud practiced by Bergson" (193).

In this argument we see Lewis's characteristic mixture of misrepresentation of details (for Bergson, the "individual conscience" is *not* the same as the personality[32]) and justice to the total argument. What we must notice now, though, is how far Lewis goes in agreeing with Bergson in this instance. For once, Lewis himself admits the similarities in their views: "It is *art* that relieves this oppression of the crushing weight of the 'stable' world; breaks it up and uncovers the intense reality. That is M. Bergson's account of art, and it would also in effect be mine. But he goes on to explain that its function is to 'send to sleep' the resistance of the active personality. Again I think he is quite right" (191–92). Even this degree of agreement is a little surprising in light of Lewis's usually vitriolic treatment of Bergson, but then in this matter Lewis is in his home territory: as a novelist and a painter, he knows more about art than Bergson does, so he can confidently show us where Bergson is right and where he goes wrong.

But their agreement goes even further, as the language of Bergson's passages makes clear. These statements make good examples for Lewis precisely because his own terms are so nearly the same as Bergson's. For Lewis, too, language is stable and impersonal and belongs to "our common world in which we all meet and communicate" (191). It is not brutal, of course; in Lewis's eyes, as he tells us again and again, these qualities are virtues. Aside from the disagreement implied by this value term and their different attitudes toward personality, then, Lewis comes close to echoing his former teacher. Certainly he has adopted Bergson's assumption that language, stability, impersonality or objectivity, and the individual personality form a natural family belonging to the world of common sense. Their difference here is simply that Lewis embraces what Bergson has rejected.

We see the same kind of relationship even more clearly in the second passage (the first in Lewis's text), which appears immediately after Lewis has called Bergson the chief source of the time-philosophy and explained that until recently he had known him very little. Mentioning that it is indexed as

The Enemy Opposite

"the apogee of the sensible object," Lewis quotes a long passage of Bergson's that, he says, "will give a hint at least of what my argument signifies where it relates to him":

> "For the ancients, indeed, time is theoretically negligible, because the duration of a thing only manifests the degradation of its essence; it is with this motionless essence that science has to deal. Change being only the effort of a form toward its own realization, the realization is all that it concerns us to know. No doubt the realization is never complete; it is this that ancient philosophy expresses by saying that we do not perceive form without matter. But if we consider the changing object at a certain essential moment, at its apogee, we may say that there it just touches its intelligible form. This intelligible form, this ideal, and, so to speak, limiting form, our science seizes upon. And possessing in this the gold-piece, it holds eminently the small money, which we call becoming or change. This change is less than being. The knowledge that would take it for object, supposing such knowledge were possible, would be less than science.
>
> But, for a science that places all the moments of time in the same rank, that admits no essential moment, no culminating point, no apogee, change is no longer a diminution of essence, duration is not a dilution of eternity." (167)[33]

This passage comes from *Creative Evolution,* but significantly, Lewis neglects to tell us so. He is frequently careless about his citations, but this is the only time he fails to identify one of his major exhibits with more than a remark about how it is indexed. Such a lapse is indeed "a hint at least" of the relationship between Lewis and Bergson.

What this passage signifies as it relates to Lewis's argument is that once again Lewis has taken over Bergson's categories, accepting what Bergson discards, rejecting what

Bergson endorses. This time the issues are change and stability, subject and object. Lewis follows Bergson in regarding as central this opposition between the modern and the classical world views based on their scientific and metaphysical attitudes toward time and change. Like "the ancients" Lewis regards change as negligible; his "rounded *thing* of common-sense" is the "apogee or perfection" of "classical science" (168). (In fact, earlier in *Time and Western Man* Lewis has suggested the same metaphor and pun: "Time for the bergsonian or relativist... is the glorification of the life-of-the-moment, with no reference beyond itself and no absolute or universal value; only so much value as is conveyed in the famous proverb, *Time is money*. It is the *argent comptant* [ready money] of literal life, in an inflexibly fluid Time" [27].) Bergson's description illuminates for us what Lewis means when he claims to stand for the classical world: if Lewis insists at times that this kind of opposition is inaccurate, that "the age of Plato swarmed with empirical, sensationalist philosophers, from Protagoras downwards" (158), he still consistently adopts Bergson's generalization as his working definition. At one point, for example, Lewis argues, "The world of classical 'common-sense'—the world of the Greek, the world of the Schoolman—is the world of nature, too, and is a very ancient one" (186). Moreover, Bergson's description suggests that what Lewis means by space and stability is much the same thing as what Bergson means by the classical ideal; if time and change stand against this ideal, space and stability stand for it.

When we look further in *Creative Evolution* to see how Bergson would prefer that this classical "object" be described, we find him offering what turns out to be a very revealing metaphor—revealing not only because of what it shows us about Bergson, but also because both Alexander and Lewis use similar but significantly different metaphors. According to Bergson, the natural "mechanism of our ordinary knowledge"—of "perception, intellection, language"—"is of a cinematographical kind." "Suffice it to say that the intellect represents becoming as a series of states, each of which is homogeneous with itself and consequently does not change." Ordinarily, he believes, we conceive of movement by breaking it into individual static states: "We take snapshots, as it were, of the passing reality." In this tendency we are like the Greeks, who, Bergson explains, "trusted to nature, trusted the natural propensity of the mind, trusted language above all"; and, like them, "we end in the philosophy of Ideas when we apply the cinematographical mechanism of the intellect to the analysis of the real." Finally, he argues, the difference between ancient philosophy and the procedures of modern science (remember that for Bergson modern science is still nineteenth-century mechanism) is one of *degree,* not kind:

> *It is the same cinematographical mechanism in both cases,* but it reaches a precision in the second that it cannot have in the first. Of the gallop of a horse our eye perceives chiefly a characteristic, essential or rather schematic attitude, a form that appears to radiate over a whole period and so fill up a time of gallop. It is this attitude that sculpture has fixed on the frieze of the Parthenon. But instantaneous photography isolates any moment; it puts them all in the same rank, and thus the gallop of a horse spreads out for it into as many successive attitudes as it wishes, instead of massing itself into a single attitude, which is supposed to flash out in a privileged moment and to illuminate a whole period. (my emphasis)

But even the cinema does not recognize the flux between frames, and for Bergson, this limitation is the failure shared by the intellect, ordinary perception, modern science, and classical metaphysics. Neither the sculptured image of classical art nor the succession of images in film is for him an adequate vision of the true nature of change. Instead, he believes, we must place ourselves inside the moving reality to grasp its essence.[34]

In a different context (describing the "singular universal"), Alexander offers a metaphor similar enough to point to the blind spot in Bergson's analogy. Where Bergson treats the snapshot and the sculpture as images of the same kind, Alexander emphasizes the difference between a photograph and a painting: "We may next take a more highly organized individual, say a person whose life may be regarded as arranged on a certain plan. . . . It is such a plan of a man's personality which an artistic portrait endeavours to express, whereas a photograph gives only a picture of the man at a passing moment, unless by artistry or technique the hardness of the momentary outlines may be softened and the photograph approximate to a portrait."[35] To portray the essence of a personality, a painter combines all changing moments into a single unmoving image. The art image, the sculptured horse, is *not* the same as a film or a frame of film; both may remove time from their object, but they do so in significantly different ways.

Both of these metaphors lead straight into Lewis's strongest suit, since he wishes to maintain that his philosophy is that of a visual artist. Through their choice of images, Bergson and Alexander implicitly confirm Lewis's view that the art image and the artist's vision are natural metaphors for personality, timelessness, the classical essence, and the natural tendency of the human perception and intellect—all the things Lewis sees himself as defending.[36] In this matter, again, Lewis chooses not to quote Bergson or Alexander directly; instead, he silently adopts their images and revises them to make his own metaphorical comments on the time-philosophers' vision.

A couple of examples will illustrate Lewis's perspective. For instance, he describes how Bergson's view would change the classical sculpture of the Parthenon by reminding us about the influence of Bergson upon the Italian Futurists. After noting (accurately) that his long-time enemy "Marinetti... was a *pur-sang* bergsonian" (213), he tells us, "One of the tasks he set [for the Futurists] was to start making statues that could open and shut their eyes, and even move their limbs and trunks about, or wag their heads" (216). Elsewhere, describing the philosophical implications of the time-cult, Lewis writes, "The notion of the transformed 'object' offered us by this doctrine is plainly in the nature of a 'futurist' picture, like a running dog with a hundred legs and a dozen backs and heads. In place of the characteristic static 'form' of greek Philosophy, you have a series, a group, or, as Professor Whitehead says, a *reiteration*" (181).[37] This metaphor is particularly clever, I think, because it perversely collapses the successive images of a film into a single image. Such an analogy spatializes movement even more emphatically than does Bergson's cinema. Moreover, Lewis implicitly reminds us here that with a few historical exceptions like the Futurists, the graphic arts have always portrayed movement by suggestion rather than by attempting to spell it out with multiple or superimposed images.

Lewis also recasts Bergson's description of the "cinematographical mechanism." He explains, "The traditional belief of common-sense, embodied in the 'naïf' view of the physical world, is really a *picture* [informed by what we know from experience].... And it is this picture for which the cinematograph of the physics of 'events' is to be substituted. ...people are to be trained from infancy to regard the world as a *moving* picture. In this no 'object' would appear, but only the states of an object" (408).[38] If for Bergson the cinematographic perception of reality has too little movement, for Lewis it has far too much. Lewis inverts Bergson's blindness: in Bergson's eyes the static image of classical art and the successive images of film are essentially the same; in Lewis's, the film and Bergson's vision of continual, unbroken flux are indistinguishable. The metaphor of the cinema suggests to Bergson all that has been left out of the reality. But to Lewis it suggests only the disintegration of the stable image of reality: "With the thousand *successive* pictures we thus obtain," he argues, "we shall have—only *successively*, nothing all at once, except a punctual picture and momentary sensation—the perceptual picture of common-sense" (409). Once again, the space-philosopher adopts the time-philosopher's description of the metaphysical alternatives and alters it to argue the opposing view.

This example of a shared metaphor and the two long passages Lewis quotes from Bergson about art and the classical world view are not isolated resemblances but parts of a larger pattern of relationships. The key to this pattern lies in a casual remark about Bergson Lewis makes when he is introducing Whitehead. This is the third passage I have called especially significant; it is the least direct and the most revealing of the three. Again, Lewis does not identify the source as *Creative Evolution* (or any other of Bergson's books), and again, he distances himself by working through another philosopher. In this case he does not even quote Bergson's words. He writes: "The greater part of Professor Whitehead's analysis, in his *Science and the Modern World*, turns on what, as he starts by announcing, was the main objective of Bergson's criticism. Bergson had said that the intellect 'spatialized' things. It was that 'spatialization' that the doctrinaire of motion and of mental 'time' attacked. It is that, too, that Whitehead is busy confuting; only he acquits the intellect of this villainy, where Bergson pursues it with his hatred and abuse" (168). Throughout his argument Lewis continues to refer occasionally to this idea of Bergson's, always separating himself from it by enclosing "spatializing" in quotation marks. But he never stops to examine this aspect of Bergson's argument—the aspect Whitehead regarded as its "main objective." Even in the chapter on "Space and Time" he does not clearly explain what Bergson means by the intellect or its spatializing tendencies. What we find when we look at *Creative Evolution*, though, is that in this matter Lewis's distance from his former teacher is again more apparent than real. His quotation marks imply that he questions Bergson's view of the intellect, but in fact, that view is basic to Lewis's own philosophy.

When Bergson says that the Greek "framework marks out the main lines of a metaphysic which is, we believe, the natural metaphysic of the human intellect," he means no compliment. According to him the intellect is only half of consciousness—and the less interesting half at that. He explains: "Intuition and intellect represent two opposite directions of the work of consciousness: intuition goes in the very direction of life, intellect goes in the inverse direction, and thus finds itself naturally in accordance with the movement of matter." Intuition, or instinct, is the "natural direction" of the mind, and leads to "progress" in the form of "tension, continuous creation, free activity." The natural sphere of intuition is *durée* or lived time. Intellect, on the other hand, inverts this natural direction, and leads to "extension, to the necessary reciprocal determination of elements externalized each by relation to the others, in short, to geometrical mechanism."[39] Intellect is at home in space. In short, we could say, for Bergson intuition is to intellect as time is to space; and his "main objective" in *Creative Evolution* is to persuade us that intuition and time or duration are not only more natural but also more productive and life-enhancing than their antitheses.

Consequently, Bergson is more interested in exploring the potential of intuition than in defining the limitations of intellect. Still, he does fully describe both sides of this central opposition. What is interesting to a reader of Lewis is the terms Bergson associates with intellect and space. A selection of quotations will indicate their character. First, he links intellect, space, and matter:

> Thus, concentrated on that which repeats, solely preoccupied in welding the same to the same, intellect turns away from the vision of time. It dislikes what is fluid, and solidifies everything it touches. We do not *think* real time. But we *live* it, because life transcends intellect.
>
> Intelligence is, before anything else, the faculty of relating one point of space to another, one material object to another...
>
> The more consciousness is intellectualized, the more is matter spatialized.[40]

Second, he associates intellect with language, perception, and the senses:

> We take snapshots, as it were, of the passing reality ...Perception, intellection, language so proceed in general.
>
> The aspect of life that is accessible to our intellect—as indeed to our senses, of which our intellect is the extension—is that which offers a hold to our action.[41]

And finally, he adds to these terms distinctness, clarity, and stability:

> So intelligence even when it no longer operates upon its own object, follows habits it has contracted in that operation: it applies forms that are indeed those of unorganized matter. It is made for this kind of work. With this kind of work alone is it fully satisfied. And that is what the intelligence expresses by saying that thus only it arrives at *distinctness* and *clearness.*
>
> It must, therefore, in order to think itself clearly and distinctly, perceive itself under the form of discontinuity. Concepts, in fact, are outside each other, like objects in space; and they have the same stability as such

objects, on which they have been modeled. Taken together, they constitute an "intelligible world," that resembles the world of solids in its essential characters, but whose elements are lighter, more diaphanous, easier for the intellect to deal with than the image of concrete things: they are not, indeed, the perception itself of things, but the representation of the act by which the intellect is fixed on them.[42]

In all its major characteristics, Bergson's world of space and intellect is Lewis's—the sensible, intelligible world of clear, distinct, stable objects and ideas. And the world of time that Lewis himself pursues "with his hatred and abuse" is Bergson's preferred intuitive, instinctual world of interpenetration and constant flux.[43]

Disguising these fundamental resemblances, not surprisingly, Lewis and Bergson have different uses and interpretations for certain value terms. Both, for example, claim to preserve continuity against discontinuity. Bergson, to whom change is essential, believes that the intellect sees reality as discontinuous because it is blind to flux; Lewis, to whom the essence of reality is stability, believes that Bergson's vision of change blinds him to continuity. Lewis would agree with the accusation that he sees objects and ideas as discontinuous in space, but he would call them clear and distinct and insist that he preserves the more important continuity of stable self-identity. In this case Lewis and Bergson simply mean different things by the same word; each chooses to emphasize a different kind of continuity.

Similarly, both Lewis and Bergson claim to describe the natural human tendency. Bergson argues that the intellect inverts the natural direction of consciousness and that intuition follows it; Lewis argues that the common sense view he supports is the natural view of the world. In this case Bergson actually supplies Lewis with justification for his claim. If at one moment he calls the intellect "unnatural," at another, as we have seen, he explains that the classical world of unchanging essences is the natural world: "The Greeks trusted to nature, trusted the natural propensity of the mind, trusted language above all, in so far as it naturally externalizes thought.... In spatial movement and in change in general they saw only pure illusion."[44] With this description Lewis agrees: if his world-view is natural to the senses, the intellect, and language, it is better than any alternative Bergson could offer. Again, each appeals to one aspect of human nature and rejects another.

A third difference between Lewis's and Bergson's oppositions is a little more complex. This is the value each puts on the terms *action* and *life.* In general, Bergson sees himself as opposing action, by which he means practical action, and endorsing life. "The essential function of our intellect, as the evolution of life has fashioned it," he explains, "is to be a light for our conduct, to make ready for our action on things." Or again: "Our intellect has been cast in the mold of action. Speculation is a luxury, while action is a necessity." Against this limited function he places the unlimited potential of intuition to create. Intellect means work, but "the more we study the nature of time, the more we shall comprehend that duration means invention, the creation of forms, the continual elaboration of the absolutely new."[45] In other words Bergson devalues intelligence by associating it with life. But according to Lewis, Bergson's claims for intuition are fraudulent: "There is no serious question at all that on the score of *life-value,* and as far as the advertisement of this particular warm and, with Bergson, ecstatic, appeal is concerned, the boot should be on the other leg" (174). This assertion comes in the same paragraph where Lewis calls Bergson a "perfect philosophic ruffian" who "pulls every emotional lever on which he can lay his hands."

For Lewis, as for Bergson, "action" is a term of disapproval, but Lewis argues further that the time-philosopher's "life" means nothing other than action for its own sake, despite its pretense of creativity. In a chapter entitled "The Popular Counters, 'Action' and Life," he contends (with supporting evidence from Bertrand Russell[46]) that Bergson's philosophy was primarily a practical one, suited to the "man-of-action," not the "man-of-peace":

> An immense snobbery centering around the counter 'life' had been built up to the bursting point when the War began; and at the end of four years of that few people could have been found to exclaim any more about 'life' for the moment. For it was then plain to the meanest intelligence for a month or two, that what that sort of 'life' signified was death. All the sickly ecstasies of *élan vital* were drugs on the market. It was on the ecstatic 'life' cry that Bergson was allowed formerly to provide the first (continental) wave of the High-Bohemia with an appropriate philosophy, showing it plainly that it was the roof and crown of things, and that the contemptible 'intellect' was less than the dust beneath its chariot-wheels. (216)

Lewis is right, I think, that Bergson's doctrine does imply that activity is more alive—and hence more desirable—than contemplation. Moreover, Lewis's corollary argument that this doctrine suggests an enthusiasm for even violent activity is not as extreme as it might initially seem. Bergson does use metaphors of violence with disturbing frequency in speaking of the life-force. For example, this is how he characterizes the implications of his world-view:

> All organized beings, from the humblest to the highest, from the first origins of life to the time in which we are, and in all places as in all times, do but evidence a single impulsion, the inverse of the movement of matter, and in itself indivisible. All the living hold together, and all yield to the same tremendous push. The animal takes its stand on the plant, man bestrides ani-

mality, and the whole of humanity, in space and in time, is one immense army galloping beside and before and behind each of us in an overwhelming charge able to beat down every resistance and clear the most formidable obstacles, perhaps even death.[47]

In the context of Lewis's values, such a description damns itself. An "immense army" is not a happy metaphor for the life force. So allowing Bergson his claim that intuition means life, but insisting that "what that sort of 'life' signified was death," Lewis again inverts Bergson's position, transforming a term of praise into an insult.

The one important value term that both Bergson and Lewis wish to appropriate for their side of the opposition between intellect and intuition is *creativity*. Both see themselves as opposing the sterility of nineteenth-century mechanism; but each believes that his view best reveals the sources of true creativity and that the other subverts those sources. Bergson will say, for instance, "The intention of life... is just what the artist tries to regain, in placing himself back within the object by a kind of sympathy, in breaking down, by an effort of intuition, the barrier that space puts up between him and his model."[48] But once again, he also supplies the terms with which Lewis can refute him. Bergson writes, "Suppose we let ourselves go and, instead of acting, dream. At once the self is scattered; our past, which till then was gathered together into the indivisible impulsion it communicated to us, is broken up into a thousand recollections made external to one another. They give up interpenetrating in the degree that they become fixed. Our personality thus descends in the direction of space." Lewis quotes this passage,[49] and commenting only that for the time-philosopher, "This 'dreaming' is to be very much reprehended" (436), he allows the reader to recognize how Bergson's apparent self-contradictions undermine his argument—and so, indirectly, support Lewis's.

Against Bergson's claim Lewis would insist that we create

only when we dream rather than act. "The production of a work of art is, I believe, strictly the work of a visionary" (198), he explains. Furthermore, such creation can only take place in the kind of intellectual, spatial world Bergson sees as restrictive: "And I suppose that no one would deny that for the greatest achievements of the intellect, whether in art or in science, tranquillity and a stable order of things is required... if you say the contrary, you are merely asserting, like a good little egalitarian, that people *should not be* philosophers, men-of-science, or artists—that they should give up all those vain things, and plunge into the centre of the flux of life—*live* and not think" (164).[50] Of course this avowal is a little disingenuous, if only because Lewis knows full well that not everyone would agree that art, like science, is an achievement of the intellect; but at the same time, Bergson is equally disingenuous in his apparent conviction that intelligence always moves in the opposite direction from art. Here again, we see Lewis and Bergson agree on everything but a value term. For each, this time, creativity must be regarded as belonging to his position alone.

Everywhere, Lewis's philosophical position is a sort of mirror image of Bergson's. *Creative Evolution* argues that intellect inverts the more natural intuition; *Time and Western Man* implies that Bergson and his followers invert—and pervert—everything that is valuable to our human experience, everything that results from our senses, our thoughts, and our dreams. Noisily, Lewis reverses Bergson's values. Silently, at the same time, he appropriates Bergson's categories, constructing his central opposition of time and space to agree in almost every respect with that of his former teacher.

What to make of this relationship is not an easy question for Lewis's readers. In some respects the way he hides his considerable debt to Bergson is clearly justifiable. Contradictory values are in themselves a crucial difference—

certainly one that it would be reasonable for Lewis to see as more significant than any structural similarities. And, too, his secrecy has a fairly obvious strategic function. Lewis might well have reasoned that his readers would take his argument less seriously if he acknowledged this influence, since an autonomous space-philosophy seems more authoritative than one defined so largely by negating the time-philosophy it attacks. In *Time and Western Man* he argues repeatedly that one of the time-cult's chief weaknesses is its unanimity, that modern philosophers agree with each other far more than they ought, and that it is Bergson "more than any other single figure that is responsible for the main intellectual characteristics of the world we live in, and the implicit debt of almost all contemporary philosophy to him is immense." Lewis consequently had a considerable—and legitimate—tactical interest in disguising his own implicit debts to this "perfect philosophic ruffian."

Yet this action is also clearly at odds with Lewis's frequent claims that as a critic he is unusually honest about his personal biases—so much at odds as to suggest that perhaps in these claims he protests too much. Juxtaposed against this advertised honesty, Lewis's treatment of Bergson looks like a case of aggressively self-confident bad faith. He may succeed in exposing what he calls "the particular system of intellectual fraud practiced by Bergson," but in doing so he exposes himself to the same kind of unmasking.

None of us, of course, can be entirely free of our precursors, and no one would expect any of us to be entirely honest about our debts. As critics have increasingly realized (it hardly seems necessary to point to Harold Bloom's pioneering theory of the "anxiety of influence"), every writer has special strategies for concealing and revealing these crucial influences—strategies from which we in turn may learn important things about the ways these writers think. In Lewis's case we find that the way he deals with Bergson is by no

The Enemy Opposite

means an isolated phenomenon. Instead, similar patterns of strongly suggestive similarities, vigorously denied or disguised, can be discovered throughout his books, in what he says about Nietzsche, or Joyce, or Spengler, or—as we have seen—Pound. To a considerable extent, indeed, such relationships are inextricably built into Lewis's project as a critic: when he defines himself as the Enemy *opposite*, he takes on the demanding structural obligation to stand alone in absolute contradiction to everyone else in his culture. Not even his fundamental philosophical principles escape this demand. As the examples of Pound and Bergson reveal, these patterns of hidden oppositions—and the Enemy's distinctive ways of distracting us from them—are central to the structure of Lewis's thought.

The "Domestic Adversary"

By now we have seen how Lewis structures his arguments around a series of clear oppositions: time and space, inside and outside, thought and feeling. We have seen how he structures some of his central principles as paradoxes—personality and mind, idealism and concrete reality. And we have seen how he structures his stance and some of his premises by opposing himself to others—Ezra Pound, Henri Bergson. In all of these structures, we can see the shape of the Enemy Horseman; in all of them, we are reminded of Lewis's description of his "most essential ME." Here again is part of this important passage:

> I have allowed these contradictory things to struggle together, and the group that has proved the most powerful I have fixed upon as my most essential ME. This decision has not, naturally, suppressed or banished the contrary faction, almost equal in strength, indeed, and even sometimes in the ascendant. And I am by no means above spending some of my time with this domestic Adversary.... And luckily in my case the two sides, or micro-cosmic 'opposites,' are so well matched, that the dominant one is never idle or without criticism. (*TWM* 6)

Opposition and dominance: the Enemy Horseman's enormous head and torso dominate but do not destroy the grid of crossed diagonals that structure his horse. The drawing and this description represent an equilibrium of tensions, not an absence of tensions. What they tell us is that Lewis knows that the interests of his "most essential ME" are not his only interests—that his dominant position is never free from the criticism offered by his own internal Enemy. This is the final major structure of opposition in Lewis's thought: the voice of his Domestic Adversary.

If we look in detail at some of the contradictions a close reading discovers, we can discern how this undercurrent of self-criticism functions. And, significantly, we will hear both voices—the dominant and the hidden—within a single book: there is no question here that this kind of self-contradiction simply marks a change of mind. Casually, here and there, sometimes in commenting about someone else's beliefs, sometimes in explaining his own, Lewis gives us the arguments we would need to counter even his most fundamental premises.

Lewis's principle of individual personality and mind, as we have seen, is central to his thinking. But even this principle is countered by traces of criticism. In the book where he argues most strongly for the philosophical primacy of mind, *Time and Western Man,* he also explains that what we call the "mind" is a "stolen, aristocratical monopoly of personality" (318) and "an artificial, pumped-up affair—just as the 'male' is a highly unstable and *artificial* mode of life" (324). Lewis does not only reveal his own social and sexual politics in such comments. He also calls the basis for his position artificial and unstable—terms of condemnation throughout his criticism. Elsewhere in the same book, he describes this basis as being artificial in the same way an optical illusion is unreal: "When you analyse the notion of the 'self,' it is true, it falls to pieces. But the means you use to effect this disintegration are of the same nature as those you would employ to demonstrate the unreality of an optical illusion" (420).[51] Just after he makes this analogy (an odd one for someone who insists that he stands for the concrete, *physical* world), Lewis admits and then sets aside one of the main philosophical weaknesses of his position: "These regions, I am aware, are guarded over by the hideous problem of self-evidence and subjective truth: but if

The "Domestic Adversary"

we stopped to settle accounts with every traditional dragon that we encountered, we should prolong this essay indefinitely." This dragon, of course, is capable of destroying—or at the very least, of greatly complicating—his argument. So the Domestic Adversary puts in his word but does not silence the "most essential ME."

Men Without Art offers a curious corollary to this example. In a book devoted largely to arguing that satire is all art that tells the *truth,* Lewis also points out, "There is the 'truth' of Satire and there is the 'truth' of Romance," "the 'truth' of the intellect" and "the 'truth' of the average romantic sensualism," and asks: "What is 'the truth' regarding any person? What is the objective truth about him?—a public and not a private truth? What is that in a person, or in a thing, that is not 'satire,' upon the one hand, or 'romance,' upon the other? Is there such a purely non-satiric, non-romantic truth, at all?" (122). The Lewis who believes in the purity of mind would surely answer yes, there is a purely objective truth; the Lewis who recognizes the inevitability of the personal in everything would surely answer no, all truth is subjective; the Lewis who holds these contradictory beliefs together with the paradox of the not-self would surely answer that at bottom these truths are the same. But the Domestic Adversary recognizes and maintains the contradiction: "Such questions may at all times with advantage be asked," he asserts, and answers, "There is, in both cases, *another* truth, that is all. But both are upon an equal intellectual footing I think" (*MWA* 122). Such an answer, clearly, would have enormous destructive force if it were carried throughout Lewis's whole work.

Lewis is equally clear, though less direct, about the dark underside of the personality as such, which he calls at one point "a vein of picturesqueness, an instinct for the value of the *person* in the picture" (*TWM* 92). In the same pages which introduced the Enemy (the part of *Time and Western Man* that first appeared in *The Enemy*), he cautions: "The less you are able to realize other people, the more your particular personality will obsess you, and the more dependent upon its reality you will be. The more you will insist on it with a certain frenzy.... Your 'individualism' will be that mad one of the 'one and only' self, a sort of instinctive solipsism in practice" (*TWM* 24–25). Although the point of this passage is to distinguish this solipsistic individuality from "political 'individualism' " which "expresses belief in the desirability of *many* individuals instead of *one*," certainly it also reminds us that if anyone insists on the reality of his personality, it is Lewis. (Significantly, Northrop Frye suggests that Lewis is "an almost solipsistic writer, whose hatreds are a part of him because he understands nothing of what goes on outside his own mind."[52]) And one result of that insistence in his case does seem to be some difficulty in realizing other people as something other than the enemy. In another context, he remarks, "The insistence on sensation-at-all-costs, then, like the incessant emphasis upon 'virility,' or 'sex,' or 'stimulation,' suggests an unaccountable consciousness rather of an absence than of an abundance of life" (*TWM* 382). Again, Lewis's insistence on the self and on the "masculine" principle of mind may suggest exactly the same interpretation.

In one way or another, we can find similar traces of Lewis' interior argument with all of his other important values. To counter his assertion that his values are essentially those of a visual artist, we read this: "But is there such a thing as 'an artist'? Or to what degree is there such a thing? Am I not, when I employ that term, just using an empty theoretic counter, to which no particular meaning can be attached? If there is no pure art, can there be any 'artist' *tout court*?" (*MWA* 272). To counter the central distinction between time and space, the Domestic Adversary reminds us, "Space and Time are mere appearances... riddled with contradictions that bar them from anything but a relative reality" (*TWM* 444). And, in *Paleface*, he writes: "Under

The "Domestic Adversary"

more normal conditions I should probably be ranged upon the other side of the argument. I am really driven into the position of the Devil's Advocate to some extent" (19–20). Thus, he explains, "I of course can find [for the White Man] the necessary arguments to dispose of his passionate critics, and I am only too glad to, for his opponents are a stupid crew for the most part—just 'to amuse myself' I would help my Paleface. But all the same I recognize that his case is dangerously open to attack" (69). This is the voice of the Domestic Adversary, who always somewhere reminds Lewis and his readers that "all the same" his "case is dangerously open to attack."

Sometimes, of course, it is impossible to guess how much or how little Lewis realizes the deconstructive force of his own remarks, and certainly that force varies. To some extent such self-criticism simply results from his habit of conceptualizing everything as polar opposites. Any recognition of the simplification involved in creating such pairs would naturally undermine their authority. And although Lewis both intuitively and deliberately uses oppositions, he clearly recognizes their limitations. Thus when he asserts that the time-mind and space-mind are "the poles of the human intelligence," always "confronted, eternally hostile to each other," he continues with this qualification: "or at least eternally different."

But the voice of the Domestic Adversary also sometimes calls our attention to the fundamentally self-contradictory nature of many of Lewis's ideas. All those relationships he describes as "paradoxical," for instance, are suspect: there, I think, we see Lewis confronting a real opposition within his own thinking and trying to control its potentially explosive force by containing it as *paradox*—the category of apparent contradictions that we recognize on some deeper level not to be contradictory at all. This tactic does have the virtue of bringing the difficult terms into the open and at least temporarily recognizing them as the terms of real oppositions; in this, it is more honest than any alternative of attempted compromise or mediation could be. Yet, of course, calling a contradiction a paradox does not automatically stop it from being a contradiction. Thus Lewis may assert that the personality is (a) the ultimate reality and (b) as unreal as an optical illusion; he may explain the apparent inconsistency by referring us to the paradox of Berkeley's concrete and vivid illusions; but to a considerable extent such a solution only works on the level of rhetoric. The Domestic Adversary marks Lewis's own awareness that this is so.

One possible way of understanding this pattern of "micro-cosmic 'opposites' " is offered by Fredric Jameson, the only critic so far who has focused on it as problematic. Jameson, whose provocative polemic against Lewis's "fascism" is an extensive analysis of self-contradictions in Lewis's thought, offers historical/ideological explanations of their significance. For instance, he writes, "The 'ideal' of the strong leader or 'strong' personality in Lewis remains precisely that—a dead letter, a contradiction in terms, an ideal and impossible synthesis of incompatible characteristics, a merely logical possibility which no narrative—let alone real history itself—can concretely generate. Lewis' narratives know this, whether he does or not..." In the novels the "self" Lewis defends in his nonfiction—the stable subject or ego—disintegrates entirely. Not surprisingly, Jameson sees the novels as the truer expression of Lewis's vision: "One part of Lewis' mind—the political and journalistic—is powerfully locked into the ideological closure of ethics and has become a virtual machine for issuing judgements and anathemata. The narratives, on the other hand, may be seen as the experimental or laboratory situation in which the very problem of making such judgements is itself foregrounded, and in which the impossibility of the ethical becomes itself the implicit center of the text, whose operations systematically and critically undermine this older 'habit,' this henceforth historically outmoded system of positioning the individual subject." This double vision Jameson sees as a sign of Lewis's problematic ideological position: the "ideal of the 'strong personality' " is the "central organizational category of Lewis's mature ideology," but—he cautions us—"ideology is not...a coherent system of ideas, but rather the desperate response to a contradictory situation. The notion of the 'strong personality' in Lewis is then not to be read as a 'belief,' a conceptual value or conviction, but rather as a symbolic act in its own right, which has then taken on the reified appearance of a 'thought' or an 'opinion.' " The contradictory situation in Lewis's case, Jameson believes, is the real erosion of the (petty bourgeois) individual's economic and political autonomy—an erosion against which intellect is powerless.

Given his Marxist premises—"In our time, ethics, whenever it makes its reappearances, may be taken as the sign of an attempt to mystify"—and his assumption that Lewis is blind to his own contradictions, Jameson's negative judgment is inevitable.[33] If we do not share those premises, or perhaps more important, if we give Lewis credit for knowing what he was doing, we might argue from Jameson's insights to a less negative description. In the nonfiction, perhaps, Lewis pleads for the central values of intelligence and personality; in the fiction he questions these same values by exploring their opposites. Between the nonfiction and the fiction, the dominant principles and the undercurrent of self-criticism change places.

Another historical, but less political, explanation for Lewis's self-contradictions is indirectly suggested by Michael Levenson in *A Genealogy of Modernism*. Levenson (who mentions the "modernist urge towards dualistic opposition and radical polarities") looks in detail at the theories of T. E. Hulme and Ford Madox Ford and argues that their many apparent inconsistencies reveal the presence of two opposing but intertwined intellectual traditions. In the works of Mill, Arnold, Pater, and Babbitt, Levenson traces the development of two beliefs: that the individual self, in all its subjectivity, is the only criterion for judgment; and that the only way to avoid complete anarchy is by appealing to external, impersonal order, discipline, and the State. Because so many of Hulme's and Ford's theories closely resemble Lewis's, Levenson's analysis suggests an historical explanation for several of the contradictions we have examined. The question of "truth," for instance: Hulme, he argues, continues both sides of the Arnold-Pater-Babbitt tradition, first by following Bergson—but only for a while—in believing that truth is relative and personal; then, when he comes under the influence of the French neoclassicists Maurras and Lasserre, by deciding that truth is independent and objective. The opposition that is diachronic in Hulme, I think, exactly matches the synchronic opposition in Lewis, in whom we can trace the influence not only of all these English and French writers, but also of Hulme himself. But Lewis responds to the difficulties in reconciling such different beliefs by complicating his own thought through paradox and an undercurrent of self-criticism. Similarly, Levenson cites Arnold's theory of the "best self" as an attempt to combine his belief in the primacy of the individual with his desire for outside control; in contrast to our "everyday self," Arnold argues, "by our *best self* we are united, impersonal, at harmony." This "best self" is "right reason," and we learn to know it through culture.[54] Lewis's theory of the not-self offers a similar solution, but because the chasm between individual and shared authority has grown wider between Arnold's day and Lewis's, his personality/mind paradox is more complex and even more problematic.

To these explanations we must, I think, add Lewis's. Once again, we find the best evidence is indirect: in three remarkable instances—all from the *Man of the World* books—Lewis describes the contradictory structure of an-

The "Domestic Adversary"

other writer's mind in terms that strongly suggest the structure of his own. The self-reflexivity of these passages is clearest if we hold in mind Lewis's "most essential ME," his "micro-cosmic 'opposites,'" and his "domestic Adversary."

First, this description of D. H. Lawrence from *Paleface:*

> But Mr. Lawrence's explanation is that he has 'a little ghost inside' him, which 'sees both ways.' And this arrangement he recommends to us. We should all get such little optical ghosts. I will quote the whole of this passage:
>
>> 'The consciousness of one branch of humanity is the annihilation of the consciousness of another branch . . . .
>>
>> [This] is the eternal paradox of human consciousness. To pretend that all is one stream is to cause chaos and nullity. To pretend to express one stream in terms of another, so as to identify the two, is false and sentimental. The only thing you can do is to have a little ghost inside you which sees both ways, or even many ways. But a man cannot *belong* to both ways, or to many ways. One man can belong to one great way of consciousness only. He may even change from one way to another. But he cannot go both ways at once. Can't be done.'—(*Mornings in Mexico,* 105, 106.)
>
> All this appears to me exceedingly sound. But, having regard to the locality in which it is uttered, what has taken its author there, and what he elsewhere undoubtedly is proposing to us, it is certainly puzzling. The little two-way-looking ghost is the solution, of course, or the excuse for this glaring paradox. But that is scarcely satisfying. (154–55, my ellipsis)

Of course this description seems to Lewis "exceedingly sound": Lawrence's interior ghost is very similar to his own

The Enemy Opposite

"micro-cosmic 'opposites,'" though without the vocabulary of struggle. Both Lawrence and Lewis argue that it is impossible truly to *reconcile* opposite forms of consciousness within one self. But Lewis is, naturally, reluctant to give Lawrence full credit—since this passage falls in the midst of his long attack on Lawrence's primitivism—and so he also points out that this is a "scarcely satisfying" solution to a "glaring paradox." Here is an instance of double self-reflexivity: the Domestic Adversary points out a problem in the idea of the Domestic Adversary itself. And typically, Lewis leaves the subject with just this hint.

The second passage—his argument about Shakespeare from *The Lion and the Fox*—is more extensive, and accordingly more revealing. Here he offers a double explanation: Shakespeare's doubleness, "the forces of disintegration at work in his mind," results from both his historical position—on the cusp between the medieval and the modern, the Christian and the pagan—and the structure of his mind. Consider these passages:

> Out of one half of his mind, we might say, the modern world could be seen issuing, with its mean, colourless and violent *hubris* (on whom nature retaliates by gigantic, dull and muffled wars). Out of the other and civilized half we could almost step into the attic theatre—taking, if you like, the crude and humble mediaeval stage on the way.

Here Shakespeare's mind mirrors the historical contradiction (in terms, incidentally, that strongly suggest John Holloway's very interesting analysis of Lewis's concern with the violence of the modern world[55]).

> As the tragic and comic were mixed in Shakespeare's plays, so they were mixed in his mind: and at some time one was in the ascendant, then the other would have its turn. But neither was ever absent; it dogged its

The "Domestic Adversary"

> other half like a shrinking or growing shadow.... keeping this in mind we shall be less surprised at the fundamental contradiction that is evident everywhere through them.

Here is Shakespeare's mind described in exactly the same terms as Lewis's—with the added diagnosis of "fundamental contradiction...everywhere" in his writing.

> The mirror is held up to nature, and there are two fighting forms reflected there—mazdean, moral or not-moral; at all events, a dark and a light, a black and a white....
>
> To be a "mirror" at all, it could be pointed out, is ethically dubious. It could be shown that any mirror that was really a mirror, and which told the truth, would have been smashed long ago. And then it could be suggested that this particular mirror was a very lively one, giving a very purged, not to say peculiar, view of the hegelian "contest" in progress. But in these pages it will be contended that Shakespeare entered furiously into the contest of the two halves of which he was composed. He was alternately as black as night and as white as snow, or both at the same time. Renan describes himself as a "tissue of contradictions, one half of me engaged in devouring the other half, like the fabled beast of Ctesias who ate his own paws without knowing it": a description that could very well be applied to Shakespeare. The perfection and equilibrium of his mind is the proof of the beautiful matching of the opposing forces. (21–23)

The parallels here are especially rich. Like Shakespeare, Lewis enters into the contest of his two halves (here is the combative vocabulary of the "contrary factions" warring with one another); and he is alternately black or white or both (note, too, Lewis's characteristic vision of polar opposites). Like Renan, Lewis also could be described as a "tissue of contradictions," one half devouring the other. Even the final sentence matches Lewis's "And luckily in my case the two sides, or micro-cosmic 'opposites,' are so well matched" that he, too, is "at the centre of the balance." The effect of these similarities is quintessentially the effect of the Enemy: on the surface, a straightforward though binary description of another artist; below the surface a bit of self-advertisement or praise (Lewis is *like* Shakespeare) and a bit of acute self-analysis.

The final passage to consider is from *The Art of Being Ruled*. This is a description of Georges Sorel—like Bergson and Nietzsche, a thinker with whom Lewis has a complex relationship of influence:

> [Sorel] seems composed of a crowd of warring personalities, sometimes one being in the ascendent, sometimes another, and which in any case he has not been able, or has not cared, to control.... The 'cause' matters very little to him—the 'battle' is everything. And yet in the midst of this detachment you have to allow for some deep, and indeed rather mysterious, sectarian passion. And intellectually he is a sensitive plate for the confused ideology of his time. He is a semitaur who sees red both ways, the bull-nature injects the human eyes with blood. He is, in brief, a symptomatic figure that it would be difficult to match.... he is a fabulous hybrid, attacking himself, biting his own tail, kicking his own heroical chest, contunding his own unsynthetic flesh, and showing his wounds with pride—self-inflicted, *self* in everything. (132–33; Lewis cites Hulme's translation of Sorel's *Réflexions sur la violence*)

Again: the same vocabulary as in Lewis's self-portrait; the same mix of detachment and passion; the same image of self-consumption. Here Lewis adds the descriptions of the

The "Domestic Adversary"

"*self* in everything" and the bloody-eyed bull—two more acutely self-reflexive insights. And here we find the two wonderful summary statements, both equally applicable to Lewis: "Intellectually he is a sensitive plate for the confused ideology of his time.... He is, in brief, a symptomatic figure that it would be difficult to match."

It is the undercurrent of acute and critical self-awareness that these passages reveal, I believe, that makes Lewis such an interesting figure. As always, he provides an apt description himself: "If I speak of myself it is not out of vanity. Every complexity is to be found in me. So if I demonstrate upon myself, it is because I am a good subject."[56] That he recognizes the complexity of his own mind (and, of course, of the issues he cares about) and that he struggles as he does to control this complexity through the structure of the Domestic Adversary make him endlessly intriguing—as a puzzle, as a powerful and unusual mind, as a "sensitive plate," as a symptomatic figure.

PART 3:
The Enemy Criticism

The Enemy Versus James Joyce:
Literary Criticism

THE ARGUMENT

Of all Lewis's art and literary criticism—some ten volumes worth—one of the most notorious and most misunderstood pieces is the "Analysis of the Mind of James Joyce." This rudely stated, comprehensive attack on Joyce as a "time-mind" and *Ulysses* as the quintessential "time-book" raises many questions, some of which may be identified in the range of other critics' comments about it. Wagner, for instance, concludes that "calling Joyce a 'time-philosopher' was a *deliberate* misunderstanding," and that "unless we allow for the idea of malice, Lewis's criticism of Joyce as a 'time-philosopher' is almost inexplicable." Kenner, whose work on Joyce, especially *Joyce's Voices,* derives in part from Lewis's ideas, refers to his "near misses" and calls him "the most helpful of devil's advocates"; Kenner's earlier *Dublin's Joyce* asserts even more emphatically that Lewis's is the "most brilliant misreading in modern criticism." And Joyce himself admitted that Lewis had written "by far the best hostile criticism that had appeared," but also added, "Allowing that the whole of what Lewis says about my book is true, is it more than ten per cent of the truth?"[1] These judgments disagree about the fairness, the accuracy, and the adequacy of Lewis's view, but they agree that his criticism is somehow extraordinary.

In all of the Enemy criticism, as we have seen, two different forces are at work. Speaking as the Enemy, Lewis demonstrates flamboyant hostility to the objects of his scrutiny, a deliberately extreme bias, a strong impulse towards self-dramatization, and occasional underground maneuvers designed to hide similarities and exaggerate differences between himself and his targets. At the same time, he believes his function is to try to *change* things he dislikes, and so he tries to reveal what he believes to be hidden and destructive influences underlying the arts, both in general and in the works of specific artists, primarily those he identifies as "strongly established leaders, of mature talent"—Lawrence, Hemingway, Stein, Pound, Joyce. As Lewis explains in *Time and Western Man,* "What I am concerned with here, first of all, is not whether the great *time-philosophy* that overshadows all contemporary thought is viable as a system of abstract truth, but if in its application it helps or destroys our human arts" (129). So he examines Joyce as an exemplary time-writer. Read in this context—as part of his larger argument—Lewis's analysis of Joyce makes sense. It also makes a good example of his critical practice. From the way the Enemy deals with Joyce, we can learn not only how Joyce looks from the perspective of an intelligent heretic, but also a good deal about where Lewis is weakest as a critic and where he is most acute.

Lewis begins his criticism with an important warning: "What I have to say will not aim at estimating [Joyce's] general contribution to contemporary letters" (91; unless I note otherwise, all page references in this discussion are to *TWM*); and he later explains, "Had I undertaken to write a general criticism of Joyce I should not have passed on this impression uncensored—in its native sensational strength—but have modified it, by associating it with other impressions more favourable to the author" (118–19). Instead, he reminds us, he is writing as a highly partisan critic of the time-cult. "I regard *Ulysses* as a *time-book*," he announces, "and by that I mean that it lays its emphasis upon, for choice manipulates, and in a doctrinaire manner, the self-conscious time-sense, that has now been erected into a universal philosophy" (100).

Lewis, of course, means by "time" everything opposite to what he means by space: time is what is *not* distinct personality, the conscious mind, vision, common sense, stability, order. This is the broad context we must keep in mind. But in the critique of Joyce, Lewis's argument about time can be more narrowly organized into three categories. One: *Ulysses* subtly manifests one of the main characteristics of the time-cult, the substitution of a simulacrum for a real thing—in this case a simulated Irishness for real cultural differences. Two: it shows a certain obsession with time in its usual sense—an obsession much like that which Lewis sees in modern philosophy and theoretical science. Three: its mixture of technical sophistication and conceptual conventionality illustrates the tendency of the time-philosophy to dissolve the distinctions between subject and object.

ONE: IRISHNESS.

Joyce, Lewis explains, "has a very keen preoccupation with the Past" (106). The problem is in his setting: "The local colour, or locally-coloured material, that was scraped together into a big variegated heap to make *Ulysses*, is—*doctrinally even more than in fact*—the material of the Past. It is consciously the decay of a mournful province, with in addition the label of a twenty-year-old vintage, of a 'lost time,' to recommend it" (99–100, my emphasis). Real national differences have virtually disappeared from the modern world, Lewis argues, so the Irishness of *Ulysses* is at best an archaic survival, at worst a romantic sham.

Lewis objects to this "material of the Past." The best modern artists, he asserts, ought to create *new* materials, not rely on old ones: "There is nothing for it to-day, if you have an appetite for the beautiful, but *to create new beauty.*

You can no longer nourish yourself upon the Past; its stock is exhausted, the Past is nowhere a reality. The only place where it is a reality is in *time,* not certainly in space" (99).[2] Far too much contemporary art, Lewis believes, involves some kind of return to the past—Pound's historical past, Picasso's or Lawrence's primitivism, Stein's or Matisse's or Proust's interest in childhood and the child-like. And far too often this art is advertised as the "new." "I am not therefore suggesting that where art is concerned other periods, races and countries should be banished," he has explained earlier; but "let us call a spade a spade; let us call what the spade digs up old, very old; not new, very new" (53, 52). *Ulysses* is everywhere hailed as a great original work of art; Lewis wants to demonstrate that beneath its "challenging novelty" it too participates in this return.

But Lewis's main reason for criticizing Joyce's archaic Irishness is that he sees it as a particularly neat illustration of a wide-spread political situation. *Ulysses* adumbrates a "problem set throughout the world to-day": "Everywhere the peoples become more and more alike. Local colours, which have endured in many places for two thousand years, fade so quickly that already one uniform grey tint has supervened.... Simultaneously, and in frenzied contradiction, is the artificially fostered nationalism rampant throughout the world since the War. So while *in reality* people become increasingly one nation...they *ideologically* grow more aggressively separatist, and conscious of 'nationality' " (95–96). Joyce, Lewis points out, participates in this contradiction. Though he had no use for Irish nationalism, especially in its politically militant forms, Joyce "is ready enough, as a literary artist, to stand for Ireland": "Although entertaining the most studied contempt for his compatriots...it will yet be insisted on that his irishness is an important feature of his talent; and he certainly also does exploit his irishness and theirs" (95).

What Lewis most wishes to impress on us is that all these

things—Joyce's Irishness, the "newness" of modern art, the endemic artificial nationalism—share the same structure. Not surprisingly, the structure he sees takes the form of a complicated opposition. "That sort of contradiction is paralleled throughout our life," Lewis explains. "There is no department that is exempt from the confusions of this strategy—which consists essentially in removing something necessary to life and putting an ideologic simulacrum where it was" (96). Everywhere he recognizes "that trap of an abstraction coloured to look concrete, and placed where once there was something but where now there is nothing" (99). Here the immediate context of these remarks is particularly important: Lewis moves directly into a brief summary of the argument of Book 2 of *Time and Western Man*—where he will echo and expand upon the paradoxical contrast between the abstract and the concrete.

Joyce is valuable to Lewis in large part because he supplies the occasion for the image of the simulacrum. In *The Enemy*, which did not include the theoretical Book 2, Lewis depended on this image and the following summary to suggest his philosophical argument; in the complete *Time and Western Man*, they introduce that argument and give the reader a schematic framework with which to begin the more complicated analysis of modern philosophy. So for Lewis the issue of Joyce's Irishness provides what he calls elsewhere a sort of "skeleton key" to his whole argument. Once we have seen in what sense the Dublin of *Ulysses* only *simulates* what it appears to *be*—how this novel is romance pretending to be realism—we should be able to recognize the same pattern when it recurs in the more theoretical doctrines of the time-philosophers.

TWO: TIME.

Lewis's second major reason for calling *Ulysses* a timebook is focused more directly on the novel itself. He believes that Joyce is more concerned than he ought to be about time itself—and about time's closest cousin, flux. This is the argument that has given rise to most of the confusion about Lewis's criticism of Joyce: as Wagner complains, "Few if any critics, however unfriendly to Joyce in the intention... have chosen the basis of 'time' on which to arraign Joyce's *oeuvre*. Most critics realize the reverse to have been true." Yet understood on its own terms, Lewis's point is both simple and reasonable. When he writes that Joyce "has a very keen preoccupation with the Past," he goes on to say, "He does lay things down side by side, carefully dated; and added to that, he has some rather loosely and romantically held notion of periodicity" (106). These traits, though, mean less in Joyce's work than they might in another artist's: "But I believe that [what] all these things amount to with him is this: as a careful, even meticulous, craftsman, with a long training of doctrinaire naturalism, the detail—the time-detail as much as anything else—assumes an exaggerated importance for him" (106). More important than such details is the way Joyce collapses time into a kind of timelessness. The "all-life-in-a-day scheme," Lewis argues, constitutes a "fanatically observed" and "barbarous version" of the classical unities of time and place (100).

Lewis does not say what he might, that this aspect of Joyce's work distorts our everyday or classical sense of time both by compressing and by expanding it. Because we learn so much about the characters' pasts through their thoughts, this one day and one place expand temporally more than spatially; Bloom's and Stephen's whole lives are present in the novel more vividly than, say, the rest of Western Europe. The "adventures" of the Circe chapter, Lewis admits, "take us still further from the ideal of the Unities, and both Space and Time temporarily evaporate. But on the whole the reader is conscious that he is beneath the intensive dictatorship of Space-time" (100). In one sense *Ulysses* arrests time by gathering it all into one moment—the moment of one day. But to Lewis, this way of understanding time is finally equivalent to its apparent opposite, an emphasis on the constant passing of time—since in both cases time itself is the important thing. (Here, of course, we might also hear the Domestic Adversary speaking: Lewis, too, is much concerned, even obsessed, with time, though in ways he sees as significantly different. As they were in his attack on Pound's sense of advertisement, these differences are a matter of perspective.)

To make clear how the timelessness of Joyce's novels is not the same as the "classical" timelessness he prefers[3], Lewis quotes from *A Portrait of the Artist as a Young Man* a statement that ties Joyce's timelessness with flux: " 'So timeless seemed the grey warm air, so fluid and impersonal [Stephen's] own mood, that all ages were as one to him' " (128). Joyce seeks to arrest time by collapsing the distinctions between past and present; his timelessness is psychological. "So," Lewis concludes, "we arrive at the concrete illustrations of that strange fact already noted—that an intense preoccupation with *time* or 'duration' (the psychological aspect of time that is) is wedded to the theory of 'timelessness.' It is, as it were, in its innate confusion in the heart of the reality, the substance and original of that peculiar paradox—that so long as *time* is the capital truth of your world it matters very little if you deny time's existence . . . or say there is nothing else at all" (128). The very quality of Joyce's work that leads many critics to call it timeless leads Lewis to identify it as just as much a time-book as any of Stein's, Proust's, or Bergson's more obvious ones.

THREE: SOPHISTICATION/CONVENTIONALITY.

Lewis's third major argument against Joyce is the most complex. It is really two arguments—or two families of points—joined by what Lewis offers again as a kind of paradox, though in this case he wants us to stay aware of the contradictions. On the one hand, *Ulysses* is technically progressive, a trait that causes both the novel's greatest strength and several of its major weaknesses: if it is a "considerable achievement of art" (95), it is also the "very nightmare of the naturalistic method" (108) and the "sardonic catafalque of the victorian world" (109). On the other hand, it is conceptually conventional, all too full of clichés of one kind or another. In detailing these accusations, Lewis offers two kinds of explanations, one kind deriving from Joyce's personality, the other kind deriving from the time-philosophy.

About Joyce's technical sophistication there has never been much critical disagreement. Consequently, Lewis can simply assert Joyce's stylistic skill as a given, and then focus not on the strengths of that skill but on its weaknesses. The key to Joyce's technical virtuosity, he says, is that he is essentially a craftsman: "What stimulates him is *ways of doing things*" (106). The evidence, of course, is all the styles in *Ulysses,* and as we might expect, what interests Lewis is how these styles are imitative rather than original. Joyce echoes Rabelais, Stevenson, Sterne, Dickens, and Nashe (92, 121–23); he shows the influence of Lewis himself (especially his prewar play *Enemy of the Stars*), Eliot, Pound, Stein, and Freud (121, 123, 127). So many resemblances, Lewis concludes, show us Joyce's "unorganized susceptibility to influences" (91).[4]

Lewis is most bothered by what he sees as the claustrophobic conjunction of two techniques: naturalism and stream-of-consciousness. Lewis believes that Joyce's acute eye for detail and meticulous craftsmanship have led him into a "fanatic naturalism" in which details overwhelm "all contour and definition." "The amount of *stuff*—unorganized brute material—that the more active principle of drama has to wade through, under the circumstances, slows it down to . . . [a] sluggish tide . . . The newspaper in which Mr. Bloom's bloater is wrapped up, say, must press

The Enemy Versus James Joyce: Literary Criticism

on to the cold body of the fish, reversed, the account of the bicycle accident that was reported on the fated day chosen for this Odyssey; or that at least is the idea" (108). Joyce has spent his skill and energy in an outdated literary technique; the result is a novel too stuffed with details to maintain clear outlines or to support the "more active principle of drama" appropriate to literature. He may be better than anyone else at capturing the material details of everyday life—a skill Lewis would certainly in principle admire—but he makes the whole endeavor look "obsessional."[5]

Lewis further suggests how the "naturalistic nightmare" also results from Joyce's use of stream-of-consciousness. This technique embodies much of what Lewis dislikes in the time-cult—its interest in the subconscious, unconscious, or prelogical rather than the conscious; the emotional rather than the intellectual; the process rather than the product of thought. Joyce, he argues, who has naturally a "highly developed *physical* basis," has been weakened by the psychological approach: by adopting the "telling from the inside" method, he "imposes a softness, flabbiness and vagueness everywhere in its bergsonian fluidity" (120). He explains more clearly in *Satire and Fiction*: "As developed in Ulysses, [the internal method] robbed Mr. Joyce's work as a whole of all linear properties whatever, considered as a plastic thing—of all contour and definition in fact. In contrast to the jelly-fish that floats in the centre of the subterranean stream of the 'dark' Unconscious, I much prefer, for my part, the shield of the tortoise, or the rigid stylistic articulations of the grasshopper.... The ossature is my favourite part of a living animal organism, not its intestines."[6] As a matter of principle, as we have seen, Lewis values the everyday, common sense, visual outsides of things and people; as a matter of practice, accordingly, he opposes the modernist interest in insides.

In this criticism Lewis does not mean that *Ulysses* has no structure. Rather, he thinks that its structures make the reader feel trapped and smothered—"not in the open air, but closed up inside somebody else's head" (108):

> The author... takes you inside his head, or, as it were, into a roomy diving-suit, and, once down in the middle of the stream, you remain the author, naturally, inside whose head you are, though you are sometimes supposed to be aware of one person, sometimes of another. Most of the time you are being Bloom or Dedalus, from the inside, and that is Joyce. Some figures for a moment bump against you, and you certainly perceive them with great distinctness—or rather some fragment of their dress or some mannerism; then they are gone. But, generally speaking, it is *you* who descend into the flux of *Ulysses,* and it is the author who absorbs you momentarily into himself for that experience. That is all that the 'telling from the inside' amounts to. All the rest is literature, and dogma; or the dogma of time-literature. (120)

In Joyce's hands stream-of-consciousness joins with naturalism to become "the method of confining the reader in a circumscribed psychological space into which several encyclopaedias have been emptied" (107).

It is when Lewis comes to examine Joyce's characters that he discovers what he considers the novel's conceptual inadequacy—the second half of his third major argument against Joyce. Just as he reveals the traditional elements beneath Joyce's technical innovations, Lewis argues that *Ulysses* is everywhere vitiated by its underlying conventionality.

Though he praises Joyce's overall awareness of "purely verbal clichés," Lewis still detects in both *Portrait* and *Ulysses* various lapses into triteness. "Buck Mulligan," he remarks, " 'turned abruptly *his great searching eyes* from the sea,' etc. Great searching eyes! Oh, where were the great searching eyes of the author, from whom no verbal cliché may escape, when he wrote that?" (115). Such clichés are "tell-tale": they betray the novel's more serious underlying clichés of character. Some of Lewis's objections are to the minor figures—Buck Mulligan, the "stage Irishman," and Haines, the "stage Anglo-Saxon" (113)—but his major argument is that Stephen and Bloom are equally conventional. "But if [Haines and Mulligan] are clichés, Stephen Dedalus is a worse or a far more glaring one. He is the really wooden figure" (113–14). Although Stephen comes in for the bulk of Lewis's abuse, Bloom is "an unsatisfactory figure, too, but of an opposite sort and in a very different degree. He possesses all the recognized theatrical properties of 'the Jew' up-to-date...but such a Jew as Bloom, taken altogether, has never been seen outside the pages of Mr. Joyce's book" (117–18). Lewis expands very little on Bloom's specific flaws; like most subsequent critics, though, he sees Bloom as representing sensuality in the central contrast between the novel's two major characters.

This central contrast is what really exacerbates Lewis's distaste for Stephen and reluctance to praise the much more likeable Bloom. The sensual Bloom seems to him to win "the reader's sympathy every time he appears" (117). But Stephen, who represents the intellectual principle, is a "frigid prig," a "mean and ridiculous figure" (116). Whenever the two come into conflict, Dedalus loses, thus, "to the dismay of the conscientious reader, betraying the principles he represents" (117). Naturally Lewis wants Stephen's intellectual principles to triumph over Bloom's sensuality, but he finds Stephen himself far less admirable than his misdirected counterpart. Here Lewis sees another version of his own central contrast between the time-mind and the space-mind—with the wrong side winning.

These criticisms could be developed in at least two ways into a kind of praise—or, at least, neutralized. Lewis adopts neither. One is Kenner's solution: he agrees with Lewis that Stephen is a prig, but goes on to argue that Joyce intended him to be one, that Stephen's characterization is ironic. Lewis recognizes this possibility, but rejects it as an inadequate excuse: "From this charge Joyce would probably attempt to escape by saying that with Dedalus he was dealing with a sentimental young man. But that unfortunately does not explain his strange fondness for his company, nor his groundless assumption that he will be liked by us" (126). Such a solution also leaves untouched Lewis's objection that Stephen represents and betrays the intellectual—or the classical—principle. The second option is the now common view that neither character alone represents an adequate vision of life, and that the novel suggests a balance between the two. To this explanation, I think, Lewis would object with some justification that the balance is uneven, that Stephen is far too "mean and ridiculous" to hold his own against his opposite.

We must remember, too, how Lewis is directed by his definition of his role as a critic: "In such a crisis, all the weight of our intelligence should be thrown into the scales representing our deepest instincts." His deliberate polemical bias restrains him from suggesting that Joyce might successfully stand on both sides of the scales at once; his commitment to defending intellect prevents him from accepting any compromise between mind and sensuality. Instead, he derives from such flaws as Stephen's priggishness a general judgment about Joyce: "Where a multitude of little details or some obvious idiosyncrasy are concerned, he may be said to be observant; but the secret of an *entire* organism escapes him. Not being observant where entire people (that is, people at all) are concerned, he depicts them conventionally always, under some general label" (118). And he concludes, "It is in tracking this other sort of cliché—the cliché of feeling, of thought, and in a less detailed sense, of expression—that you will find everywhere beneath the surface in Joyce a conventional basis or framework" (126).

Lewis sees the time-cult's influence in Joyce's treatment of

The Enemy Versus James Joyce: Literary Criticism

nationalism, his interest in time and timelessness, and his explorations of his characters' consciousness; even the conjunction of empty characters and rich details reflects the time-philosophy. Because the characters in *Ulysses* are too lifeless and the things that surround them are too much alive, the distinction between mind and matter is obscured from both directions: "For it is in the fragmentation of a personality—by isolating some characteristic weakness, mood, or time-self—that you arrive at the mechanical and abstract, the opposite of the living. This, however, leaves [Joyce] free to achieve with a mass of detail a superficial appearance of life" (118). Joyce tends to see both personality and the material world as a series of fragments or events; he depicts the changing reality of the time-philosopher rather than the stable classical reality.

To explain the contrast between Joyce's technical sophistication and conceptual naiveté, Lewis also proposes a description of the artist's personality. "Two opposite things were required for this result," he writes. "Mr. Joyce could never have performed this particular feat if he had not been, in his make-up, extremely immobile; and yet, in contradiction to that, very open to new technical influences. It is the *craftsman* in Joyce that is progressive; but the *man* has not moved since his early days in Dublin" (109). Joyce's strength simultaneously limits him: "There is not very much reflection going on at any time inside the head of Mr. James Joyce. That is indeed the characteristic condition of *the craftsman*, pure and simple" (106).

Moreover, Lewis suggests, this conjunction is not coincidental: "Daring or unusual speculation, or an unwonted intensity of outlook, is not good for technical display, that is certain, and they are seldom found together. The intellect is in one sense the rival of the hand, and is apt to hamper rather than assist it" (112). As a technician Joyce is unlikely to be a thinker. This conclusion not only encloses very neatly much of Lewis's view of Joyce. It is also an Enemy maneuver: it turns a superficially neutral comment into a criticism of another artist and an implicit defense of Lewis's own work. One of the most common—and accurate—complaints about Lewis's books is that they lack technical polish; but in the light of this opposition between hand and mind, that very roughness would signal their intellectual vigor, their "daring or unusual speculation," their "unwonted intensity of outlook."

In Joyce's case this condition accounts for his susceptibility to the time-cult and his usefulness as an exhibit for Lewis. "The craftsman is susceptible and unprotected":

> He is become so much a writing-specialist that it matters very little to him *what* he writes, or what idea or world-view he expresses...Strictly speaking, he has none at all, no special point of view, or none worth mentioning. It is such people that the creative intelligence fecundates and uses; and at present that intelligence is political, and its stimuli are masked ideologies. He is only a tool, an instrument, in short. That is why such a sensitive medium as Joyce, working in such a period, requires the attention of the independent critic. (107)

Ulysses expresses the world-view of modern politics and the time-philosophy; Joyce has inadvertently allowed his novel to become infused with fashionable doctrines. "And I am sure," Lewis says, "that he would be put to his trumps to say how he came by much of the time-machinery that he possesses" (106): "So though Joyce has written a time-book, he has done it, I believe, to some extent, by accident" (109–10). The example of Joyce reveals how much the time-cult affects even the most serious and innovative recent literature. For despite his natural "elasticity and freedom" (91), his admirable "highly-developed *physical* basis" and essential sanity (107), and his largely classical aesthetic principles, most of the weaknesses in *Ulysses* point to parallel weaknesses in other aspects of modern culture.

If in a way Joyce is right that Lewis spoke only "ten per cent of the truth" about his book, if in a way Wagner is right that the "Analysis of the Mind of James Joyce" is "a *deliberate misunderstanding*," if in a way Kenner is right that it is a "brilliant misreading," surely it is also crucial that we first recognize how Lewis's purposes are quite specific, how his analysis is openly partisan and limited, how he criticizes not to elucidate but to provoke change. All readings, as we know from Harold Bloom, are misreadings: that Lewis's is deliberate, even advertised, is surely a strength, even if we set aside the question of its brilliance. Wagner is certainly wrong when he calls Lewis's argument "malicious" and "almost inexplicable"; on its own terms, understood in the determining context of Lewis's philosophical and cultural arguments, it makes very clear sense. When we know how the Enemy criticism is structured, we are free to enjoy the vigor of this now iconoclastic attack—and to respond to the specific points about *Ulysses* on their own (considerable) merits—without being blinded to the justice of Lewis's underlying thesis.

THE CRITICAL CONTEXT

In her 1948 introduction to the collection *James Joyce: Two Decades of Criticism,* Seon Givens dismissed Lewis's analysis as one among "the personal diatribes which supply little except curiosity value." But if on a cursory reading, Lewis's criticism may look like a personal diatribe, a closer and more sympathetic reading, as we have seen, reveals a systematic, intelligent, and insightful analysis of certain important aspects of Joyce's work. We have still to see how Lewis compares to Joyce's other critics. When we look at what has been written about Joyce—both by Lewis's contemporaries and by more recent writers—we find that the Enemy's ideas remain highly individual at the same time as they are echoed and paralleled with remarkable frequency. We find, indeed, that his place in the tradition of Joyce criticism very neatly endorses his axiomatic faith that an aggressively personal criticism need not be solipsistic or irresponsibly idiosyncratic.

We might expect that Lewis would resemble other early unfavorable critics of Joyce's work, especially of *Ulysses*. After all, as Robert Deming says in his introduction to the Critical Heritage volumes on Joyce, Lewis's was "the first major and significant blow at Joyce's rising reputation."[7] Surprisingly, though, he has as little in common with Joyce's attackers as with his supporters. Both in what it says and in what it doesn't say, Lewis's "Analysis of the Mind of James Joyce" stands largely alone in the criticism appearing before 1930. There is one important exception: the charge that *Ulysses* is monotonous appears often in early reviews and analyses, expressed usually in terms of the critic's boredom or Joyce's failure to discriminate which details to include in his fictional encyclopedia. To this complaint Lewis adds some vivid and memorable metaphors (this book is "like a gigantic victorian quilt or antimacassar"; it "will remain, eternally cathartic, a monument like a record diarrhoea" [109]); more important, he is unusual in trying to account for the flaw of excessive, undigested detail. His explanations, both of Joyce's personality and of the destructive conjunction of nineteenth-century realism and the time-philosophy, are distinctively Lewis's own.

Of his major complaints about the novel, though, this is the only one echoed by others. Oddly enough, very little is said in early criticism about the merits of Stephen and Bloom as characters. On the whole, Joyce's admirers call them remarkably faithful and complete portraits of human nature and consciousness; his detractors call them libels on

The Enemy Versus James Joyce: Literary Criticism

humanity, blasphemous and obscene. But perhaps because, as Marshall McLuhan comments, most of Joyce's critics "approach their subject in an awkward and diffident spirit,"[8] Lewis's comments are unusual in their mixture of confidence and relative emotional detachment. If he dislikes both Stephen and Bloom, he is not shocked or disgusted by them. On the more general issue of Joyce's intellectual originality and rigor, he is equally isolated, though there are some who agree with him in part. Perhaps the closest is Rebecca West, another critic Givens dismisses with Lewis. West, whose perspective was similarly serious and avant-garde, also sees in *Ulysses,* and especially Stephen Dedalus, evidence of Joyce's "gross sentimentality," incongruously mixed with his technical experimentation: "James Joyce, confident in his own revolutionary quality, because his sentences wear the cap of liberty, weakens his masterpiece by executing it with hands made tremulous by the most reactionary sentimentality."[9] But again, Lewis is set apart by his effort to place his criticism in a larger philosophical and cultural context.

Equally individual are the things Lewis doesn't say. He dismisses in one short paragraph "the scandalous element in *Ulysses,* its supposed obscenity" (110), and he does not even mention the difficulty or obscurity of either *Ulysses* or *Work in Progress.* These two omissions alone make Lewis's attack vitally different from nearly every other negative criticism of Joyce. (Even West, who is not bothered by the obscurity, dislikes the obscenity.) If in their general outlines, his views associate him with critics too old-fashioned to value experiment in the arts, Lewis's neglect of the most obvious ways in which he could attack Joyce points to his special motives and criteria. Because he believes Joyce's work is important, Lewis thinks its flaws must be taken seriously, not simply deplored; because he believes artistic experiment is vital to cultural health, he devotes himself to analyzing in detail the *kinds* of experiments Joyce is making.

For all his hostility, this fundamental seriousness brings Lewis far closer to Joyce's admirers than to his detractors.

Yet in other respects Lewis's views do not much resemble those of other early critics of Joyce. The most revealing comparisons are with his two other friends and fellow classicists, Eliot and Pound, both of whom had praised *Ulysses* in print before 1927. Lewis deliberately disassociates himself from their positions, not by challenging them directly but by casually dismissing their ideas among those he regards as trivial or incorrect. Thus he shrugs off with a single sentence one of the main concerns of Joyce's admirers—most notably, at that time, Valery Larbaud and Eliot: "As to the homeric framework, that is only an entertaining structural device or conceit" (121). Unlike these critics (and many who have followed), Lewis had no interest in explication. We would never find him writing what Eliot does in his 1923 essay, "*Ulysses*, Order and Myth": "All that one can usefully do at this time, and it is a great deal to do, for such a book, is to elucidate any aspect of the book... which has not yet been fixed."[10] Although Lewis might agree that this is a useful task, we know that he believes the role of the critic is to point out things that should be *changed*. Of course, Eliot criticizes to change in other essays; he calls his 1923 piece on Joyce an "appreciation."

Beyond this basic difference in purpose, though, Lewis also has a kind of vested interest in discrediting a view of Joyce that would value his return to the past, while Eliot clearly had a personal interest in promoting the use of myth. Lewis hints at this difference when he includes Pound's and Eliot's historical concerns among the things that have influenced Joyce. Eliot praises Joyce's "mythical method" as "a step toward making the modern world possible for art," a step toward classic order and form; Lewis, by dismissing this very method as trivial, points to the major difference between his vision of the classic—and of the best

The Enemy Versus James Joyce: Literary Criticism

direction for modern art—and the vision of these contemporaries.

Lewis differs from Pound in a similarly indirect way. "Another writer with whom [Joyce] has been compared, and whom he is peculiarly unlike, is Flaubert" (92), Lewis writes. But just this comparison had been the main theme of Pound's praise of Joyce for some ten years. In a published "Paris Letter" of 1922, for example, Pound had written, "Joyce has taken up the art of writing where Flaubert left it. . . . in Ulysses he has carried on a process begun in Bouvard et Pécuchet; he has brought it to a degree of greater efficiency, of greater compactness. . . Ulysses has more form than any novel of Flaubert's."[11] Even earlier, he had said about *Portrait* and Lewis's *Tarr*, "I would say that James Joyce produces the nearest thing to Flaubertian prose that we have now in English, just as Wyndham Lewis has written a novel which is more like, and more fitly compared with, Dostoievsky than is the work of any of his contemporaries" (*Pound/Joyce* 89). So when Lewis dismisses the similarity between Joyce and Flaubert, he is implicitly denying Joyce his half of Pound's praise and leaving his own half intact—in a typical Enemy maneuver. He continues this denial in two other brief remarks: "Contact with any of [Joyce's] writing, must, to begin with, show that we are not in the presence of a tragic writer, of the description of Dostoievsky or of Flaubert" (92), he says; and "all you have got to do is to compare the frigid prig [Stephen] . . . with one of the principal heroes of the russian novels, and a spiritual gulf of some sort will become apparent" (116). Lewis turns Pound's comparison into a contrast—in this case, I think, one that enriches his argument about Joyce's unsatisfactory characters. The heroes of nineteenth-century Russian novels are in a class of their own; even if his own character Kreisler had not been compared to these figures, Lewis would be able to use this contrast to support his criticism that Joyce created stock characters.[12] Lewis inverts Pound's praise in two other similar ways. Pound argues in several pieces that Bloom continues and improves on Bouvard and Pécuchet; Lewis writes, "Where Bloom is being Bouvard and Pécuchet, it is a translation, nothing more" (121). And Pound's vision of *Ulysses* as the culminating product of nineteenth-century realism is transformed into Lewis's argument that Joyce was the extreme version of Zola-like naturalism. By comparing him to Zola rather than Flaubert, Lewis emphasizes Joyce's tendency toward obsessively detailed description, and, again, revises Pound's praise into criticism.

Despite all their apparent differences, though, Lewis and Pound ended up in general agreement about Joyce. In a curious testimonial to the power of Lewis's arguments in *Time and Western Man*, Pound echoed more and more of his views in the following years. In 1931 he wrote that he preferred *The Apes of God* to *Finnegans Wake*, which he did not like at all (*Pound/Joyce* 240); in 1933 he joined Lewis in dismissing the Homeric parallels as "mere mechanics" that "any blockhead can go back and trace." In the same essay, Pound quoted a remark of Lewis's and modified it:

> Mr Wyndham Lewis' specific criticism of *Ulysses* can now be published. It was made in 1922 or '23. "Ungh!" he grunted, "He [Joyce] don't seem to have any very new point of view about anything." Such things are a matter of degree. There is a time for a man to experiment with his medium. When he has a mastery of it; or when he has developed it, and extended it, he or a successor can apply it.
>
> *Ulysses* is a summary of pre-war Europe, the blackness and muddle of a "civilization" led by disguised forces and a bought press, the general sloppiness, the plight of the individual intelligence in that mess! Bloom very much *is* the mess! (*Pound/Joyce* 251)

The Enemy Versus James Joyce: Literary Criticism

At about this time, according to Forrest Read, "Joyce became a focus for Pound's impatience with passéism and the stream of consciousness" (*Pound/Joyce* 255). Apparently, Pound was finding that the things he did not like about *Finnegans Wake* were much the same as those Lewis had not liked about *Ulysses*—and about what *Ulysses* revealed of "the mind of James Joyce."

In one of his war time radio talks, following Joyce's death, Pound returned to these matters in what seems to me a very perceptive account of his praise, Lewis's criticism, and Joyce's achievement. "And I went out with the big bass drum," he said, "cause a masterwork is a masterwork, and damn all and damn whom wont back it, without hedgin."

> Well Mr. Lewis made the BOUNDARY line, DEFINED the limit of Mr. J's Ulysses. (I said HUSH, at the time) I said wait till they *see* it.
>
> After the tree has *grown* you can begin prunin the branches.
>
> Well old Wyndham grumped: as follows, he said about J's Ulysses "Don't seem (Meaning Mr Joyce doesn't seem) to have a very NEW pt. of view about anythin". In the old style of painting, say Rembrandt or Durer or Carpaccio, or Mantegna when a painter starts painting a picture he damn well better NOT git a new point of view till he has finished it.
>
> Same way for a masterpiece of lit. new pt. of view shd BE either before a man starts his paintin: his recordin contemporary Anschauung, contemporary disposition to life, or AFTER he is thru his portrayin.
>
> That was Ulysses LIMIT, it painted a dying world, whereof some parts are eternal.

Joyce, Pound agreed, "had no philosophy, not so you would notice it"; Lewis, on the other hand, had "philosophical views," however "wrong headed" (*Pound/Joyce* 267–68). Of course Pound shared a great many of Lewis's quirks, and so we must read his agreement partly in the light of their mutual biases. But he is right, I think, both about the merit of Lewis's criticism and about its circumstantial limits.

Critics who agree with Lewis are not, moreover, limited to his friends. We find his judgments echoed even by some of his enemies—with the differences in attitude we would expect. Seon Givens, for example, who dismisses Lewis in 1948, echoes him in 1963: Joyce, she says, "was the very first to put on paper a creative expression of twentieth-century time.... He had a grasp of time in the psychoanalytic sense—no beginning or no end, a palimpsest of emotion and reconditioning; he speculated about the physicist's time; he had an uncanny grasp of his own time. It *was* fragmented; it *was* nightmarish."[13] Givens does not mention Lewis in this praise of Joyce—in fact, in the 1963 edition of the collection, this passage immediately follows the earlier introduction where she says Lewis is of no interest—but certainly the idea is his. Givens merely claims as a strength what Lewis had seen as a weakness.

Harry Levin's *James Joyce: A Critical Introduction* does much the same thing, as Lewis points out in *Rude Assignment*. In one instance Levin calls Lewis malicious at the same time that he repeats his point: Bloom's "staccato diction, as the malice of Wyndham Lewis did not fail to observe, makes a startling appearance in the very first novel of Charles Dickens." More subtly, Levin echoes Lewis's view of Joyce's characters and conceptual clichés, but this time he does not acknowledge that Lewis made the point first. "Characterization in Joyce," he says, "is finally reducible to a few stylized gestures and simplified attitudes"; and again, "*Ulysses* is not so rich in psychological insight as in technical brilliance." Conceptual conventionality and technical sophistication—this was Lewis's judgment fourteen years before it was Levin's. Levin simply chooses to focus on

Joyce's strength and minimize his weakness; Lewis does the opposite.

Indeed, if we read Levin with Lewis in mind, we find echoes on point after point: "Bloom, on the whole, is our sensorium, and it is his experience that becomes ours.... Bloom's mind is...a motion picture" (remember Lewis's use of film as a metaphor for the time-cult's vision); Joyce's "blurred sight looked for compensation in augmented sound" (Lewis says the time-cult substitutes sound for vision); "The plethora of Joyce's detail is a last exuberant outpouring of naturalism," but "action is impeded by the accumulation of details"; and, most comprehensively, "It is suggestive to note that Bergson, Whitehead, and others... were thinking in the same direction. Thus the very form of Joyce's book is an elusive and eclectic *Summa* of its age: the *montage* of the cinema, impressionism in painting, *leitmotif* in music, the free association of psychoanalysis, and vitalism in philosophy." This could be a summary of the argument of *Time and Western Man*. But if Levin has been influenced by Lewis's argument (as it would certainly seem he has), he buries his indebtedness (in his bibliography he calls Lewis's attack "well timed and badly aimed, penetrating and exasperating"); here the Enemy provokes another critic into an Enemy move.[14]

If Givens and Levin hint at Lewis's influence on Joyce criticism, Hugh Kenner's work acknowledges and embodies that influence. As Kenner says in the acknowledgments to *Dublin's Joyce*, "But it is to Wyndham Lewis's chapter in *Time and Western Man* that I owe the challenge of incontrovertible facts that would square neither with the received image of Joyce nor, as he interprets them, with my own conviction of the value of Joyce's work." Kenner's general pattern is to begin from one of Lewis's specific criticisms, point out its limitations, and then incorporate it into a positive interpretation of Joyce's work. Usually, this new interpretation depends on reading Joyce as ironic or parodic; Joyce does all the things Lewis accuses him of doing, says Kenner, but he does them all deliberately. "James Joyce's central technique," in Kenner's view, is the "parody of the once vital to enact a null apprehension of the null"—a positive restatement of Lewis's claim that Joyce's Dublin is a simulacrum of the no-longer-real.

Kenner agrees with Lewis about Joyce's characters, especially Stephen, but from a different perspective. "All his characters are walking clichés, because the Dubliners were"; and Stephen Dedalus is "the egocentric rebel become an ultimate." Repeating Lewis's observations, Kenner suggests that "the Stephen of the first chapter of *Ulysses* who 'walks wearily,' constantly 'leans' on everything in sight, invariably sits down before he has gone three paces, speaks 'gloomily', 'quietly', 'with bitterness', and 'coldly', and 'suffers' his handkerchief to be pulled from his pocket by the exuberant Mulligan, is precisely the priggish, humourless Stephen of the last chapter of the *Portrait*."[15] As Richard Deming puts it, "Wyndham Lewis and Hugh Kenner founded the 'Stephen-hating school' wherein Stephen Dedalus's callowness and sentimentality, as well as Joyce's irony, were established."[16] Lewis, we might say, identifies the problem; Kenner redefines it as evidence of Joyce's sophistication.

This is also the pattern behind Kenner's more recent *Joyce's Voices*. Lewis cites Joyce's description of Stephen's Uncle Charles (from *Portrait*) as "repairing" to the outhouse, having "brushed scrupulously" his hair, and accuses Joyce of slipping into the prose of "works of fiction of the humblest order or...newspaper articles" (126). Kenner works from this observation into an argument that Joyce deliberately manipulates his language to reflect the characteristics of the figures being described; he calls his idea the "Uncle Charles Principle," and credits Lewis with discovering but failing to understand this crucial—though certainly subtle—aspect of Joyce's art. Kenner also points out that Lewis's examples of this kind of cliché in *Ulysses* come only from the first chapter (as Lewis himself says) and explains that they are part of the whole chapter's parody of precisely those conventions Lewis identifies. As Kenner recognizes, Lewis's primary interest in such clichés is that they are "telltale"; still, Kenner's explanations appropriately modify Lewis's complaints with a delicacy (if not ingenuousness) uncharacteristic of the Enemy. Again, Kenner begins with Lewis's discovery and then reverses his judgment.[17]

In another instance of the same pattern, Kenner points to the basic contrast between his views and Lewis's. After agreeing with Lewis that *Ulysses* is "at one level" a "huge and intricate machine clanking and whirring for eighteen hours... Its characters walking clichés, as Wyndham Lewis had the want of tact to point out... Its psychological insights dry, hard, somehow obvious, devoid of Freudian romance," Kenner suggests, "If you were to project an auctorial personality behind *Ulysses*, you would find, in fact, if you insisted on feeling for a personality, just the personality sketched by Wyndham Lewis in his brilliant misreading of the book... Joyce has been at great pains to build up this persona behind his book." But, Kenner says, Lewis erred by mistaking this "mind that informs *Ulysses*" for "the mind of James Joyce." Such a solution clearly depends on a kind of subtlety foreign to the aggressive boldness of the Enemy criticism. As Kenner writes, "With these master-keys in his hand Lewis might have written the definitive exegesis. It pleased him however to use *Ulysses* rather than seek to reveal it."[18]

Kenner's analyses show us rather clearly how Lewis's specific critical and polemical purpose limited his flexibility— and also how that purpose sharpened his eye for Joyce's flaws. Lewis cannot suspend his censure of Joyce's conceptual framework to appreciate his technical accomplishment, but he does see through that dazzling surface to the possibility of an underlying conventionality; he cannot accept irony, but he does recognize the boundaries of Joyce's characters; he cannot write "the definitive exegesis," but he does offer to other critics "the challenge of incontrovertible facts."[19] Certainly, to succeed in issuing such a challenge is an important achievement—one that might well content Lewis in his capacity of gadfly or Enemy. Even if a critic like Kenner ends up thinking Lewis was wrong, Lewis has still provoked Kenner to think.

All of these critics—Pound, Levin, Kenner—show us the kinds of influences—hidden and acknowledged—Lewis has had on later criticism. But how do the Enemy's views compare with those of critics perhaps not directly influenced by him? Rather surprisingly, nearly all of Lewis's observations can be found, in one form or another, in the much more favorable analyses of other major critics. Despite his Enemy stance, what Lewis finds of interest about Joyce has consistently concerned others. The differences are not surprising: often, different contexts and purposes allow other critics to work with more care and balance; and almost always, what Lewis sees as Joyce's failings, others see as neutral or positive achievements.

A characteristic instance is a 1945 piece by Frederick Hoffmann about Joyce's interest in psychoanalytic theory and his experiments with stream-of-consciousness writing. Like Lewis, Hoffmann deals with this as a technique with possibilities and limitations; unlike Lewis, he details these possibilities, both in general and in Joyce's writing, and relates them to psychological theory. His basic premises about Joyce and about *Ulysses* closely resemble Lewis's: he quotes Eugene Jolas as saying that " 'Joyce had a passion for the irrational manifestations of life' "; and he explains that although "*Ulysses* is not a document of the Unconscious," still "the salient esthetic fact is its emphasis upon the psyche rather than upon externality." Like Lewis, too, Hoffmann looks at the fragmentation of personality and the disintegration of traditional categories of time and space. Stream-of-consciousness writing, he says, is "based on the assumption that personality is not static" but fluid and unstable; each "level" of stream-of-consciousness "has its own system of references to space and time"; as one moves deeper into the unconscious, one finds the "rational space-time continuum" being gradually obscured and replaced by private systems of different kinds.[20] Lewis, of course, says exactly the same things.

Hoffmann finds all this interesting and important, and so he gives it the sympathetic—though not uncritical—attention Lewis refuses. His article may be more useful to Joyce's readers, consequently; it certainly offers more information about psychoanalytic theory. And yet Lewis's very refusal to accept the premises of stream-of-consciousness—or the value of exploring the unconscious—can itself raise important questions. Hoffmann contributes to what is by now the received wisdom about psychoanalysis and modern literature. But Lewis—again—challenges us to question and possibly to reevaluate that wisdom.

A second critic who resembles Lewis in illuminating ways is Edmund Wilson. In his discussion of *Ulysses* in *Axel's Castle* (1931), Wilson covers much of the same ground Lewis does, and, like Lewis, finds things to criticize in Joyce's work. Wilson regards the Homeric parallel as relatively important; he admires Joyce's characters; and he praises the "psychological truth" of the novel. "With *Ulysses*," Wilson affirms, "Joyce has brought into literature a new and unknown beauty"—a direct contradiction of Lewis's polemical assertions that the products of the time-cult are the opposite of new beauty. But beyond these disagreements, Wilson's and Lewis's ideas are very similar. Both, for instance, argue that the realistic, external setting in the novel tends to dissolve under the pressure of the psychological; both compare this effect to Proust's relativism. Wilson, though, approves. More important, the two men agree that

Ulysses embodies the "new phase of the human consciousness," in Wilson's words, or the "time-mind," in Lewis's. Wilson compliments Joyce in terms that closely parallel Lewis's condemnation:

> Joyce is indeed really the great poet of a new phase of the human consciousness. Like Proust's or Whitehead's or Einstein's world, Joyce's world is always changing as it is perceived by different observers and by them at different times.... Such a world cannot be presented in terms of such artificial abstractions as have been conventional in the past: solid institutions, groups, individuals, which play the parts of distinct durable entities—or even of solid psychological factors: dualisms of good and evil, mind and matter, flesh and spirit, instinct and reason; clear conflicts between passion and duty, between conscience and interest. Not that these conceptions are left out of Joyce's world: they are all there in the minds of the characters; and the realities they represent are there, too. But everything is reduced to terms of "events" like those of modern physics and philosophy.

But again, Wilson's conclusion about all of this is quite unlike Lewis's: in his view these "events" add up to "a picture, amazingly lifelike and living, of the everyday world we know."[21]

These two critics also come very close to agreeing about the flaws of Joyce's book. "*Ulysses* suffers from an excess of design rather than from a lack of it," Wilson argues: "Joyce has as little respect as Proust for the capacities of the reader's attention; and one feels, in Joyce's case as in Proust's, that the *longeurs* which break our backs, the mechanical combinations of elements which fail to coalesce, are partly the result of the effort of a supernormally energetic mind to compensate by piling things up for an inability to make them move." In too much of the book, he believes, Joyce has "half-buried his story under the virtuosity of his technical devices." Though Wilson (who has the benefit of Stuart Gilbert's exegesis) sees as an excess of design what Lewis sees as an excess of "unorganized brute material," both find the texture of detail uncomfortably dense. In Wilson's words, "There is tremendous vitality in Joyce, but very little movement"; in Lewis's, the novel is made sluggish by "the amount of *stuff*...that the more active principle of drama has to wade through." So far, Wilson's judgments are much like Lewis's—even if his critical voice does not sound like the Enemy's.[22]

The significant difference between the two—or the one that has become significant in subsequent Joyce criticism—is in the metaphor with which Wilson associates this flaw. The positive aspect of Joyce's lack of movement or drama, Wilson thinks, is that *Ulysses* (at least on re-reading) seems "something solid like a city which actually existed in space and which could be entered from any direction." Joyce's "force, instead of following a line, expands itself in every dimension (including that of time) about a single point."[23] Following Wilson's lead, as William Chace points out, other critics like Harry Levin and S. L. Goldberg have seen *Ulysses* as essentially spatial[24]—in what regularly looks like a direct contradiction of Lewis's identification of the novel as a time-book. But this contradiction is more apparent than real.

Critics' reasons for describing *Ulysses* as spatial fall into two general categories. Some focus on the reader's experience of the novel. Joseph Frank has argued this view most clearly in his discussions of spatial form in modern literature. Along with other major modernist artists, he believes, Joyce attempted to create a work that would reach its full meaning all at once in the reader's mind; *Ulysses*, in other words, shares the same aesthetic as Pound's Imagist poems.[25] Lewis would probably agree with most of what Frank says about the intentions of modern writers, but when he calls *Ulysses* a time-book, he is simply not talking about the same thing. Lewis is *not* arguing that a reader's experience of *Ulysses* is temporal where it should be spatial. (The closest he comes to addressing this issue, in fact, is his complaint that the book moves too slowly—that Joyce has too little sense of dramatic movement.[26]) Instead, he is arguing that Joyce's work shares the metaphysic of the cultural complex he calls the time-cult.

Other critics focus on the attitude toward time within the world of the novel. This view is expressed, for instance, by Anthony Burgess in his *ReJoyce:* "The whole book has a spatial scheme in which time has been divested of its bullying hurry-along authority... Time is the great enemy, and books like *Ulysses* and *Finnegans Wake* triumphantly trounce it. Time has to be put in its place." Others, like Harry Levin, make the same point by saying that the world of the novel is "timeless," or, like Frank Kermode, that it is "intemporal."[27] Lewis himself, we have seen, counters this argument by pointing out that Joyce's timelessness is thoroughly bound up with relativist and psychological theories of time. Burgess and Levin indirectly endorse Lewis's view; both describe Joyce's timelessness or spatiality as the result of his concern with time.

All these disagreements are primarily about terminology and the judgments carried by terminology. Lewis, like these later critics, has his own reasons for using space and time as descriptive and evaluative terms. But to a surprising degree, critics after Lewis agree with him about the important characteristics of Joyce's novel—that it is concerned with time and timelessness and spatiality, and that its ways of dealing with these things have much in common with the conceptual changes occurring in modern science and philosophy. Some, like Frank and Burgess, focus on Joyce's reaction to these changes, suggesting that he uses the new concepts to construct an escape from time. Others, like Kermode and Lewis, focus on Joyce's participation in these changes, pointing out that to escape from time, Joyce has chosen to use the new concepts.

The long critical debate on this one issue has clearly helped to distort readers' understanding of Lewis's arguments. Because critics like Frank and Kermode—and there are many others—have given their attention to time and space in modern literature, Lewis's analysis has come to seem like a contribution to the same debate. But it is not: only a very small part of his view of Joyce has to do with Joyce's use of time and space proper. That his concerns are much wider, and that he uses these terms as shorthand, anyone who reads the whole of *Time and Western Man* can see. But the chapter on Joyce read alone leaves Lewis's larger context unclear, and so in a sense invites misunderstanding.

The importance of reading Lewis's criticism in context has led to more general problems as well. Most obviously, it has kept him out of critical anthologies. His analysis of Joyce does appear in edited form in the *Critical Heritage* collection, but these volumes are exceptional. Since *Time and Western Man*—like Lewis's other volumes of literary criticism—is not readily available, Lewis's contributions to the critical tradition have been obscured for this reason alone. William Chace's comment in his introduction to the Twentieth Century Views volume on Joyce is one of the more favorable references to Lewis's criticism: "The most important of the early iconoclasts was Wyndham Lewis, whose boisterous and overwritten attack on what he thought was the formlessness of Joyce's work is not now much read." Chace goes on to summarize Lewis's argument very briefly and to indicate its importance for other critics; but he does not include Lewis in his collection. And he cannot be faulted for this. Not only does Lewis's "Analysis" lose much of its coherence when it is removed from *Time and Western Man,* but because it is packed with digressions about the time-cult, it would also need to be substantially edited and annotated to make clear sense. In this respect Lewis's obscurity results both from his own patterns of argument and from the importance of self-sufficient essays in modern criticism.

Much the same thing can be said about the effect of Lewis's polemical slant—and the extent to which his critical judgments are Enemy attacks. As C. H. Sisson remarks in his introduction to the collection *Enemy Salvoes,* "The relative obscurity of Lewis's critical writing... is due partly to the fact that the immense success of Eliot's apologetics has turned people's minds away from other methods of criticism."[28] The dominant tone of twentieth-century literary critics has been far different from the Enemy's flamboyant exaggerations and gaudy insults. Consequently, we are more likely to echo Chace's "over-written"—or even Leavis's "brutal and boring"—than to enjoy what Kenner calls Lewis's "epithetic sparkle." The inadequacy or inappropriateness of our expectations is not Lewis's fault. But his analysis of Joyce makes it clear that his critical stance also has significant inherent limitations. Because he throws his weight so enthusiastically on one side of the balance, he frequently seems to see only one side of the issues he is arguing. And because he alienates many readers with his rhetoric, he fails to convince them of the same points another more tactful critic might argue with more success.

Yet at the same time, Lewis can also succeed in his own way. For some readers Lewis can offer a challenge—sometimes one of "incontrovertible facts" that do not square with other impressions, sometimes simply one of uncommon and powerful arguments that demand either agreement or refutation. Lewis's role as an Enemy is all the more important because it is so unusual in modern criticism. As a literary critic, Lewis may finally be strongest, ironically, as an opposite—not as the opposite of those he analyzes, but as an opposite against whom we can define our own judgments.

The Enemy Versus the Zeitgeist: Cultural Criticism

THE ENEMY VERSUS MOSZKOWSKI

To explain his temerity in dealing with matters outside the arts, Lewis writes: "It has been suggested...that I should be better advised to ignore such things [as mathematical physics], and only attend to what happens in my own field. Now that I should be delighted to do if these different worlds of physics, philosophy, politics and art were (as, according to my view, they should be) rigidly separated" (*TWM* 9–10). But in the time-cult, of course, these worlds are not distinct; in fact, they are so full of parallels and influences as to seem not just unified but uniform. And so, Lewis finds, his analysis of the state of the arts must expand into an analysis of a culture.

In his concentrated attack on the time-cult in *Time and Western Man,* Lewis considers the theories of culture presented in three books: Spengler's *Decline of the West,* Whitehead's *Science and the Modern World,* and Alexander Moszkowski's *Einstein, The Searcher.* Spengler, with whom Lewis deals at length, and whom he calls the "philosopher of the Zeitgeist," sees politics as the basis of culture; Whitehead sees science as the source not only of the modern world but of all cultures; Moszkowski, in his praise of Einstein's genius, indirectly suggests that philosophy (which is itself sometimes political) lies beneath even scientific theories. Each of these men serves Lewis as a spokesman for the primacy of one of the three main aspects of what he calls culture's "theoretic plane"—politics, physics, and philosophy. By examining their views, Lewis suggests and questions several different explanations of the ties among these fields. In each case he finds himself in partial agreement at the same time that he recognizes the inadequacy of any simple solution to a highly complex problem. And in each case, he hints at what his own account would be but backs off from any direct statements.

The discussion of Moszkowski comes first in *Time and Western Man,* but it is quite possibly the last Lewis wrote. It appears in the "Preface" to counter criticism of Lewis's interdisciplinary approach—as a tentative justification for speaking of a scientist like Einstein as if his ideas were like a philosopher's or an artist's. So in a sense it encloses the critique of the time-cult. Although it is short (much shorter than the chapters on Spengler), and although Lewis does not regard Moszkowski (unlike Whitehead) as of much real importance, this discussion nevertheless introduces in a particularly succinct form all of the major issues Lewis will confront every time he considers the nature of cultures. It also raises many of the questions Lewis will find impossible to answer in his own tentative solutions.

Moszkowski is not himself especially interested in the sources of the Zeitgeist, although he tacitly assumes its existence in his book about Einstein. But he does make a few comments Lewis finds useful in dealing with the relationship between scientific discoveries and contemporary political and philosophical theories. The question is this: Suppose we should find that a scientific theory significantly parallels a philosophical or political system current at the time of the discoveries on which that theory is built. Does such a parallel suggest that the scientist's work has been somehow directed by nonscientific concerns? If so, to what extent does the role of these external influences undermine the validity—the truth—of the discoveries or of the theories? The answer Moszkowski suggests in the case of Einstein seems to Lewis simultaneously compelling and repellent: he finds he must agree with Moszkowski's description of the situation, but he is torn between agreeing and disagreeing with his interpretation.

According to Moszkowski, Lewis tells us, scientific discovery and philosophy " 'are intimately interwoven with one another, and are only different aspects of one and the same process.' " Bergson's philosophy and the discoveries of Planck and Einstein, Moszkowski thinks, are so similar not by coincidence, but because they result from " 'a demand of the time, exacting that the claims of a new principle of thought be recognized.' " Moreover, science parallels politics: " '[Einstein's] principle of relativity is tantamount to a regulative world-principle that has left a mighty mark on the thought of our times. We have lived to see the death of absolutism: the relativity of the constituents of political power, and their mutability according to view-point and current tendencies, become manifest to us...the world was far enough advanced in its views for a final achievement of thought which could demolish the absolute also from the mathematico-physical aspect' "(*TWM* 15, 16; Lewis's ellipses).[29] To Moszkowski, these similarities apparently mean that a certain kind of scientific idea can best succeed when society is ready for it, or as he says, when "the time is ripe." He clearly does not think that science is made any less "true" by its affinities with less exact disciplines. On the contrary, he seems to regard the analogues to relativity theory as evidence of Einstein's genius. For Moszkowski, science, philosophy, and politics simply progress together.

Now certainly Lewis agrees that Einsteinian physics parallels contemporary political and philosophical constructs: *Time and Western Man* and the other *Man of the World* books are to a large extent based on their similarities. And he agrees that Bergson's philosophy somehow prefigured relativity theory. But if on the whole he accepts Moszkowski's descriptions of the state of affairs, he is much less sanguine about its implications. For Lewis, the general thrust of the analogies Moszkowski sees is to undermine any claims of science to truth. "If Moszkowski's reading of Relativity could be shown by some competent person to be true," Lewis says, "then immediately we should know that the Relativity physics we had been taught to admire was not an achievement of the first order, and that we had been taken in, however much amused in the process. For such an *ad hoc* universe as would result from a desire to 'banish absolutism,' or equally on the other hand to 'establish absolutism,' and impose terrestrial politics upon the stars, would indeed be scientifically a farce, however intelligent a one. But," he concludes, "so many eminent men of science have accepted Einstein's theory, that Moszkowski, as far as Einstein is concerned, must be wrong" (*TWM* 17–18). Where Moszkowski is happy to see the similarities between Einstein and Bergson as an illustration of the united front of progress in the modern world, Lewis views them suspiciously as signs of an insidious influence on a field—science—that ought properly to be impervious to outside forces. Moszkowski offers his views as praise of Einstein; Lewis would consider them a kind of insult. And so he concludes his discussion of Moszkowski by rejecting his ideas.

Yet he is far from rejecting these ideas out of hand; in fact, he finds himself in so much agreement with Moszkowski (or with his interpretation of Moszkowski) that this final dismissal comes to seem as much a gesture of faith as an intellectual decision. For one thing, he welcomes Moszkowski's view of the ties between science and philosophy as an endorsement of his own attack on the tyranny of the time-cult over modern thought. Moreover, in light of his thorough dislike of the time-complex, it is not surprising that he takes advantage of this way of questioning Einstein's authority as an independent, objective thinker—and consequently the authority of philosophers and others who

The Enemy Versus the Zeitgeist: Cultural Criticism

have built upon Einstein's theories. In this respect, I think, we can read Lewis's section on Moszkowski as a rhetorical maneuver that allows him to suggest a point of view he does not want to endorse openly himself. With Moszkowski as his foil, Lewis can raise but not answer a question about the credentials of relativity physics, and thus undermine one of the time-cult's foundations—without actually attacking either Einstein or his mathematics. Similarly, he can suggest that the time-cult may be based on a science that in turn may be politically and philosophically motivated—without directly arguing this view, and without implying that all cultures and all sciences must be motivated in the same way. With one hand, he disassociates himself from Moszkowski on the grounds that "many men of science have accepted Einstein's theory"; with the other hand, he allows Moszkowski to argue a point that is much in line with the substance of his own book. Lewis, we could say, uses Moszkowski as the voice of his Domestic Adversary.

But Lewis also has more disinterested reasons for leaning toward Moszkowski's relativistic point of view. He not only agrees with Moszkowski's description of the modern situation; he also agrees that earlier scientific paradigms have resembled the politics and philosophies contemporary with them. Both men use the example of Newton, whose theories are of course far more congenial to Lewis than are Einstein's. Generally speaking, Lewis argues, "It is mere superstition to suppose 'a mathematician' to be a sort of divine machine. In any reasonable, and not romantic, account of the matter, we must suppose the mathematical physicist not entirely unaffected by neighbouring metaphysical thought" (*TWM* 13–14). So, he concludes, "With the Moszkowskis and Spenglers we reach the point at which the system of the mathematical physicist becomes suspect, in exactly the same way as for long now we have been accustomed to regard with suspicion the system of the philosopher" (18). Lewis goes further here than Moszkowski: he points out that Moszkowski's own logic requires that scientific discovery and theory be regarded not as wholly objective or empirical but as partly determined by the scientist's preconceptions and biases. By extending Moszkowski's argument, Lewis makes it seem more extreme than it really is. Although this is not an unusual kind of rhetorical procedure for the Enemy, in this case, I think, he exaggerates not so much to attack his opponent as to try to clarify a possible explanation of cultural resemblances.

Lewis's interpretation of Moszkowski allows him to raise some difficult theoretical questions. Can we cast doubt on a scientific theory by attacking its philosophical premises? Or can we discredit a theory only through empirical testing? On the whole Lewis would answer that indeed a scientist's work can be vitiated by his personal presuppositions. He certainly thinks motives matter in such applied sciences as behavioral psychology, and he is inclined to think they also matter in the purer, more abstract sciences as well. After all, physicists are no less subject to preconceptions than anyone else; and, Lewis points out, in so metaphysical a field as relativity theory or quantum mechanics, the data are likely to be open to multiple interpretations.

In this belief Lewis aligns himself with the "relativist" side of the debate over another question: In what way (if at all) can scientific theories be refuted or proven? This question and its implications have occupied philosophers of science throughout this century; that Lewis was aware of the initial terms of the debate is clear in his scattered references to Pierre Duhem, who with W. V. O. Quine first argued that there can be no crucial experiments—experiments that establish the validity of a theory beyond all doubt. Significantly, Lewis's appeal to Duhem in the discussion about Einstein is encased in a paraphrase of Moszkowski: "Some of the 'intuitions' don't come off, owing to the unfortunate prevalence of the negative instance, but some do, like Relativity, though all subject, Moszkowski energetically does *not* think, to Duhem's law of reversal, whereby *any* physical system can be knocked over, and can rely on *no* experiment, however 'crucial' " (*TWM* 16–17). Lewis would remind us that like Ptolemy, Copernicus, or Newton, Einstein may himself be improved on or overthrown by someone else's theory.

Now this line of thought is consistent with Lewis's emphasis on personality. The belief that we cannot divorce an idea from its source is a sort of converse of his opinion that people must be held responsible for their ideas. And his corollary argument that an impersonal and wholly objective criticism is impossible would extend logically enough into a similar argument about a wholly objective scientific theory. But at the same time, these views are decidedly at odds with his equally fundamental belief in the essential disinterestedness of the individual mind and its access to some stable truth. (Curiously, this ambivalence in Lewis also parallels one of the major philosophical splits within modern physics itself. One view, that held by Einstein, is that absolute truth exists and is potentially accessible to our knowledge. The second view, that held by Neils Bohr and Max Planck and derived from quantum mechanics, is that the presence of the observer itself alters reality in such a way that our access to knowledge is wholly a question of probabilities. This, I think, is one of the ways in which Lewis's complicated mind mirrors the complications of his time.) With his interpretation of Moszkowski and his appeal to Duhem, Lewis places himself in the awkward position of implying that complete independence and authority are impossible even for a thinker in a field as "pure" as mathematical physics—a position that would contradict Lewis's faith in the purity of the "not-self" and the potential universality of mind. In this position, too, he would seem to agree with the time-cult's belief in the subjectivity of knowledge—the "everything is relative" attitude he condemns as the vulgarized product of Einstein's theories.

And so in a number of direct and indirect ways, Lewis backs off from a position with which he seems substantially to agree. For instance, he encloses his reference to Duhem in a kind of double negative: instead of simply explaining Duhem's ideas, he disagrees (through his sarcasm) with Moszkowski, who would in turn disagree with Duhem. And, I think, he realizes that he is on shaky ground in attacking physics with philosophy—particularly since he is no scientist. Significantly, this is the closest he ever comes to questioning relativity physics itself. In criticizing Moszkowski, a second-rate biographer and popularizer of science, he is on familiar ground; but criticism of Einstein would take him out of his depth.[30] Thus he concludes by bowing to the greater authority of other scientists—although even in this concession he avoids saying that Moszkowski's general view of the relationship between science and other disciplines is incorrect. He says simply, "Moszkowski, *as far as Einstein is concerned,* must be wrong."

Lewis's own conclusion about the time-cult—or as close as he comes to one—is that it results from Einstein's work. As he explains (borrowing the new terminology), "A great many *effects,* a whole string of highly characteristic disturbances, *come out of* einsteinian physics, then.... The cause, if a cause we must have, is einsteinian physics" (*TWM* 12). He chooses to regard Einstein's work as the basis of his culture, I believe, because if anyone can approach pure disinterested thought, it is more likely to be a mathematician than a politician or a philosopher: of all the people Lewis sees as involved in the time-cult, Einstein would seem to be the least affected by preconceptions or inappropriate motives. Before Lewis brings Moszkowski into the discussion, then, he states his faith that "the physical inves-

The Enemy Versus the Zeitgeist: Cultural Criticism

tigations as to the structure of our universe which culminated in Einstein, were, for all any one need suppose to the contrary, as innocent as that...of any human *arrière-pensée*. Nor, further, were they necessarily at all metaphysical in origin" (13). Yet even in the attempt to "make his position clear," he is strangely ambivalent. He brackets his relativistic argument with disclaimers, but these disclaimers carry less conviction than does the argument they would deny.

Lewis does not acknowledge the fundamental self-contradiction in these remarks about Einstein. But he does realize that he has argued two opposing views, and he does what he can to reconcile them. At the end of this introductory foray into the problems of the Zeitgeist, he offers a tentative resolution of the conflict:

> It is only by fully accepting the evident fact that many men of science, or philosophers, are politicians, and their supposed 'pure' theoretic mind in reality merely a very practical one...that we can show that *all* theory and all theoretic men are *not* involved in those proofs and arguments.......There are no doubt good and bad times: in the bad ones these influences may be more powerful. The immense influence exerted on our lives by these 'discoveries' cannot leave us indifferent to the character of the instruments that are responsible for them—namely, the minds of the discoverers. But it is only the less fine instruments that can be influenced in that way and lend colour to spenglerism, that is our argument. This essay is among other things the assertion of a belief in the finest type of mind, which lifts the creative impulse into an absolute region free of spenglerian 'history' or politics. (17–18)

This is a solution we see over and over in Lewis's speculations about cultural unity. There are good times and bad times; there are first-rate and second-rate minds; and all cultures need not be as uniform as the time-cult. If he is not entirely certain about the quality of Einstein's mind, he has no doubt that the modern world in general is dominated by the second-rate. As I have said, this position is quite clearly a statement of faith—"the assertion of a belief in the finest type of mind"—as much as it is a recognition of the imperfection of reality. But if Lewis chooses a belief he himself recognizes as idealistic, he goes further in this instance and tries to devise an explanation that will accommodate both what he sees as the reality and what he desires as the ideal. If we look carefully beneath the analyses of the time-cult, we will find the Enemy's own model of culture.

THE CULTURE MODEL

In his role as culture critic, Lewis is far from alone. We can see him as part of two different though overlapping contexts: 1) the British tradition including such writers as Burke, Coleridge, Arnold, and Ruskin, and continuing into this century with Shaw, Eliot, F. R. Leavis, and Raymond Williams; and 2) the group of culture critics writing between the two world wars including such figures as Ortega y Gasset, Charles Maurras, Irving Babbitt, Julian Benda, and Oswald Spengler, all of whom follow arguments earlier developed by Burke, Taine, Nietzsche, and other European precursors. Lewis's ideas show the influence of both the British and the European traditions—not least because he had read so widely among these writers.[31] Yet his vision of culture is also distinctively his own.

Lewis's most visible culture model is the one he offers in *The Art of Being Ruled*. This is a simple two-part model, not so much of culture as of social politics: there is a small class of true individuals capable of independent thought, and there are the unthinking masses who wish for nothing better than to be ruled. Lewis has several names for these groups—names that clearly indicate some of his sources: following Nietzsche, they are "masters" and the "herd"; following Bergson, they are "persons" and "things"; following Goethe, they are "Natures" and "puppets."[32] Such a vision is conspicuously authoritarian and has, for a contemporary reader at least, obviously distasteful practical implications; and, of course, it is difficult not to draw connections between this kind of thinking and Lewis's notorious political views. Fredric Jameson does so explicitly. This kind of culture critique, he says, always hides its own class interests behind the pretense of disinterested idealism:

> Where [Lewis's] polemics become formally and ideologically revealing are those moments in which the idealist framework of the culture critique is briefly and with fitful, energetic impatience unmasked. At such moments, indeed, the rhetoric of conservative thought, which has ended up believing in its own official solicitude for Culture, gives way to the unpleasant and embarrassing cynicism of protofascism itself, which knows its intellectual practice as something other than the disinterested guardianship of universal values. In these moments, an embattled and Darwinian defense of the subject's own threatened position and individual vested interests breaks through the universalizing pretense of philosophical discourse; and the rights of privilege are openly affirmed against the threat to the self of some genuinely universal vision of human society.

Or as Raymond Williams says, "The concept of a cultivated minority, set over against a 'decreated' mass, tends, in its assertions, to a damaging arrogance and scepticism."[33]

Because this is the only model Lewis states directly (and because it is so blatantly problematic), it has been the focus of attention for his readers and critics. Nevertheless, it is not the model of culture underlying most of his Enemy criticism. One of the problems in the two-part description—in terms of Lewis's Enemy principles—is that it puts artists and thinkers into the "master" group, where the potential purity of the "not-self" is muddied by issues of worldly power (since the masters are also the rulers). As a response to this unsatisfactory situation, Lewis evolved a second model. Still informed by the same influences, though now drawing more heavily on the British tradition, this more complex version accords more completely with the Enemy stance and the Enemy principles—both in its surface characteristics and in its submerged contradictions.

It is the second model that underlies the *Man of the World* books following *The Art of Being Ruled*—the rest of the Enemy criticism. Lewis never clearly explains this model; he never defines "culture" or "cult"; and he never describes his ideas about cultural unity or change. But just as we could discover his space-philosophy through his attack on the time-philosophy, here we can reconstruct this model from indirect evidence: from occasional remarks about the relationship between the time-cult and other cultures, from scattered comments about such things as the cultural role of the artist or the scientist, and most important, from the kinds of questions he asks and criticisms he makes of other writers who more explicitly address theoretical issues.

What we find is a three-part model of culture. At the bottom is the "social plane"; in the middle are the "middlemen," those who have "second-rate" minds; on the top are the "first-rate" minds in whom the "pure speculative impulse" lives. Given this structure we can understand what distinguishes good cultures from bad ones, the decadence of the time-cult from the ideal Lewis would prefer. What changes is the balance of power.

The social plane consists of common men and women who are generally uninformed about the ideas they receive and use. It is a rather vaguely defined group. At times, it seems to combine the mindless masses, for whom Lewis has only disdain, with the purveyors of what we might call popular culture—artists like Anita Loos, the author of *Gentlemen Prefer Blondes* (see *TWM* 75), who in Lewis's eyes simply exploit the work of more serious and innovative creators. But most often, Lewis thinks of this level much more generously, as including his own reading audience of "general educated persons" and almost all artists. This is why in *Time and Western Man,* for instance, he divides his subject into the "literary, social and artistic plane" and the "philosophic and theoretic."

When he expresses his wish that different fields should remain rigidly separated, he explains how he sees the role of the artist in the social plane:

> To receive blindly, or at the best confusedly, from regions outside his own, all kinds of notions and formulae, is what the 'creative artist' generally does. Without knowing it, he receives into the central tissue of his work political or scientific notions which he proceeds to embody, if he is a novelist, in his characters, if he is a painter, or a poet, in his technique or emotional material, without in the least knowing what he is doing or why he is doing it. But my conception of the rôle of the creative artist is not merely to be a medium for ideas supplied him wholesale from elsewhere, which he incarnates automatically in a technique which (alone) it is his business to perfect. It is equally his business to know enough of the sources of his ideas, and ideology, to take steps to keep these ideas out, except such as he may require for his work. When the idea-monger comes to his door he should be able to tell what kind of notion he is buying, and know something of the process and rationale of its manufacture and distribution. (*TWM* 10)

As this passage indicates, the difference between the good times and the bad on the social level is one of self-awareness. In the good times, artists (and ordinary people) go to the trouble to inform themselves about ideas and ideologies; in the bad times, they simply accept them without question. This is why Lewis has embarked upon his critique of his culture: because "it would not be easy to exaggerate the naiveté with which the average artist or writer to-day, deprived of all central authority, body of knowledge, tradition, or commonly accepted system of nature, accepts what he receives in place of those things" (*Paleface* 104). And this is why he specifically criticizes Pound for being a fashion-follower and Joyce for being more concerned about his craft than his metaphysics.

The second level consists of the "idea-mongers," those with essentially practical minds who deliberately use ideas for their own purposes—and, in the process, usually distort them. At its most innocent, this group includes those in industry who exploit scientific discoveries in practical ways. But it also—and for Lewis most significantly—includes people motivated by politics and religion, "the influences that are most able to distort and cancel the pure speculative impulse" (*TWM* 248). Often we hear the Enemy's invective in Lewis's descriptions of this level: "The merely political revolutionary is thus, for the most part, an *interpreter* only of a creative mind. And he is, of course, very often, a very bad and corrupt interpreter; often he is a startlingly vulgar, peculiarly unscrupulous and self-seeking one."[34] These political middlemen are strong in the bad times and weak in the good. In his own time, Lewis thinks, too much power lies in the wrong hands—neither the thinkers' nor the workers', but the manipulators'. He explains, again:

> The finest creations of art or of science, to-day as ever, only more so, reach the general public in a very indirect fashion. If that contact could be more direct it

would be much more sanely 'stimulating'.... It is upon the essentially political middleman, the imitative self-styled 'revolutionary,' that I direct my main attack. It is he who pollutes on the way the prime issue of our thinking, and converts it into a 'cultural' or 'scientific' article, which is a masked engine of some form of political fraud, which betrays the thought of its originator. (*TWM* 150)

In a culture with fewer middlemen, those on the social level will receive ideas more directly, before they have become diluted or polluted; the responsibility of the artist and the general public to know about ideas will be easier to meet, and there will be fewer hidden political motives to entrap them.

Science seems to be especially corruptible. "When we say 'science,'" he cautions us, "we can either mean any manipulation of the inventive and organizing power of the human intellect: or we can mean such an extremely different thing as the *religion of science,* the vulgarized derivative from this pure activity manipulated by a sort of priestcraft into a great religious and political weapon"; "So pure science is one thing; its application another; and its vulgarization a third" (*ABR* 4, 27). Comparing science and magic, Lewis writes, "'Science gives as much power as was formerly given by magic,' we started by saying. But it does not give it to the true magician, to the maker of the spells and the engineer of the machinery. Nor, still less, does it give it to the Everyman who handles the machinery and magical properties. There is *a third character in the plot:* and he alone is invested in all the marvellous power of Science" (*TWM* 311, my emphasis). Because science confers power, those who want power manipulate scientific discovery for their own ends.

Lewis also includes most of the time-cult's philosophers in this group of middlemen. Philosophic thought is at least as vulnerable to political pressures as scientific thought. Now, he explains, "By 'politics' to-day we must understand something very much wider than what was formerly meant" (*TWM* 163). "Politics and philosophy in Europe are traditionally a little too close together" (*TWM* 261–62); thus Bergson is "the first servant of the great industrial caste-mind"—or at best, "simply a very common but astute intelligence—naturally, and without other inducement, on the side of such a society, instinctively endorsing its ideals" (*TWM* 214). Not all modern philosophers seem to Lewis as political as Bergson, but he does think that because they depend so much on science, they are too much infected by its corrupt power.

In his objections to this state of affairs, Lewis is in sharp contrast to Spengler, for instance, who holds that philosophers *should* be practical people involved in politics and other affairs of the real world; Spengler is also content to observe the involvement of scientists in the world of action. In fact, Spengler's description of cultural ties would tend to put nearly everyone in this middle group—philosophers and scientists, politicians, artists, mathematicians, economists.[35] In the case of the time-cult, Lewis is inclined to agree, though what Spengler accepts, Lewis deplores. Certainly he believes the uniformity of modern culture stems from its ties between science and philosophy:

> When I speak of an 'orthodoxy of thought,' therefore, or a philosophic orthodoxy, I refer to this strict uniformity that ensues from the scrupulous following of the datum provided by the instruments of research, by philosophy and by all speculative thought. And the identity of philosophy or of speculative thought with politics is largely owing to the fact that both depend more and more absolutely upon machines of greater and greater precision, on machines so wonderfully complex and powerful that they usurp to a great extent

the functions of independent life. But philosophy and speculative thought is, further, an emotional interpretation, and not entirely a soulless imitation, of technical discovery. (*TWM* 165)

It is on the level of the practical and often political middleman, Lewis believes, that philosophy and science come together.

It is because the connections among properly separate fields occur on this level that Lewis sometimes (and more often in later years) refers to the members of this group as the "Zeitgeist"—or personifies the "Zeitgeist" as if it were one of these politicizing middlemen. In *The Art of Being Ruled* he says, "The Zeitgeist has nothing to do with the workshop or laboratory, but is a phenomenon of the social world.... At all times he is a *salon*-spirit, the spirit of fashion" (431). (In *Paleface* he explains how "fashion" is "the emanation of some person, or some small inner ring of people" [120].) And in *The Doom of Youth,* he remarks, "Zeitgeist [is] the term we employ to indicate whoever it may be possessing the political power and wealth necessary to compel us to believe and do what he wants, and so make of our "Time" whatever he desires it to be."[36] These people—the ones with power and wealth, the ones who tie politics to science and philosophy and the arts—are the controlling "they" of Lewis's occasional paranoic sense of a conspiracy: the "third character in the plot."

The level of pure thought, finally, is made up of the true revolutionaries, those who originate all really new ideas of all kinds. This level has clear analogues in the British and European traditions of culture critiques: it resembles, for instance, Coleridge's clerisy and Arnold's class of scholars and artists; it anticipates Eliot's cultured elite and Leavis's minority culture; and—perhaps most directly—it parallels Benda's *clercs,* "all those whose activity essentially is *not* the pursuit of practical aims, all those who seek their joy in the practice of an art or a science or metaphysical speculation, in short in the possession of non-material advantages, and hence in a certain manner say: 'My kingdom is not of this world.' "[37] Or as Lewis says, "Nature does in every generation endow a handful of people with invaluable and mysterious gifts, in the special fields of science, and of art, or in character and general ability, making them fertile and inventive where other people are for the most part receptive only."[38] Like Benda, Lewis includes in this third level, at least ideally, scientists, philosophers, and artists.

Because "revolution is *first* a technical process" (*TWM* 138), the group of pure thinkers is most likely to include scientists—mathematicians, chemists, and physicists. (It does *not* include such "soft" scientists as psychologists or behaviorists.) Lewis explains, "I believe that it requires a really very foul or else very fanatical person to live with ideas, and consistently to betray them: and secondly, the ideas themselves are apt to be refractory, and to have some say in the matter. The material of theoretic thought, at least, is not 'personal,' if its manipulator is" (262). Scientists whose work is both technical and theoretical may thus be able to avoid personal distractions. Consequently, Lewis is inclined to place science at the base of culture: "The *ideal* basis for an epoch would certainly be the instruments of research, invented for the advancement of the common good; and certainly the impulse behind all 'revolution'—the will, that is, to pass from one epoch to another and better (of course)—is the work of the man of science" (160; my emphasis). Here Lewis is agreeing with Whitehead's argument in *Science and the Modern World,* though unlike Whitehead he continues with the caution that "unfortunately the best-organized and most powerful minorities will [i.e., want] a different thing to [from] the common good; and the more irresponsible power they obtain, the more their chosen interpreters (who are not, however, the great and inventive minds, but rather the opportunist and interpretative) expound the discoveries of science in a sense vaguely favourable to that power" (160). Ideally, at least, science can be pure.

In an ideal culture, philosophers will also belong to this level. Lewis explains: "In order to be humane and universally utilizable, philosophy must be abstracted from these special modes and private visions. *There must be an abstract man, as it were, if there is to be a philosopher*" (332). (Here Lewis again disagrees with Spengler, who argues that "higher thought" possesses no "everlasting and unalterable objectiveness."[39]) But of course, since philosophy is so much less technical and so much more personal than pure science, philosophers are less likely to attain this degree of abstraction. Here, too, the uniformity of philosophic thought in the time-cult demonstrates its failure. Pure thought is individual, and so ideal philosophers would necessarily resemble each other much less than do those who base their work on relativity physics.

Finally, this third level includes true artists. Art, Lewis explains, "is a constant stronghold... of the purest human consciousness" (*TWM* 39). "In art, as in everything else, all revolutionary impulse comes in the first place from the exceptional individual" (41); "From this point of view the true man-of-science and the artist are much more in the same boat than is generally understood" (199). Lewis places artists in this group—or the best artists—partly because of the large role technical problems play in the arts (as in the sciences), and partly because he sees artistic creation as occurring in a trance or a dream state. Art, too, is like magic: "The production of a work of art is... strictly the work of a visionary" (198). The artist must take care to maintain his creative isolation: "What it is really essential to press upon the attention of the reader is this: that the least distraction on the part of a great intelligence from his task of supplying pure thought, is fatal; its result is the same as in the case of a plastic or other artist when he allows himself a similar distraction" (309–10). Ideally, an artist can remain free from impure motives and impulses and maintain what Lewis calls a direct access to reality. (Again, this is of course not a new idea with Lewis, but a clear legacy from the romantics.)

In the good times this group of scientists, philosophers, and artists—the level of the "first-rate"—is strong; in the bad times, it is dominated by the impure thought of the middleman. As a critic, then, Lewis seeks "to dissociate from the pure revolutionary impulse of creative thought all those corrupt imitations which confuse so much the issue" (*ABR* 429). When this group of pure thinkers is strong, culture is diverse since it evolves directly from individuals; when it is weak, culture is uniform since the work of individuals is diverted into narrow practical channels.

This three-level model presents a few immediate problems. The most conspicuous internal problem is that the model contradicts itself on the role of art and artists. Given Lewis's insistence on his own identity as a painter, this is not an insignificant difficulty. Lewis seems to see the artist as both the beginning and the end of a culture—as both the source and the result of the spirit of an age. He explains the difference between politics and art in a way that makes this problem clear:

> If you want to know what is actually occurring *inside*, underneath, at the centre, at any given moment, art is a truer guide than 'politics,' more often than not. Its movements represent, in an acuter form, a deeper emotional truth, though not discursively. *The Brothers Karamazov*, for example, is a more cogent document for the history of its period than any record of actual events.... So if art has a directer access to reality, is truer and less artificial and more like what it naturally grows out of, than are politics, it seems a pity that it should take its cue from them. (*TWM* 136–37)

But listen to the voice of the Domestic Adversary describing much the same idea:

> But is there such a thing as 'an artist'? Or to what degree is there such a thing?... For artistic creation must express *something*... If it is the famous 'personality of the artist' to which expression is given, in the art-form, why then that precious 'personality' has been built up out of a number of components, has it not: which, closely enough inspected, would be found to betray a political complexion. (*MWA* 272–73)

"All art must be a political expression to some extent," he admits; "all creative activity at the best of times must have been influenced, if not controlled, by political necessity" (*ABR* 420, 430). As the truest historians of their period, artists respond to what is around them; they are susceptible to influences. But then they cannot at the same time be as free from influences and as independent of their Zeitgeist as Lewis wishes them to be.

We can look at this contradiction in two ways. To some extent it is a dilemma that Lewis has inherited with the romantic notion of the artist's special nature and role. Compare this passage from Ruskin, for instance: "The art of any country *is the exponent of its social and political virtues.* The art, or general productive and formative energy, of any country, is an exact exponent of its ethical life. You can have noble art only from noble persons, associated under laws fitted to their time and circumstances." As Raymond Williams points out, "The question of the 'goodness' of the artist is, however, at times ambiguous. At times, he must be good in order to reveal essential Beauty; at other times he is good *because* he reveals essential Beauty—other criteria of goodness are irrelevant."[40] From this perspective the contradiction is not Lewis's own.

But the problem is also typical of Lewis's own thinking: it repeats in a slightly different form his arguments that one can be personal and impersonal at the same time, that individual "eye" can be the same as "common sense," that the self and the not-self are fundamentally one. But what in those arguments he can present and justify as paradox, here resolves into clear contradiction. Because the artist receives impressions from society and culture, he or she can express the Zeitgeist: the artist is therefore part of the first level. Because the artist is free from the superficial impressions of the Zeitgeist, he or she can express the true nature of reality: the artist is therefore part of the third level. Nor is this a contradiction that can be solved with a distinction between first- and second-rate artists—though such a distinction can mask the contradiction.[41]

A similar problem underlies the ideal role of the scientist. Although Lewis wishes the scientist to represent pure speculative thought, as we have seen, he has serious doubts that such purity is possible. This scepticism has two different sources. One, he doubts that any real person can maintain the necessary isolation: "You cannot insist enough, it seems to me, on the human factor in the man of science. Scientific discovery or the teaching of science is one thing, and the man of science as private man, reflecting on his functions and applying his discoveries or selling them to other people, is another" (*ABR* 266). Two, as a Berkeleyan idealist, Lewis believes that we create our world through perception, thought, and memory—not that there is a real world we can hope to experience without these aspects of personality and mind. He asks about the scientific discoverer: "Is he not directed to some extent in that by what he *wants* to discover? Has he not often a blind eye for what he does not want; and does he not *always* interpret what has been discovered, by himself or other men, as he *wants* to understand it, or as somebody else requires him to?" (*TWM* 161). His own answer to this question, again, is that "It is mere superstition to suppose 'a mathematician' to be a sort of divine machine. In any reasonable, and not romantic, ac-

The Enemy Versus the Zeitgeist: Cultural Criticism

count of the matter, we must suppose the mathematical physicist not entirely unaffected by neighbouring metaphysical thought" (13–14). Even in his own terms, the basis for Lewis's ideal culture is "superstitious" and "romantic." And for this classicist, "the *'romantic' is the opposite of the real* (22, Lewis's emphasis). Again, this is another manifestation of the fundamental conflict in Lewis's thinking between his insistence that we must always recognize the role of personality in thought and his belief that we can think impersonally.[42] And his affirmation of the potential purity of the scientist over his belief that his ideal is superstitious and romantic repeats his philosophic choice of Berkeleyan illusion over realistic nihilism.

The difficulty in Lewis's culture model extends even further than these internal contradictions. It shares with all culture critiques a problem of perspective: from what position does the critic analyze his culture without being shaped by it? As that of an artist belonging to level three, presumably, Lewis's vision of culture would be free of any personal or worldly influences. (Thus this characteristic assertion: "I advance the strange claim... to act and to think non-politically in everything, in complete detachment from all the intolerant watchwords and formulas by which we are beset. I am an artist and my *mind,* at least, is entirely free."[43]) Yet as that of an artist belonging to level one, his vision would be specialized, partisan, and personal—and this is the advertised perspective of the Enemy.

Moreover, of course, Lewis's ideal culture—his Golden Age—is highly unlikely to occur in the real world. And if it did exist, it would hardly be a culture at all in our usual sense of the word. It would be strongly individualistic, and consequently very diverse; there would be almost no influences among its creative members, since each would work independently of everyone else. It would be a culture with little or no unity. Furthermore, it would be ahistorical. Its members would be no more influenced by their predecessors than by their contemporaries. It might change as its individual members changed, but its perspective, ideally, would be that of the static pure present, not an historical perspective.

Lewis's allegiance to the value of personality and his philosophical preference for stasis over time and motion lead him to create a model based on the timelessness of mind and the independence of individual genius; they do not allow him to embrace either cultural unity or unified cultural change as anything other than symptoms of disintegration and decadence. Again, Lewis himself seems to recognize the inflexibility of his scheme. He remarks, at one point, "When you get well into the centre of the consciousness of any time (and we have just illustrated this by the greek consciousness), there is certainly a unity there, for, if for no other reason, it is after all a time" (*TWM* 256); and he cautions us, "So we must in this investigation remember... that, though a 'new thing in philosophy,' nevertheless some and indeed a great deal of merging and interpenetration is to be found everywhere in the world of thought of any time whatever" (257). These statements appear right in the middle of his critique of the unity of the time-philosophy, and we must recognize them as important qualifications of his own judgments of both modern culture and his ideal culture; here once more is the voice of the Domestic Adversary.

As we might expect from all these structural resemblances between Lewis's three-part model and his critical and philosophical principles, this view of culture is also remarkably consistent with his stance as the Enemy. To attack the spirit of one's age as he does in this role, one must argue that any Zeitgeist is secondary to individual achievements. Thus his continual sense of difference leads Lewis to oppose the concept of a Zeitgeist and to insist not only that it is *possible* to think without being pressured by cultural fashion, but also that independent thought is *essential* to culture.

The Enemy Versus the Zeitgeist: Cultural Criticism

Here again we see the negative side of this position: this kind of self-justification suggests Lewis's uncertainty about his authority as an outsider. Raymond Williams's remarks about Orwell's exile status will illuminate Lewis's situation as well: "The exile, because of his own personal position, cannot finally believe in any social guarantee: to him, because this is the pattern of his own living, almost all association is suspect. He fears it because he does not want to be compromised (this is often his virtue, because he is so quick to see the perfidy which certain compromises involve). Yet he fears it also because he can see no way of confirming, socially, his own individuality; this, after all, is the psychological condition of the self-exile." (And, Williams notes, "The cost, in practice, [of Orwell's adoption of this stance] was a partial abandonment of his own standards: he had often to curse, wildly, to keep others away, to avoid being confused with them.")[44] Lewis's Enemy, too, is forced by the logic of his self-exile to defend himself: his sense of being opposed by his own actual culture compels him to imagine an ideal one where he would feel at home.

Yet we can also see this model as a successful extension and justification of the Enemy stance. On Lewis's analysis the person who acts alone will be the one responsible for real change: "All revolutionary impulse comes in the first place from the exceptional individual" (*TWM* 41). As Nietzsche says, "The time will come when... we shall no longer look at masses but at individuals who form a sort of bridge over the wan stream of becoming"; "The aim of mankind can lie ultimately only in its highest examples." But in an age of uniformity like ours, these individuals will look like heretics. "All effectual men are always the enemies of every time," argues Tarr; "All activity on the part of a good mind has the stimulus of a paradox."[45] "Truth," Lewis proclaims, "is always 'heretical': and it is always the truth of a minority, or of an 'isolated mind'... the truth-bearing individual is always ahead of the rest of the world, although

The Enemy Opposite

no one could claim that they willed him, and strained towards him, in order to reach his higher level. Rather he *drags them up* by the scruff of the neck" (*TWM* 466–67). With this, perhaps the ultimate Enemy maneuver, Lewis-the-Enemy becomes Lewis-the-"truth-bearing individual": his very opposition to the dominant thought of his time proves him not wrong but right.

Conclusion

Lewis based his vision of culture on an ideal of pure thought—an ideal that he clearly does not always believe possible. He describes himself as defending the view of common sense; yet he realizes that this common sense is rapidly becoming a part of the dead past, and that the views he attacks are the common sense of those who believe them. He thinks that each of us creates our own world through our perceptions; yet he denies the relativistic vision of his contemporaries. He sees the world he chooses to believe in as an illusory surface disguising a real abyss—the abyss revealed by the time-cult. Quite clearly, he explains that he chooses to live in an illusion and to act as if he did not recognize the reality that illusion contradicts. And he admits that "Western Man" is "the completest myth," but then, asking "whether you should not erect that myth into a reality," he devotes himself to its defense.

He insists that he hates violence, that he wants peace. Yet he creates the figure of the Enemy, who fights battles, snipes at his foes, arms himself against and for attack. And all of his novels explore the workings and consequences of violence—often violence for its own sake, gratuitous violence. He defines himself as the defender of human individuality and of the complexities of personality against the mechanizing and leveling forces of modern society; but the characters in his novels are machines, and even his Enemy "Horseman" has a bestial mask instead of a human face.

As a critic Lewis regularly attacks in others his own characteristics. He criticizes Pound for being an impresario and for loving dramatics, while he is himself self-consciously

The Enemy Opposite

flamboyant and is always engaged in advertisements for himself. He attacks Joyce for being obsessed with the problem of time and for being romantic about his classical framework, but he writes the very long *Time and Western Man* to explore the same problem, and his own proposed solution is a rather romantic notion of a pure classical present. He opposes Bergson for distinguishing between clock time and lived time, and yet he bases his own position on Bergson's distinction; he accuses Bergson of polarizing intellect and instinct, space and time, and then he constructs his philosophy around the same poles. He even argues against Gertrude Stein that the least mannered, most translucent prose is the language of the liveliest, most acute intellect—in the midst of his own highly individual and decorative style.

All of these contradictions, it is clear, add up to a central structure in Lewis's work. The "Horseman" portrays this tension between opposition and dominance; the Enemy dramatizes it; the principles and practice of the criticism develop and reveal it. And the conflicts this structure expresses, it is also clear, are quintessentially modern. As others have recognized, Lewis's great importance is that he is at once a powerful critic and a powerful representative of his time. According to Kenner, Lewis "had not so much opposed as dramatized the history of his time"; William Pritchard, similarly, writes, "He was as a man and a writer very much of his time; and perhaps that is why he devoted so much energy to dispraising it." Jameson notes, "A consistent perversity made of him at one and the same time the exemplary practitioner of one of the most powerful of all modernistic styles and an aggressive ideological critic and adversary of modernism itself in all its forms." Northrop Frye suggests, "Such books as *The Apes of God* or *The Human Age* can hardly be written without a personal descent into the hell they portray, and Lewis has made that descent, and taken the consequences of making it, with a perverse

Conclusion

but unflinching courage."[1] And Lewis himself wrote, "I am a man of the 'transition,' we none of us can help being that" (*Paleface* 83).

As we might expect, there is evidence within his own books of Lewis's paradoxical position in his culture. On this matter, too, the Domestic Adversary traces the path for our argument.

Here we must look at Lewis's statement about the cause of the time-cult. On the whole, he decides, it is a logical product of an ailing society, a dying world. Speaking of the "cult of childhood," he writes that he would

> trace this impulse to its source in the terrible and generally hidden disturbances that have broken the back of our will in the Western countries, and have already forced us into the greatest catastrophes. Whether these great disturbances are for the ultimate good of mankind or not, no one can claim that they are pleasant, or that they do not paralyse and weaken the system they attack. Many complaints break out in consequence in the midst of our thinking; and the instinctive recoil of the stricken system makes it assume strange shapes. (*TWM* 69)

Later he asserts that "all 'creative' or 'emergent' life doctrines we must regard as semi-magical prescriptions for the *power* we have lost, like a sort of stimulant for the impotent" (*TWM* 315). And he agrees with Spengler that "there is a fearful state of chaos throughout the world"—but observes it "with far more anguish than does Spengler" (*TWM* 307). Such descriptions reveal Lewis's belief that he and his contemporaries share a sense that their world has been paralyzed by "terrible and generally hidden disturbances." "We are in a world in which we are all in some sense outlaws, at the moment," he explains, "for our traditions have all been too sharply struck at and broken and no new tradition is yet born" (*Paleface* 87–88).

The Enemy Opposite

"instinctive recoil of the stricken system." As he says in *Men Without Art,* "An artist...must today be penetrated by a sense of the great discontinuity of our destiny" (126). And his description of the way Shakespeare mirrored the complexities of his time again points to his understanding of his own role: the critic's task, he tells us, is "to show the forces of disintegration at work in [Shakespeare's] mind," to show "the fundamental contradiction that is evident everywhere through [his plays]," for "Shakespeare did, indeed, perfectly express his time, only he expressed it a little too perfectly to be its child" (*L&F* 22, 21). And much later, in *Rude Assignment,* he summed up: "I have confessed how I have not been free of vacillation. I saw a culture I was born into being dissolved or picked to shreds by an antlike process. I have had romantic rebellions. It seems to me that I should have forgotten the Past entirely.... The place occupied by Western culture is being rapidly filled by something else!" (193). With its cult of the individual and its claim that an artist has a more direct access to reality than do others, the Enemy criticism is indeed a romantic rebellion—or, as the defense of a culture of the past, a romantic reaction. Lewis sees the time-cult as a reaction to cultural chaos; and he sees himself as the defender of culture against the chaos he fears has already triumphed. From this perspective his own role would seem to be a sort of finger-in-the-dike operation, similar to what he condemns in Proust and Joyce as "the ardent recapitulation of a dead thing—though so recently dead, and not on its own merits a very significant one" (*TWM* 101). Thus he plays the same role with his defense of Western culture as he accuses Joyce of playing with *Ulysses.* Over and over again, Lewis offers a kind of mirror image of the visions he criticizes. All are responses to a "fearful state of chaos"; all are "prescriptions for the power we have lost."

Perhaps the clearest sign of Lewis's hidden kinship with the time-cult is in the metaphor he offers to describe the "sort of contradiction [that] is paralleled throughout our life." As we saw in his criticism of Joyce, he finds everywhere in the modern world the "strategy" of "removing something necessary to life and putting an ideologic simulacrum where it was" (96). Pointing out that "everywhere the peoples become more and more alike," Lewis observes that in reaction to the reality, aggressive nationalism arises. Surely we could make the same analysis of the Enemy's aggressive individualism and personality. He proposes an especially suggestive explanation of the role of personality in such a world:

> But the transition society of to-day, no doubt inevitably, is essentially an actor's world. The successful personality of the moment is generally an actor-mind (Mussolini): with all the instincts bred behind the footlights, the apotheosis of the life-of-the-moment, of exteriority, display and make-up; and of an extreme instability, fundamental breaks and intermittences, the natural result of the violent changes of, and the return of great chaotic violences into, our time. In the arts themselves this tendency issues in the form of prodigious virtuosity. The work of one person will consist of the schematic juxtaposition of a series of disconnected stylizations... (*TWM* 365)

Though of course he does not intend this as a self-portrait, it comes very close to being one. Even the symptom of prodigious virtuosity has its counterpart in Lewis's remarkable productivity in painting and drawing, in fiction, and in social, political, philosophical, literary, and art criticism.

What is even more interesting is the wording of Lewis's summary of this pervasive modern substitution of the unreal—the simulacrum—for the real: "It is headlong into this sheer delusion... that we are running, every time that we essay to found our view of things upon some harmonious and precise picture. We fall immediately into that trap of an abstraction coloured to look concrete, and placed where once there was something but where now there is nothing" (*TWM* 99). What is Lewis's stable classical world but such a harmonious and precise picture? "The traditional belief of common-sense," he says, "is really a *picture*." And what is his choice of the serene world of traditional common sense over the nihilistic world of modern philosophy but a deliberate effort to found his view of things upon some harmonious and precise picture? He knows that his ideas of the self, of the personality, of individuality, of the mind are artificial constructs; he knows that his dream of an ideal world depends on an illusory purity of thought. Yet he insists that these things should shape our lives as if they were real.

Lewis's participation in the world he deplored seems to me the key both to his expression of his culture and to his insight into its fundamental structural weaknesses. Certainly, I think, the Enemy's strengths as a critic of his society depend directly on his simultaneous position within and without that society: Lewis would not have recognized so clearly the assumptions of the time-cult if he did not in part share them, nor would he have seen what he did about the implications of these assumptions if he had not explored them for himself and recognized the danger they posed to traditional values. To be torn, as Lewis was, between the old ways of seeing and the new would seem not only a reasonable but an intelligent response. His power lies in his recognition of "the desirability of a new, and if necessary shattering criticism of 'modernity' " (*Paleface* 106) and in the wholeheartedness of his attempts to explore the complexities of his changing world. His integrity lies in his willingness to let us see how this criticism, this exploration, has involved him in an interior struggle between "micro-cosmic opposites."

Once again, Nietzsche provides us with an illuminating parallel. He warns, "Whoever fights monsters should see to

Conclusion

it that in the process he does not become a monster. And when you look long into an abyss, the abyss also looks into you."[2] But here is one of Nietzsche's critics, quoted, curiously, by Julien Benda:

> Is it not the criterion of a philosophy which may be called rational without reserve and equivocation, that it should remain incorruptibly faithful to itself? On the other hand, *the systems which begin by accepting contradictions, reserving the right to add that they are capable of surmounting them or of 'living' them, lodge their enemy in their midst.* Their punishment is that their antithesis still resembles them; and that is what has happened to Nietzsche.[3]

This, too, has been the strength and the fate of Wyndham Lewis's Enemy.

Notes

INTRODUCTION

1. My first epigraph is from Pound's editorial notes in his journal, *The Exile* 4 (1928):106. All four issues of this journal (1927-28) have been reprinted by the Johnson Reprint Corporation, New York and London, 1967. My second epigraph is from Barthes's *Mythologies,* trans. Annette Lavers (New York: Hill and Wang, 1972), 12. For the description of the "aggressive partisan pen," see Wyndham Lewis, *The Diabolical Principle and the Dithyrambic Spectator* (London: Chatto & Windus, 1931), vi.

2. For Pound's first remark, see *Shenandoah* (Wyndham Lewis Issue) 4, nos. 2-3 (Summer-Autumn 1953): 17 (quoted from a private letter). For his second, see *Selected Letters of Ezra Pound, 1907-1941,* ed. D. D. Paige (New York: New Directions, 1971), 222; this is also quoted by Timothy Materer in *Vortex: Pound, Eliot, and Lewis* (Ithaca and London: Cornell University Press, 1979), 35. Eliot's comment is from "Wyndham Lewis," *Hudson Review* (Wyndham Lewis Issue) 10, no. 4 (Winter 1957-58):170.

3. *The Diabolical Principle and the Dithyrambic Spectator,* 82-83.

4. Lewis speaks of this one massive project in his letters. See *The Letters of Wyndham Lewis,* ed. W. K. Rose (Norfolk, Conn.: New Directions, 1963), 136-40 (hereafter cited as *Letters*); and *Pound/Lewis: The Letters of Ezra Pound and Wyndham Lewis,* ed. Timothy Materer (New York: New Directions, 1985), 142-45 (hereafter cited as *Pound/Lewis*). Some of the books of this period were not part of this rough manuscript (*Men Without Art* was not, for instance, nor was *Hitler*), but they are all concerned with the same general analysis of contemporary culture.

5. Others have seen the Enemy as one in a series of roles and have emphasized the distinction between this dramatic fiction and the real Wyndham Lewis. Hugh Kenner, for instance, calls the Enemy "Lewis's most famous persona," describes his whole career as a sequence of personae who together form a kind of "personality," and insists that we must not confuse this "personality" with "the

London resident of the same name who created that personality and may be inadequately described as its business manager and amanuensis." See *Wyndham Lewis* (Norfolk, Conn.: New Directions, 1954), 12, vii. Geoffrey Wagner, similarly, who asserts that Lewis adopted "at least six such personalities himself" and calls the Enemy "Lewis' most recurrent mask," argues that by adopting these masks "Lewis makes it hard to take much of his criticism directly." See *Wyndham Lewis: A Portrait of the Artist as the Enemy* (New Haven: Yale University Press, 1957), 22–23. And Timothy Materer calls the Enemy the "Iron Mask" and suggests that "this mistaken identity" imprisoned rather than freed Lewis when "the Enemy persona was taken for the real Lewis." See *Wyndham Lewis the Novelist* (Detroit: Wayne State University Press, 1976), 12. My view differs from these primarily in emphasis: I agree, of course, that the Enemy and Lewis are not identical, but what seems most important to me are the many ways in which the Enemy *does* resemble Lewis.

6. The only other full-length study of Lewis's criticism is Wagner's *Wyndham Lewis: A Portrait of the Artist as the Enemy*, which also focuses on the Enemy period. Wagner's explanation of Lewis's context in Modernist neoclassicism and his explications of many of Lewis's ideas are thorough and very useful, but not always convincing. D. G. Bridson's *The Filibuster: A Study of the Political Ideas of Wyndham Lewis* (London: Cassell & Company, 1972) is also quite informative; Bridson focuses on a different aspect of Lewis's work—and different texts—than I do. In addition, there are two anthologies of Lewis's criticism, C. J. Fox's *Enemy Salvoes: Selected Literary Criticism* (New York: Barnes & Noble, 1976), and Walter Michel and C. J. Fox's *Wyndham Lewis on Art: Collected Writings 1913–1956* (New York: Funk & Wagnalls, 1969). Both of these books have good introductions and notes (the introduction to *Enemy Salvoes* is by C. H. Sisson). Jeffrey Meyers's biography, *The Enemy* (London: Routledge & Kegan Paul, 1980), covers a good deal of useful background information. Materer's *Wyndham Lewis the Novelist*, William H. Pritchard's *Wyndham Lewis* (New York: Twayne Publishers, 1968), and Thomas Kush's *Wyndham Lewis's Pictorial Integer* (Ann Arbor, Michigan: UMI Research Press, 1981) also have good discussions of Lewis's criticism. Fredric Jameson's *Fables of Aggression: Wyndham Lewis, the Modernist as Fascist* (Berkeley: University of California Press, 1979) is indirectly concerned with many issues raised by the criticism.

7. Critical responses to Lewis's self-contradictions can be divided into four categories. Many readers have found them simply exasperating, and see them as evidence of Lewis's inability to write or think coherently; Northrop Frye's "Neoclassical Agony," *Hudson Review* 10, no. 4, exemplifies this view. Most of Lewis's critics—the second group—note his inconsistencies when they arise, but on the whole set aside the questions they raise. A third and much smaller group responds by seeing his contradictions as his strength; I. A. Richards's "A Talk on 'The Childermass' " (in *Agenda,* [Wyndham Lewis Issue], nos. 7–8 [Autumn-Winter 1969–70]) and John Holloway's very interesting "Wyndham Lewis: The Massacre and the Innocents" (in *The Charted Mirror* [London: Routledge & Kegan Paul, 1960], 118–36) represent this response; both of these essays deal mainly with Lewis's fiction. Jameson is the only critic who has focused on these issues as problematic. His provocative analysis of the ideological structures and implications of Lewis's work is consistently illuminating; though I often disagree with him, his arguments and judgments are challenging.

8. See *Wyndham Lewis on Art,* 27. This passage is also quoted by Materer in *Vortex,* 115.

9. Lewis, *The Mysterious Mr. Bull* (London: Robert Hale, 1938), 142. This passage appears in a description of "Satire," but in the same section Lewis also writes, "Satire is a criticism of human society. But it is criticism undertaken with the deliberate purpose of changing what is criticized" (144).

THE ENEMY

1. This "Horseman" appeared on the cover of the first issue of *The Enemy* in 1927. In *Wyndham Lewis: Paintings and Drawings,* ed. Walter Michel (Berkeley: University of California Press, 1971), it is Number 620 (in black and white). It also served (in color) as the cover for the Wyndham Lewis issue of *Agenda.*

2. In *Paleface,* Lewis explains: "Schopenhauer's father gave him the name of 'Arthur' because Arthur is the same (he argued) in all european tongues—at least it is not exclusively german. (It is interesting to note that the 'Arthur Press' received that name for a reason of a similar order.)" (67)

3. For instance, in *The Diabolical Principle and The Dithyrambic Spectator,* Lewis explains that "every creative act of the butterfly-brush [i.e., Whistler's] was accompanied by a critical or

militant operation of the pen"—on the same page where he describes himself: "If I paint a picture or write a novel, I have to be out at once, in the saddle next minute, lance in hand (my best pamphleteering-pen, that is, in position)—or *Corona* rattling away like a machine-gun—in defense of it" (viii).

4. *Daily Herald,* 30 May 1932, in *Wyndham Lewis on Art,* 267.

5. Lewis, *Tarr* (London: The Egoist, 1918; reprinted New York: Jubilee Books, 1973. Revised version, London: Chatto & Windus, 1928; London: Calder and Boyars, 1968). In my text I quote only from the 1928 version since Lewis made these revisions during the Enemy decade; in my notes I point to differences in the 1918 version. For the description of Kreisler, see p. 141 (1928) and p. 127 (1918). In this instance the passage is the same in both versions.

6. In *Paleface* Lewis explains, "There is, of course, some exaggeration in this analysis: but it is only by over-stressing the significance of such material that the true meaning of all such writing can be laid bare for the inattentive reader" (229).

7. Lewis, *The Childermass* (London: Chatto & Windus, 1928), 37, 175. My attention was drawn to these examples by Geoffrey Wagner (see his pp. 275, 175). But elsewhere Lewis also writes: "Miss Stein is probably a clever, sober, intelligent woman, who has her head screwed on straight and has been a pupil of William James. She is *amused* by the stammering and fumbling of the poor lunatic; and, like an old child with a new toy, she imitates him" (*ABR* 418).

8. See Sherwood Anderson, *Dark Laughter* (New York: Boni & Liveright, 1925), 113. Lewis quotes Anderson accurately.

9. Lewis was also a personal friend of McAlmon's. Behind the attack on *This Quarter* seems to have been a personal dispute (with both McAlmon and Walsh) as well as an aesthetic one. See *Letters,* 156–60, and *Pound/Lewis,* 143, 156.

10. Lewis's most extended discussion of these figures is in *The Lion and the Fox*, pt. 7, chap. 3. See also Robert C. Elliott, *The Power of Satire: Magic, Ritual, Art* (Princeton: Princeton University Press, 1960), especially the chapter on Timon (pp. 141–167), which is in this matter more suggestive about Lewis than is the chapter about Lewis himself. Several other critics have discussed Lewis's affinity with Timon; see, for instance, Materer's *Wyndham Lewis the Novelist*, 24 ff, and Reed Way Dasenbrock's *The Literary Vorticism of Ezra Pound and Wyndham Lewis: Towards the Condition of Painting* (Baltimore: Johns Hopkins University Press, 1985), 174–75.

11. *Beyond Good and Evil*, trans. Walter Kaufmann (New York:

Vintage, 1966), 137, 139. For a discussion of this romantic tradition, see Lesley Johnson, *The Culture Critics* (London: Routledge & Kegan Paul, 1979), chap. 1; and Raymond Williams, *Culture and Society* (London: Chatto & Windus, 1960), chap. 2.

12. *Tarr* (1928), 169. This version is slightly but significantly different from that in the 1918 edition, which has: "Then it appeared to her that it was *he*, the enemy getting in" (186). The 1928 version adds a crucial comma after "enemy" and also moves the sentence to the beginning of a paragraph, thus clearly adding emphasis to the enemy as a name.

13. *Tarr* (1928), 222. The 1918 version (253–54) is much the same.

14. *Tarr* (1928), 221. This is significantly different from the 1918 version which has simply: "His contempt for everybody degraded him" (253). The whole analogy to the Cynic is added in the 1928 version.

15. *Beyond Good and Evil*, 36.

16. In *One-Way Song* (London: Faber & Faber, 1933), 61. In this book of poems Lewis also calls the Enemy "a great professional Outcast of the Pen" (44); the Enemy himself says, "'Outcast' is good, in a system of shark and gull, / Where all that's 'illustrious' is also Untouchable! / A solitary honour" (56); and Lewis announces, "You must salute this outcast Enemy— / Outcasted for refusal to conform / To the phases of this artificial storm" (77).

17. Lewis makes similar statements in book after book. Here are some from the less-known "tracts" of the 1930s. In *Left Wings Over Europe: Or, How to Make a War About Nothing* (London: Jonathan Cape, 1936), he explains why he has defended Germany: "Whereas you might be disposed to suspect me of partisanship— in order a little to restore the balance I have been compelled so often to insist upon the rights of those to whom all right is denied, by all parties, at present, in England—" (311); and

> If I have figured as an advocate for the German, so stupidly repressed and, in season and out of season, badgered and browbeaten, I have likewise figured somewhat as an advocate for those extremists who, rejecting as too slick and suspiciously destructive the communist solution for all our ills, yet recognize that some radical and revolutionary solution is imposed upon us. 'Fascist' thought is outcast thought, in the same way that certain countries are outcast countries. And although I am very far from being anything that could be described as a 'fascist', I consider the 'fascist' just as worthy of attention as the communist.... But it may be that I myself

have exhibited some of the characteristics of the 'extremist'. If that is so, it is hardly to be wondered at. (331)

Of course these explanations do not wholly account for Lewis's (notorious) political arguments during this period (especially, they bypass his pacifism), but it is interesting to see how closely they match the terms establishing the Enemy role.

Here is another instance of Lewis offering his isolation and contrariness as advantages, from *The Jews: Are They Human?* (London: Allen & Unwin, 1939) (whose misleading title mimics Gustaaf Reiner's *The English: Are They Human?* [1931]):

> As a person who can scarcely be suspected of mercenary intentions, or of courting popularity, my testimony—however rugged, however great its informality—may be more valuable than that of the professional humanitarian.
>
> There is only one danger. I have often been accused of opposing myself, deliberately, to anything that is popular, just in order to be "contrairy". [sic] And now it may be said of me—seeing that antisemitism is on the increase—*of course* Mr. Wyndham Lewis comes forward and utters a kind word for the Jews. That is just like him!
>
> I have not such a high opinion of the workings of the popular mind as to feel that this rôle, for which I have been cast, is such a bad one as all that. Any democracy would be a suffocating place were there not *some* people who made a habit of contradicting its emotional excesses. . . .
>
> But in the present instance it is not out of perversity that I champion, not the Jew, but an attitude of common sense regarding the Jew. (30)

By this time—1939—Lewis's habitual stance of opposition is well enough established that he must partly disassociate himself from it to give his argument credibility.

18. In *The Lion and the Fox*, he explains, "The child is made to feel that the individual in himself or in herself is the enemy. And the death or subjection of that enemy is the task of the child" (79).

19. All of the quotations from the Pound criticism are from two chapters of *The Enemy* and *Time and Western Man*, "Ezra Pound, Etc." and "The Man in Love with the Past." Both chapters are short, so I have not given individual page references. I wish to thank the *Journal of Modern Literature* for permission to use this section, which appeared in much the same form under their copyright in vol. 10, no. 2 (June 1983).

20. Both of these metaphors appear elsewhere in Lewis's work. In *Tarr* Lewis describes a minor character: "Hobson, he considered, was a crowd. You could not say he was an individual, he was in fact a set.... A distinguished absence of personality was Hobson's most personal characteristic. Upon this impersonality, of crowd origin, Tarr gazed with the scorn of the autocrat" (1928 p. 18; the same metaphor appears in the 1918 version on p. 12). And in *The Lion and the Fox*, he argues that "human beings are congeries of parasites subsisting on The Individual, subsisting on a very insufficient supply of Individuals" (136–37), and that Shakespeare was "a particularly glorious parasite on everything" (152). Like Pound, Shakespeare was "of all parasites that have ever breathed on a human back... the most fastidious, most critical of his bloody supper, possessed the greatest moderation and rectitude, and an infallible taste" (152). The analogies to Pound (and the under-the-surface contrasts with Lewis) would be consistent: like Hobson (and unlike Tarr/Lewis), Pound lacks a clear personality of his own; like Shakespeare, Pound turns this lack into an artistic strength (but here it gets complicated: Lewis sees himself as an Individual, but would certainly rather compare than contrast himself with Shakespeare). It is typical of Lewis to adapt metaphors, turns of phrase, and even arguments to different occasions in different books; he echoes himself everywhere.

21. Two comparisons should make the similarities clear—one with a hostile critic of Pound, John Gould Fletcher, and one with a friendly critic, T. S. Eliot. Fletcher, in a review of 1920, argues, just as Lewis does, that Pound lives better in the past than in the present:

> Pound, you feel sure, might quite easily have lived with Bertran de Born, or even Villon, held rhyming bouts and drinking bouts with them, and broken their pates if necessary
> ....
>
> .... Pound has never been at home in twentieth-century Europe. He can only get life out of books—from the life about him, he can obtain nothing. Something prompts him, therefore, to mock the world he sees, because he hates it; and when he mocks, the vividness utterly abandons him. The smile becomes a leer, the attitude a pose, the dependence on other men's work assumes the dimensions of intolerable pedantry. ("Some Contemporary Poets," *Chapbook: A Monthly Miscellany*, no. 2 [May 1920]: 23–25; in Eric Homberger, ed.,

Ezra Pound, The Critical Heritage [London & Boston: Routledge & Kegan Paul, 1972], 173.)

Lewis's remarks, because they are illustrated with acutely chosen quotation, are slightly more detailed than Fletcher's—as well as slightly more positive in their greater stress on Pound's genius in dealing with the past—but the points are the same. In a second article, written after the publication of *Time and Western Man*, Fletcher incorporates Lewis's argument into a restatement of the same view. But he goes further than Lewis, claiming that Pound fails even to recreate the past in his translation poems; he calls Pound a "failure as a poet" (Review in *Criterion* 8 [April 1929]: 513–24; in Homberger, 235).

Lewis's attack on Pound is also remarkably consistent with the most favorable criticism. The difference between his views and Eliot's is in their attitude, not in their observation. What Eliot praises, Lewis criticizes. In an essay of 1918, "A Note on Ezra Pound," Eliot writes that it is Pound's historical sense that makes his work important (*To-day*, September 1918; cited by Homberger, 13). Of course Lewis focuses on the same aspect of Pound's work, but he condemns it by juxtaposing it with his awkwardness in other areas. In 1928, in his introduction to an edition of Pound's *Selected Poems* (London: Faber & Faber), Eliot makes the same argument again—this time, undoubtedly, with Lewis's counterattack in mind:

> Now Pound is often most 'original' in the right sense, when he is most 'archaeological' in the ordinary sense. It is almost too platitudinous to say that one is not modern by writing about chimney-pots, or archaic by writing about oriflammes. .... If one can really penetrate the life of another age, one is penetrating the life of one's own.
>
> He is much more modern, in my opinion, when he deals with Italy and Provence, than when he deals with modern life. When he deals with antiquities, he extracts the essentially living; when he deals with contemporaries, he sometimes notes only the accidental. But this does not mean that he is antiquarian or parasitical on literature. . . . Time, in such connexions, does not matter. (xii, xiii)

Implicitly accusing Lewis of "platitude," Eliot defends his own—and Pound's—use of the past. The terms of Lewis's and Eliot's disagreement are the same, as is their observation of the evidence in the poetry. The differences are largely polemical; Lewis would have to include Eliot's fascination with tradition as one of the signs of the time-cult.

22. "Mr. Ezra Pound," *Observer* (18 January 1920), 5; in Homberger, 168–69.

23. Lewis, *Blasting and Bombardiering* (London: Eyre and Spottiswoode, 1937), 271, 279, 280.

24. In 1953 he wrote to Hugh Kenner, "In editing *Blast* I regarded the contributions of Ezra as compromisingly passéiste, and wished I could find two or three literary extremists." See *Letters*, 552. Lewis's judgment of this balance of power between himself and Pound may well be accurate (even if it is unfair), and is still a matter of some debate. In any case the function of the attack in *The Enemy* remains the same.

25. A curiously similar argument appears a few years later in *The Doom of Youth* (London: Chatto & Windus, 1932), where Lewis cites his previous membership in "a number of 'groups' " as evidence of his competence to explain the phenomenon of communist youth groups. Noting that these are rarely made up of real youths ("A desperate spasm of ambition seems to set in at about thirty or thirty-five... and a little clot of bald-headed, wall-eyed 'Youths' get together and form themselves into a 'Youth-movement' "; but remember that Lewis was himself in his early thirties at the time of Vorticism), and that they are supported by a public of "Revolutionary Simpletons," he argues that "the very idea of 'the Group' is an essentially *communist* notion" and that "Communism, or Marxism, whether right or wrong, is unquestionably the most fanatical anti-individualist creed that has ever seen the light." "Myself," he asserts, "I happen to be an individual... and as such I am not a 'group' person." Here is the really interesting comment: "I have shown, too, how the very notion of the 'group' must be suspect, unless it is integrated on behalf of mankind, and not against mankind—on behalf of exceptional talents, and not in order to enable a small herd of talented persons to masquerade as 'geniuses,' under the wing of some Zeitgeist." But how does one distinguish between these two purposes? Was Vorticism "on behalf of exceptional talents" or "to enable a small herd of talented persons to masquerade as 'geniuses' "? And this is in a book where Lewis says he is "writing *From the standpoint of genius*"! We will see more of this kind of hidden self-criticism below. See pp. 138–42 in *Doom*.

26. Noel Stock, in his biography of Pound, writes,

> Lewis's criticisms were sometimes unfair but often brilliant and perceptive... In Pound's case there was no sharp break in their friendship but a further cooling in a relationship which had been strained for several years... Pound's patience was remarkable in the face of some of Lewis's statements in *Time and Western Man*, especially as Lewis had placed his finger on a weak spot which had worried Pound himself only a few years before. Lewis maintained that there was still a gap between Pound's feeling for the past and his fire-eating utterances on contemporary affairs.

See Noel Stock, *The Life of Ezra Pound* (New York: Random House, 1970), 270. Many years later, in a letter to T. S. Eliot, Pound called his friend Lewis one of his few real *critics*:

> "Now as to ole Wyndham, whose address I have not, to thee & him these presents. While I yet cohere, he once sd/ a facefull, & apart from 3 dead & one aged arcivescovo who gave me 3 useful hints, ole W. is my only critic—you have eulogized and some minor have analysis'd or dissected—
>   all of which please tell the old ruffian if you can unearth him."

See *Pound/Lewis*, 225, and *Letters*, 394n.

27. To such passages, Lewis's comment about H. L. Mencken's readers seems apt: "Really these collections called *Americana* throw a more interesting light upon the people who are amused and delighted (apparently) by them, than they do upon the people whom ostensibly they are supposed to hold up to ridicule. As you read them you are inclined rather to glance aside and survey your *fellow-readers*, and to wonder what variety of snobbery, or superiority complex, has brought together this large 'reading-public'" (*Paleface* 130).

28. Here is his explanation from *The Doom of Youth*: "My approach will be by way of the more immediate and emotional issues. I open upon the popular plane—where the music-hall joke of 'a lady and her age' or of the 'never say *forty* to a spinster' order flourishes. There I shall at once make contact with a considerable public, I feel sure. Having captured its attention, and stimulated its emotional interest, I shall lead it on to consider, bit by bit, the more fundamental issues involved" (xiii).

29. The context is an attack on Michael Arlen's "youth" pieces in the *Daily Express*. See *The Doom of Youth*, 233.

30. Fredric Jameson argues that Lewis steadily loses control over

his antagonisms. He offers two explanations, one psychological and one ideological. One: "To the aggressive impulses Lewis found within himself we are of course indebted for the astonishing pathology of figures like Kreisler (in *Tarr*). But there is no point denying the oppressiveness with which such impulses gradually become dominant, are generalized and projected outwards as a global hostility, not merely to his own characters, but also to the quasi-totality of his contemporaries as well, not excluding his own readership" (4). This aggressivity, he argues, also sometimes leads Lewis into a style that is deliberately—provocatively, antagonistically—obscure: "On the stylistic level, such intransigence drives the more experimental texts to extremes which make some of them virtually unreadable for any sustained period of time" (4–5). And two: "Aggressivity in Lewis is therefore not some private characteristic of the novelist which diverts the narrative into the service of its own extrinsic gratifications: it is structurally inherent in the agon itself, in that utterly distinct from Hegelian or dialectical negativity, and expresses the rage and frustration of the fragmented subject at the chains that implacably bind it to its other and its mirror image" (61). Both explanations are suggestive, though I see Lewis's difficulties as intermittent rather than gradual and cumulative. *Paleface* causes more trouble for a reader than the later *Men Without Art*; *The Childermass* and *The Apes of God* are stylistically more demanding and difficult than the later *Revenge for Love*.

31. A number of other critics also address the topic of Lewis's relationship with his audience. In addition to Jameson, three seem to me of especial interest. Materer's *Vortex* compares "the strained relation to their audiences throughout their careers" of Pound, Eliot, and Lewis (see 219–24). Daniel Schenker's "A Modernist Dramaturgy: The Fictions of Wyndham Lewis and James Joyce" (Ph.D. diss., Johns Hopkins University, 1980) focuses on Lewis's and Joyce's life-long difficulties in defining—or shaping—adequate audiences for their work; Schenker reads Lewis's early story "Les Saltimbanques" as a paradigm for his attitude and his later problems (see 19–23, 52, 76–77). And Dasenbrock's *Literary Vorticism* discusses the "double bind" evident in *The Apes of God*, whose "premise . . . seems to be that it can have no readers." He suggests that "Lewis writes and publishes in the hope of being proven wrong" (see 178–80).

Meyers's biography also contains a good deal of suggestive information, both about Lewis's difficult personality and about his publishing history.

THE ENEMY PRINCIPLES

1. T. S. Eliot, "The Function of Criticism," in *Selected Essays* (London: Faber & Faber, 1951), 25, 29.
2. Lewis is speaking here of the artist (referring to Eliot's view of the artist as catalyst in "Tradition and the Individual Talent"), but the essay as a whole makes it clear that in this issue he sees the artist and critic as closely related. Moreover, of course, Lewis's criticism—like Eliot's—is explicitly that written by an artist.

Lewis also suggests an explanation for Eliot's position: "Mr Eliot...has allowed himself to be robbed of his personality, such as it is, and he is condemned to an unreal position. I see this difficulty of course, and understand that in the first instance he was moved by a desire to effect a *total* separation from what he regarded as unsatisfactory. And he has always been particularly alive to the sensation which has found a theological expression in the doctrine of original sin" (*MWA* 88).

3. In all of this, I am in disagreement with Wagner, who argues, "In nothing is [Lewis' criticism] more neoclassical than in its pretensions to impartiality" (18), and, "Only occasionally does this mask of detachment slip off" (19). Wagner's understanding of Lewis's personae would lead him to this view (since he sees Lewis as always speaking from behind one impersonal mask or another); more importantly, I think, it is an almost automatic corollary to his belief that Lewis is the quintessential English neoclassicist (18). Where Wagner stresses Lewis's detachment, I stress his involvement; but, as I will argue below, these two attitudes are at bottom combined in Lewis's own definition of personality.

Both Wagner and, more recently, Materer discuss the relationship between Lewis and Julien Benda, specifically with reference to the ideal of detachment. Materer's account in *Vortex* (184 ff.) clearly outlines the disjunction between Lewis's career-long claims to dispassionate impartiality and his actual writing, especially his political themes. Both discussions, though, neglect Lewis's equally frequent claims that he acts as a (biased) person.

4. "'Detachment' and the Fictionist," *English Review* (December 1934): 570–73; in *Enemy Salvoes*, 264–65. Here, too, Lewis explicitly contrasts his procedure against Eliot's.

5. To check my sense that Lewis's use of first-person changed, I counted the number of first- and second-person pronouns in the opening paragraphs of each chapter in *Time and Western Man* and an equal number of chapters (i.e., the first thirty-eight) in *The Art of Being Ruled* and *Paleface*. In the order of their publication (based on Jeffrey Meyers's biography), here is what I found:

—in *The Art of Being Ruled* (March 1926), exactly half of the chapter introductions (50 percent) include any of these pronouns. In this 50 percent, the average is just under 2.5 per paragraph. The average overall is 1.2.

—in *Time and Western Man* (February and September 1927), all but 6 chapter introductions (84 percent) include these pronouns. Of the 32 that do, each averages just over 4 per paragraph. The average overall is 3.4.

—in *Paleface* (September 1927 and 1929), all but 11 include these pronouns. Of the 27 that do (71 percent), each averages 4.3 per paragraph. The average overall here is just over 3.

6. In *Enemy Salvoes*, 264.

7. "Physics of the Not-Self" (1925; in *Enemy of the Stars* [London: Desmond Harmsworth, 1932]), 51–59. This essay and the concept of the not-self, not surprisingly, have produced considerable disagreement among critics. A few examples: the notes to the play and the essay in *Collected Poems and Plays*, ed. Alan Munton (Manchester: Carcanet Press, 1979) suggest that the not-self is a "self within the artist's self that is detached but active" and point to the similar "Buddha's *anatman* or no-self" (222–24); Schenker argues that the not-self is the equivalent of death and thus "rightfully despised in the end by sane individuals" (195–200); Dasenbrock says Lewis's essay "does little more than Westernize the Indian concept of the *atman*" (181); Wagner associates the not-self with "the 'anti-self' of Yeats and others" and with "Babbitt's 'distinguished person'" on whom "genuine social change" depends (40–41). Because the essay is so imprecisely written, I believe, any interpretation depends largely upon which of Lewis's other texts one uses to ground one's reading.

8. "Physics of the Not-Self," 53–54.

9. I have already quoted what follows: "For the whole virtue of accurate observation is that it is a *person* observing." Described in these terms, Lewis's position seems much closer to Eliot's. A remark of Eliot's on *The Lion and the Fox* shows that he recognized

this affinity underlying the radical difference in manner between Lewis and himself: "So far as I can see, Mr. Lewis is defending the detached observer. The detached observer, by the way, is likely to be anything but a dispassionate observer; he probably *suffers* more acutely than the various apostles of immediate action." See Eliot, *Twentieth-Century Verse*, November-December 1937 (Wyndham Lewis Double Number): III. In this review Eliot describes Lewis's criticism as detached; in *Men Without Art* Lewis argues that Eliot's criticism is far more personal than he admits. Both are right.

10. Of course, many politicians do abandon reason for emotion. The difference between detachment and impersonality, subjectivity and personality, is no easier to maintain in action than it is to describe in words. As we will see, Lewis sometimes fails in this respect to practice what he argues as principle.

11. Lewis is quite open about the political implications of this principle. He explains, for instance, "We live a conscious and magnificent life of the 'mind' at the expense of this community .... But in sympathy with the political movements to-day, the tendency of scientific (in which is included philosophic) thought is *to hand back* to this vast community of cells this stolen, aristocratic monopoly of personality which we call the 'mind' (*TWM* 318). And a few pages later he comments that " 'Mind' is an artificial, pumped-up affair—just as the 'male' is a highly unstable and *artificial* mode of life" (*TWM* 324). In *The Art of Being Ruled*, he explains that he is writing on behalf of the intellectual; but he argues there that "there is nothing 'aristocratic' about the intellect" since anyone from any social or economic class may have a good one (431).

12. Here is Jameson's description of Lewis's community:

> An absolute critique of culture finds itself grounded in the thoroughly relativized position of the painter, whose own vested interest lies in the desperate establishment of a more propitious ideological and cultural space in which to do his own work. Yet it cannot be said that he managed to keep faith with this uncomfortably honest and precarious stance. The anomalous situation of the painter finds itself slowly absolutized against its will and imperceptibly turns back into an affirmation of intellectual life in general ("intelligence") and artistic creation in particular. So an idiosyncratic and individualistic posture at length becomes indistinguishable from the most banal defenses of (Western) culture—or in more con-

crete terms, the privileges of Western intellectuals—against incipient barbarism. (126)

Jameson also calls Lewis's claim that he stands for the eye "his ultimate fall-back position" and an "untenable squaring of the circle." See pp. 17–18.

13. "The Credentials of the Painter " in *Wyndham Lewis on Art*, 218.

14. Ibid., 221.

15. Lewis describes these cognitive forms with the same metaphor he will use later in explaining his agreement with Berkeleyan idealism: they are "our drove of 'objects' " and "our static drove within" (*TWM* 414). But Lewis's use of "vision" is clearly not that of Berkeley's "Essay Towards a New Theory of Vision." Berkeley argues that vision must be distinguished from touch; Lewis deliberately uses the word to signify our entire perceptual apparatus, beginning with but not limited to the eye.

16. *Tarr* (1928), 276. There is no equivalent passage in the earlier version.

17. This phrase, Lewis says, is Berkeley's. See *TWM* 424, 425.

18. Samuel Alexander, *Space Time and Deity* (London: Macmillan & Co., 1920, rev. 1927), 1:82.

The closest Lewis comes to defining his terms for himself is when he says, "Kant's conception of Space is about identical with the popular or 'common-sense' view: it is a datum we cannot get behind, installed in the very centre of our perceptive faculty. It is independent of its content" (*TWM* 435). Though he never says so, I think he would agree to a similar description of Time.

19. Alexander, 1:222.

20. One of the many ironies of Lewis's career is that his own change of opinion about Hitler never freed him from being held responsible for his first ignorant enthusiasm.

21. *The Jews, Are They Human?*, 74.

22. Lewis, *Hitler* (London: Chatto & Windus, 1931), 128–29.

23. For another (and to some extent overlapping) discussion of this influence, see Materer's *Vortex*, 143 ff, 136 ff, and 151 ff, which examines the relationship of Yeats (briefly), Pound, Lewis, and Eliot to the larger tradition of Idealism, with particular attention to Eliot's work on Bradley. Materer quotes Eliot's early (1916) statement that "if one adheres 'to a strictly common-sense view (which may be defined, I presume, as that which insists on the reality of the more primary objects) the theories of speculative physics seem perhaps as chimerical and uncalled-for as those of

metaphysics' " (148, from Eliot, *Knowledge and Experience in the Philosophy of F. H. Bradley* [London: Faber & Faber, 1964], 162). (Materer also cites Eliot's objections to Russell, which preceded and perhaps influenced Lewis's very similar objections.) According to Materer, "Lewis's admiration for Berkeley's 'realism' anticipates later views of Berkeley's philosophy" (153). Schenker also discusses the Lewis-Berkeley connection (see his pp. 153 ff), and notes that Lewis's opposition to Bergson (see my next section) parallels Berkeley's opposition to Locke.

24. George Berkeley, "A Treatise Concerning the Principles of Human Knowledge," in *Theory of Vision and Other Writings by Bishop Berkeley*, ed. Ernest Rhys (London: J. M. Dent & Sons, Ltd.; New York: E. P. Dutton & Co., 1910, rpt. 1914), VI.

25. Berkeley, XXXIV, XL, XXX, VI.

26. Alexander, 1:44.

27. *Letters*, 488–89, written in 1949.

28. Hulme published several pieces on Bergson in the *New Age* in 1911–12 and a translation of *An Introduction to Metaphysics* in 1912. The contradiction between Hulme's enthusiasm for Bergson's romantic theories and his otherwise vehement dislike of romanticism and promotion of classicism is an odd permutation of—and perhaps influence on—Lewis's paradoxical attitudes. Michael H. Levenson's *A Genealogy of Modernism: A Study of English Literary Doctrine 1908-1922* (Cambridge, London, New York: Cambridge University Press, 1984) makes considerable sense of this apparent contradiction by examining in detail the chronology of Hulme's changing attitudes toward Bergson (39–42, 80–88). See also Alun R. Jones, *The Life and Opinions of T. E. Hulme* (Boston: Beacon Press, 1960), 57–67; and Wagner, 194–96.

29. On the theory of satire see Wagner, 215–16, 222–25.

Thomas Kush's *Wyndham Lewis's Pictorial Integer* (Ann Arbor, Michigan: UMI Research Press, 1981), so far as I know, contains the only extended discussion of Bergson's philosophic influence on Lewis. Kush, whose main interest is in the connections between Lewis's fiction and his paintings and drawings, argues, "Lewis learned from Bergson's *Creative Evolution* that the form of the body determines the condition of an organism's psyche. He used this principle as a rhetorical structure—Lewis's art is preoccupied with 'the externals,' but it still suggests the psychological impulses beneath the encrusted surface" (5). Kush's argument is similar to mine with respect to the fact of Bergson's influence, but his context and perspective are different (see 5–6 and 24–33). A few other critics have very briefly noted Lewis's relationship with Bergson: see Wagner, 186; E. W. F. Tomlin, "The Philosophical Influences" (in *Wyndham Lewis: A Revaluation*, ed. Jeffrey Meyers [Montreal: McGill-Queen's University Press, 1980]), 29–30, 34–35; Meyers, *The Enemy*, 137; and Jameson, 134–35.

30. I wish to thank *Twentieth Century Literature* for permission to use this section, which appeared in much the same form in vol. 29, no. 3 (Fall 1983).

31. See Henri Bergson, *Time and Free Will: An Essay on the Immediate Data of Consciousness*, trans. F. L. Pogson (London: George Allen & Unwin, 1910), 132, 14. Lewis must have made his own translations; he does not use the English title, and his wording is slightly different from this, the only published translation available to him.

32. Bergson distinguishes two kinds of self, explaining that "our perceptions, sensations, emotions and ideas occur under two aspects: the one clear and precise, but impersonal; the other confused, ever changing, and inexpressible because language cannot get hold of it without arresting its mobility or fit it into its common-place forms without making it into public property" (see *Time and Free Will*, 129).

33. Bergson, *Creative Evolution*, trans. Arthur Mitchell (New York: Henry Holt and Co., 1911), 343–44. Further references are cited below as *CE*.

34. *CE*, 306, 163, 306, 314, 315, 332, 308.

35. Alexander, 1:209–10.

36. In *Time and Free Will*, immediately following the passage Lewis quotes about art putting the personality to sleep, Bergson writes, "The plastic arts obtain an effect of the same kind by the fixity which they suddenly impose upon life, and which a physical contagion carries over to the attention of the spectator. While the works of ancient sculpture express faint emotions which play upon them like a passing breath, the pale immobility of the stone causes the feeling expressed or the movement just begun to appear as if they were fixed for ever, absorbing our thought and our will in their own eternity" (15). Here again Bergson and Lewis appear to agree on a matter of aesthetics.

37. Also see Wagner, 133, on the connections among Bergson, Lewis, the cinema, and futurism. Lewis's hostility to the Futurists' interest in movement was not new. In *Blasting and Bombardiering*, he tells of having argued with Marinetti in 1914 by quoting Baudelaire: "*Je hais le mouvement qui déplace les lignes!*"

Notes

(34–35). And Dasenbrock notes that the Futurists claimed Bergson's ideas as the philosophical basis for their aesthetic (49).

38. The bracketed phrase comes from the preceding paragraph in Lewis's discussion.

39. *CE*, 326, 267, 223, 223. Bergson usually, though not always, uses "mind" for the combined intellect and intuition. Mind, for him, "overflows" the intellect, as Lewis notes (436).

40. *CE*, 46, 175, 189 (Bergson italicizes this passage).

41. *CE*, 306, 162.

42. *CE*, 160–61 (Bergson's emphasis).

43. See, for instance, *Paleface*, where Lewis attacks D. H. Lawrence's primitivism by associating it with Bergson's belief that intuition is superior to intellect (cf. 159–60, 176–77, 241). Here Lewis does mention CE by name, although only in passing: "For if Behavior comes out of Evolution, does not also *Creative Evolution* and Bergson come out of Evolution?" (158).

44. *CE*, 314.

45. *CE*, 29, 44, 11.

46. Lewis cites Russell as an authoritative critic of Bergson several times. Russell's earlier attack on Bergson is very similar to Lewis's in its dislike of Bergson's anti-intellectualism and its insistence that his theories were mainly aimed at practical action: as Russell says, "There is no room in this philosophy for the moment of contemplative insight when, rising above the animal life, we become conscious of the greater ends that redeem man from the life of the brutes." Unlike Lewis, though, Russell also attacks Bergson's distinctions between space and time, subject and object, intellect and instinct, and mind and matter. See *A History of Western Philosophy* (New York: Simon and Schuster, 1945), 791–810; Russell notes here that this chapter was first published in *The Monist* in 1912.

47. *CE*, 270–71.

48. *CE*, 177. T. E. Hulme repeats this passage almost verbatim (without quotation marks) in his essay "Bergson's Theory of Art," included in *Speculations: Essays on Humanism and the Philosophy of Art* (London: Kegan Paul, Trench, Trubner & Co., 1924, 1936), 144. Lewis would probably have seen this essay.

49. *CE*, 201. When he quotes this passage, Lewis omits the phrase about the scattered self, since he would argue that the true self coheres even in the dream-state.

50. *In Time and Free Will* Bergson comes curiously close to saying the same thing as Lewis does in this passage, making the same transition from psychological and philosophical stability to social

stability: "And, in truth, for the sake of language, the self has everything to gain by not bringing back confusion where order reigns, and in not upsetting this ingenious arrangement of almost impersonal states by which it has ceased to form 'a kingdom within a kingdom.' An inner life with well distinguished moments and with clearly characterized states will answer better the requirements of social life" (139).

51. In *The Mysterious Mr. Bull*, similarly, Lewis explains, "It is on the whole not pleasant to get outside oneself and to look at oneself, for that I can vouch. One steps out of an illusion. But it is great fun, all the same. It is always fun to burst out of an illusion" (71).

52. Frye, "Neoclassical Agony," 596.

53. Jameson, 120, 56–57, 110, 111, 56.

54. For Levenson's discussion, see especially pp. 17, 26–31, 85–89, 114. For Arnold's, see for instance *Culture and Anarchy*, in R. H. Super, ed., *The Complete Prose Works of Matthew Arnold* (Ann Arbor: University of Michigan Press, 1965), 5:134–36, 144–47.

55. Holloway, "The Massacre and the Innocents," in *The Charted Mirror*.

56. *The Mysterious Mr. Bull*, 229.

THE ENEMY CRITICISM

1. For Joyce's comments, see Richard Ellmann, *James Joyce* (New York: Oxford University Press, 1959), 608. For Kenner's see *Joyce's Voices* (Berkeley: University of California Press, 1978), 69, 23; and *Dublin's Joyce* (Bloomington: Indiana University Press, 1956), 362. For Wagner's see 176, 177; his chapter "Master Joys and Windy Nous" (168–88) discusses Lewis's personal and critical relationship with Joyce at length. For other criticism of this relationship, see also the long discussion in Materer's *Vortex*, 163–84; Pritchard's *Wyndham Lewis*, 92–94; and S. L. Goldberg, *The Classical Temper: A Study of James Joyce's "Ulysses"* (London: Chatto & Windus, 1961), 101–7.

2. In this statement and others like it, Lewis seems to say that no artist who deals with the past can be creative or original. He advances the same argument against Pound. But clearly this is inadequate: as Eliot pointed out in his defense of Pound, "If one can really penetrate the life of another age, one is penetrating the life

of one's own." Nor is Lewis ever able to state his idea of true creativity in positive terms: "To create new beauty, and to supply a new material, is the obvious affair of art of any kind to-day. But that is a statement that by itself would convey very little. Without stopping to unfold that now, I will summarize what I understand by its opposite. Its opposite is that that thrives upon the *time-philosophy* that it has invented for itself, or which has been imposed upon it or provided for it" (*TWM* 110). By begging the question in this way, Lewis reveals the weakness of this criticism.

3. Lewis calls his version of timelessness a pure or classical present. Erich Auerbach's description in *Mimesis* of the Homeric perspective seems to be close to Lewis's ideal.

4. These comparisons, I think, are both accurate and fair. The fairness of the conclusions Lewis draws from them is more questionable. Certainly we could argue that Joyce knew exactly what he was borrowing and why—that his susceptibility was deliberate and highly organized. (See the discussion of Kenner below.) Similarly vulnerable is the corollary conclusion that these influences demonstrate a failure of originality, that "the virtuosity [could] be deduced from the fact of the resourceful presence of a highly critical intellect, but without much inventiveness, nor the gift of firsthand observation—thriving vicariously, in its critical exercises, upon the masters of the Past" (*TWM* 113). On the other hand, the less negative conclusion that Joyce's stylistic accomplishments are not as new as they might appear to be is easier to endorse. Even if we want to argue that his *use* of all these styles is what matters most—and what is most original about his work—we have to agree that he did not invent them all.

5. In *Rude Assignment* Lewis recalls a conversation between himself and Joyce about the elaborate facade of the cathedral at Rouen:

> I had said I did not like it, rather as Indian or Indonesian sacred buildings are a fussy multiplication of accents, demonstrating a belief in the virtue of *quantity*, I said. All such quantitative expression I have at all times found boring, I pointed out. I continued to talk against Gothic altogether, and its "scholasticism in stone": the dissolving of the solid shell—the spatial intemperance, the nervous multiplication of detail. Joyce listened and then remarked that he, on the contrary, liked this multiplication of detail, adding that he himself, as a matter of fact, in words, did something of that sort. (56)

6. *Satire and Fiction* (London: Arthur Press, 1931), 47. Lewis also offers a list of occasions on which he thinks stream-of-consciousness can be appropriate: "In dealing with (1) the extremely aged (2) young children, (3) half-wits, and (4) animals, the *internal* method can be extremely effective. In my opinion it should be entirely confined to those classes of characters. For certain comic purposes it likewise has its uses (cf. *The Childermass*) especially when used in conjunction with a full-blooded Stein-stutter."

It is important to remember how little of the structure of *Ulysses* had been noticed when Lewis was writing. William Chace even suggests that one of the *results* of Lewis's attack was Stuart Gilbert's exegesis. "Gilbert's book," Chace writes, "composed with Joyce's own help and in reaction to Lewis's attack...offers a picture of Joyce as one wholly consumed in organization and pattern...Not flux, but mastery and control." See the "Introduction" in *Joyce: A Collection of Critical Essays*, "Twentieth Century Views" (Englewood Cliffs, N. J: Prentice-Hall, 1974), 2.

7. Robert Deming, ed., *James Joyce: The Critical Heritage* (New York: Barnes & Noble, 1970), 1:24.

8. *Critical Heritage*, 2. From Herbert Marshall McLuhan, "A Survey of Joyce Criticism," *Renascence* 4 (1951): 13.

9. Rebecca West, *The Strange Necessity* (Garden City, New York: Doubleday, Doran & Company, 1928), 3, 9, 39. Like Lewis's "Analysis," West's discussion of Joyce is only part of a longer essay that ranges fairly widely, from Joyce to buying a dress to visiting museums to Pavlov's experiments.

10. *Selected Prose of T. S. Eliot*, ed. Frank Kermode (New York: Harcourt Brace Jovanovich; Farrar, Straus & Giroux, 1975), 175. Incidentally, in this essay Eliot also compares *Portrait* with *Tarr* as examples of the end of the traditional novel form.

11. *Pound/Joyce: The Letters of Ezra Pound to James Joyce, with Pound's Essays on Joyce*, ed. Forrest Read (New York: New Directions, 1967), 194. Pound does not italicize his titles in this passage. This book will be cited below as *Pound/Joyce*.

12. Isaiah Berlin describes Tolstoy's world in terms that help clarify Lewis's contrast between Joyce and the Russians:

> The celebrated life-likeness of every object and every person in his world derives from this astonishing capacity of presenting every ingredient of it in its fullest individual essence, in all its many dimensions as it were; never as a mere datum, however vivid within some stream of consciousness, with blurred

edges, an outline, a shadow, an impressionistic representation: nor yet calling for, and dependent on, some process of reasoning in the mind of the reader; but always as a solid object, seen simultaneously from near and far, in natural, unaltering daylight from all possible angles of vision, set in an absolutely specific context in time and space—an event fully present to the senses or the imagination in all its facets, with every nuance sharply and firmly articulated.

See *The Hedgehog and the Fox: An Essay on Tolstoy's View of History* (New York: Simon and Schuster, 1953), 40.
13. Seon Givens, ed., *James Joyce: Two Decades of Criticism* (New York: Vanguard Press, 1963), xv.
14. Harry Levin, *James Joyce: A Critical Introduction* (Norfolk, Conn.: New Directions, 1941), 92, 134, 88, 89, 219, 130, 89, 229.
15. Kenner also acknowledges the influence of Pound's early criticism of Joyce. Kenner's book on Lewis followed his dissertation on Joyce but preceded *Dublin's Joyce*. See vii, 19, 11, 112.
16. *Critical Heritage*, 12.
17. *Joyce's Voices*, 16–17, 69.
18. *Dublin's Joyce*, 166–68, 364. Kenner summarizes Lewis's criticism as follows:

> Lewis's critique had the disturbing merit of being neither impressionistic nor irrelevant. He took a few quick sights at the object, extracted from their living tissue with a surgical eye four or five salient facts which no one else had been able to see—a mole, a cheekbone, an ear, set them down on his canvas in abridged relationship, and turning away from the model (since he knew more than he could see) filled in the composition brilliantly with the sallow planes of a plausible parchment mask: a Portrait of the Artist as susceptible Drudge. (362–63)

19. In the introduction to their collection of recent essays, *Post-Structuralist Joyce: Essays from the French* (Cambridge: Cambridge University Press, 1984), Derek Attridge and Daniel Ferrer remark, "From the perspective of the present, there is more of value in some of the early *attacks* on Joyce which register the force of his challenge and feel no need to mitigate or disguise it. Wyndham Lewis's hostile chapter...makes a number of points about Joyce's 'sardonic catafalque of the victorian world' (109) which lead directly to current preoccupations (their negative charge

switched to positive), including his comments on the use of cliché (112–16), and the observation that 'what stimulates [Joyce] is *ways of doing things...* ' " (5)

20. Frederick Hoffmann, "Infroyce," in Givens, 398, 413, 405, 403–5; from *Freudianism and the Literary Mind* (Baton Rouge, La.: Louisiana State University Press, 1945). Hoffmann also explains that in *Ulysses*, "The demands of such intensity of narration...are so great that space and time are subjected to the pressure of the psychic world. Space values are often completely suspended, and simultaneity takes the place of conjunction. Time subserves interest, expands and contracts in accordance with the demands of the moment—until it is completely suspended in the hallucination of the nighttown scene" (415–16).

21. Edmund Wilson, *Axel's Castle: A Study in the Imaginative Literature of 1870–1930* (New York: Charles Scribner's Sons, 1931), 220, 221–22.

22. Wilson, 222, 216, 217.

23. Wilson, 210.

24. Chace, 5.

25. See Joseph Frank, *The Widening Gyre: Crisis and Mastery in Modern Literature* (New Brunswick, N.J.: Rutgers University Press, 1963), and *Critical Inquiry* 4, no. 2 (Winter 1977): 231–52.

26. Moreover, Lewis is quite clear that he does not mean to suggest that the novel should be spatial and static in the way sculpture or painting can be. When he contrasts the ideal stasis of the plastic arts with the fluidity of music, he explains, "If a definition were attempted of the position of literature among the arts, it would turn out to be in some sense a kind of half-way house. A piece of prose or poetry is not music; it does not, on the other hand, convey images with the definiteness of the plastic or graphic arts...it is not so static as some, but more static than others" (*TWM* 188). I think this understanding of the different arts may explain in part why Lewis identifies himself as a plastic artist, not a writer, in *Time and Western Man*, despite the fact that he was doing relatively little work in painting or drawing during this period of his life (so little, in fact, that he declined to write an art review for Eliot's *Criterion* because he felt so out of touch). As a visual artist, he stands for one extreme, where as a writer, he would stand half-way.

27. Anthony Burgess, *ReJoyce* (New York: W. W. Norton & Co., 1965), 178; Levin, 198; Frank Kermode, *Critical Inquiry* 4, no. 3 (Spring 1978): 587. See also Kermode, *The Sense of an Ending:*

Studies in the Theory of Fiction (New York: Oxford University Press, 1967), 178.
28. Sisson, *Enemy Salvoes*, 12.
29. Alexander Moszkowski, *Einstein, The Searcher*, trans. Henry L. Brose (New York: Dutton, 1921), 87, 89.
30. Another of Einstein's biographers, Ronald W. Clark, calls Moszkowski "a Berlin litterateur and critic who moved on the fringes of the Einstein circle"; he also calls Moszkowski's book "a vulgarization of science more unusual then than it would be today" (*Einstein: The Life and Times* [New York: Avon, 1971], 306).
31. Comprehensive discussions of the first tradition—the British—can be found in Lesley Johnson's *The Culture Critics* and Raymond Williams' *Culture and Society*. Neither of these books, however, mentions Lewis. Michael Levenson's *A Genealogy of Modernism* also deals with this tradition and implicitly includes Lewis. Jameson (see p. 128) and Wagner have both discussed Lewis's similarities with the second group of writers.

Lewis had clearly read most, if not all, of the figures I mention. He frequently acknowledges his agreement with Arnold (largely through quotation) and Benda; he mentions Nietzsche frequently, sometimes in agreement, sometimes not; and he devotes considerable direct attention to Spengler.

32. Raymond Williams, talking about Carlyle, notes "the kind of contempt for the 'masses'—Swarmery, 'Sons of the Devil, in overwhelming majority', 'blockheadism, gullibility, bribeability, amenability to beer and balderdash'—which has remained a constant element in English thought." See *Culture and Society*, 83.
33. Jameson, 129; Williams, 263.
34. *The Diabolical Principle and the Dithyrambic Spectator*, 136.
35. Oswald Spengler, *The Decline of the West*, vol. 1, trans. Charles Francis Atkinson (New York: Alfred A. Knopf, 1926), 42, 47, 378.
36. *The Doom of Youth*, 135.
37. Julien Benda, *The Treason of the Intellectuals (La Trahison des Clercs)*, trans. Richard Aldington (William Morrow & Co., 1928; New York: Norton, 1969), 43. Also see p. 191. In *Time and Western Man*, which preceded this book, Lewis quotes Benda's earlier *Belphégor*; then, in *The Diabolical Principle and the Dithyrambic Spectator*, he writes: "The problem of art, or of the intellect, and of its relation to politics, has, since I, as an artist, first propounded it in my *Revolutionary Simpleton* and in *Time and Western Man*, become popular. M. Julien Benda in France

has taken it up. M. Benda, whom I quoted in my book, is a man of resource. In his latest work (*La Trahison des Clercs*) he makes an effective use of my writings (by some oversight he has forgotten to mention my name, but that is just as well, for he arrives at conclusions very different from mine or appears to misunderstand what he has read: it is for that reason no doubt that he abstains from any mention of his sources)" (121).

38. *The Diabolical Principle and the Dithyrambic Spectator*, 128.

39. Spengler, 41.

40. Williams, 136. Williams quotes the Ruskin passage from an appendix to *Modern Painters* (Library edition), 2:38–39.

41. In the late *The Demon of Progress in the Arts* (Chicago: Henry Regnery Company, 1955), Lewis offers several remarks that point to some of the difficulties in his own earlier theory (here we hear the Domestic Adversary over the span of his career). From the perspective of his decades of writing politically and socially engaged books, both fiction and nonfiction, he criticizes the separation of the arts from social responsibility: "The absurd things which are happening in the visual arts at present are what must happen when an art becomes almost totally disconnected from society, when it no longer has any direct function in life, and can only exist as the plaything of the intellect" (46). When he is objecting to Herbert Read's art criticism, he writes, "The ideal autonomy imagined for the painter, the tendency to speak as though *what is seen* enjoys a privileged position on the earth, is characteristic of a time in which theories are substituted for anything real and solid. What, after all, is the ghastly autonomous privilege, the splendid isolation, about which I have been speaking, except a private latitude to do whatever one likes, provided no one else suffers any inconvenience? . . . Men who trumpet such theories live in the van of 'culture'; they belong to the camouflaged section of the public services, where with fanfares and resounding words, the absence of culture is gloriously concealed" (62). And he comments critically that Malraux is "inclined to endow the visual arts with mystical revolutionary attributes" (75). All these remarks are clearly critical of the culture model I examine here.

42. The ideal role of the philosopher suggests similar contradictions. Compare Hayden White's summary of Nietzsche's argument in *The Genealogy of Morals*:

> The philosophical ideal of his own time, Nietzsche said, imagines a 'pure, will-less, painless, timeless knower' with the objective of attaining a 'pure reason, absolute knowledge, ab-

solute intelligence.' But all these concepts, Nietzsche held, 'presuppose an eye such as no living being can imagine, an eye required to have no direction, to abrogate its active and interpretative powers—precisely those powers that alone make of seeing, seeing *something*.' This ideal obscures the fact that 'all seeing is essentially perspective, and so is all knowing. The more emotions we allow to speak in a given matter, the more different spectacles we can put on in order to view a given spectacle, the more complete will be our conception of it, the greater our objectivity.'

In different places Lewis offers both sides of this conceptual opposition. See White, *Metahistory: The Historical Imagination in Nineteenth-Century Europe* (Baltimore: Johns Hopkins University Press, 1973), 354.

43. *The Diabolical Principle and the Dithyrambic Spectator*, 37.

44. Williams, 290–91. Lesley Johnson, in a discussion of various sociologists' studies of the role of intellectuals, notes that " 'the traditional position of intellectuals, of being rejected by their society, has resulted in a traditional response of rejecting their society' .... the structures of dissent are the necessary context for the intellectual.... the outsider status of the modern intellectual is essential to his universalizing, critical approach." See *The Culture Critics*, 7.

45. *Tarr*, 215–16 (1928); 245 (1918); the two versions are almost identical. Tarr is answering Anastasya's comment that " 'The most effectual men have always been those whose notions were diametrically opposed to those of their time.' "

Conclusion

1. Kenner, *Wyndham Lewis*, 142. Pritchard, *Wyndham Lewis*, 19; Jameson, 3; Frye, "Neoclassical Agony," 598.

2. *Beyond Good and Evil*, 89.

3. L. Brunschvicg, *Le Progrès de la Conscience dans la philosophie occidentale*, quoted by Benda, 229–30.

INDEX

Alexander, Samuel, 76, 78, 103, 105
Anderson, Sherwood, 8, 38–39, 63
Arnold, Matthew, 43, 124, 174, 181, 221n.31
Attridge, Derek, 219–20n.19
Audience, WL's relations with, 34–46, 164, 207n.27, 208n.31

Barthes, Roland, xi
Benda, Julien, 174, 181, 182, 197, 209n.3, 221n.31, 221–22n.37
Bergson, Henri, 37, 38, 94–116, 124, 167, 168, 175, 180, 192, 312nn.23,28,29
Berkeley, Bishop George, 87–93, 122, 186, 187, 212n.15, 213n.23
Berlin, Isaiah, 218–19n.12
Bloom, Harold, xiv, 115, 147
Bridson, D. G., 199n.6
Burgess, Anthony, 162

Chance, William, 161, 163, 164, 218n.6
Culture Model, WL's, 166, 174–89, 222n.41; context for, 174, 176, 202n.11

Dasenbrock, Reed Way, 201n.10, 208n.31, 210n.7, 215n.37
Deming, Robert, 148, 156
Domestic Adversary. *See* Oppositions, Domestic Adversary
Duhem, Pierre, 170–72

225

Einstein, Albert, 165–74
Eliot, T. S., xi, 13, 27, 52–53, 55, 59, 82, 150, 174, 181, 204–5n.21, 209n.2, 210–11n.9, 212–13n.23
Elliott, Robert C.,, 201n.10
Enemy Criticism, xi–xvi, 52, 67, 128, 133–34, 144, 147, 148, 157–58, 164, 176, 184, 191, 194, 196–97; personality xi–xiii, 5–7, 13–14, 34, 45, 53–55, 59–61, 64, 75, 191, 192, 195, 198–99n.5; stance xiii–xiv, 15–23, 24, 33, 44, 45, 79, 116, 134, 164, 176, 187, 188–89, 202–3n.17; strategies xiv, 22, 24, 30, 37–38, 77, 115, 146, 151, 169–70, 190, 204n.20; voice 5–14, 24, 39, 43, 45, 97, 178. *See also* Audience; Lewis, Wyndham, style of writing

Ferrer, Daniel, 219–20n.19
Fletcher, John Gould, 204–5n.21
Fox, C. J., 199n.6
Frank, Joseph, 161, 162
Frye, Northrop, 120, 192, 200n.7

Gilbert, Stuart, 161, 218n.6
Givens, Seon, 147, 149, 154
Goldberg, S. L., 161, 216n.1

Hoffmann, Frederick, 158–59, 220n.20
Holloway, John, 126, 200n.7
Hulme, T. E., 98, 123–24, 128, 213n.28, 215n.48

Jameson, Fredric, xv, 122–23, 175, 192, 199n.6, 200n.7, 207–8n.30, 211–12n.12, 214n.29, 221n.31
Johnson, Lesley, 202n.11, 221n.31, 223n.44
Joyce, James, 7, 24, 116, 133–63, 178, 192, 194, 217nn.4,5, 218n.6, 219nn.18,19

Kenner, Hugh, 133, 143, 147, 155–58, 164, 192, 198n.5, 219nn.15,18

Index

Kermode, Frank, 162
Kush, Thomas, 199n.6, 213–14n.29

Lawrence, D. H., 63, 66, 67, 125–26, 136
Leavis, F. R., 164, 174, 181
Levenson, Michael, 123–24, 213n.28, 221n.31
Levin, Harry, 154–55, 161–62
Lewis, Wyndham. *See also* Audience; Culture Model; Enemy; Oppositions; Principles, Critical and Philosophical; Time-cult
—drawings: "Horseman," 3–4, 5, 15, 58, 64, 74, 79, 117, 191, 192, 200n.1; "Timon of Athens," 11
—exemplary figure, as, xv, 91, 126–29, 171, 192–97
—on art, 45, 65–70, 76, 90–91, 96, 99, 101, 105, 106, 14, 135–36, 177–78, 182–87, 194, 209n.2, 216–17n.2, 220n.26
—on science, 165–72, 179, 180, 182, 184, 186
—style of writing, 7–13, 55–58, 60, 62, 71, 76–77, 80, 106, 192, 210n.5
—writings: *The Apes of God*, 7, 67; *The Art of Being Ruled*, 18, 35, 40, 45–56, 54, 56, 63, 65, 81, 83, 84, 85, 92, 95, 128, 174, 176, 179, 181, 184, 185, 186; *Blast*, xiii–xiv, 11, 29, 31, 32, 206n.24; *Blasting and Bombardiering*, 28; *The Childermass*, 7–8; "The Credentials of the Painter," 67, 68; *The Demon of Progress in the Arts*, 222n.41; "Detachment and the Fictionist," 55, 59; *The Diabolical Principle and the Dithyrambic Spectator*, xi, xii; *The Doom of Youth*, 9, 41, 43, 181, 206n.25; *The Enemy:* Editorial, Preface, Epigraph, xii, 15, 17, 20–23, 32, 33, 54, 56; title, 6, 52 (for cover, *see* Lewis, Wyndham, drawings); "Enemy of the Stars," 31, 140; *Hitler*, 44, 84–85; *The Jews, Are They Human?*, 41, 83, 203n.17; *Left Wings Over Europe*, 202n.17; *The Lion and the Fox*, 11, 40, 42, 56, 126–27, 194, 201n.10; *Man of the World*, xii, 124, 167, 176,

198n.4; *Men Without Art,* 12–13, 22, 41–42, 43, 45, 52, 53, 55, 56, 57, 59, 66, 67, 68, 72, 77, 79, 82, 90, 119, 194; *The Mysterious Mr. Bull,* xiv; *One-Way Song,* 20–21, 202n.16; *Paleface,* 8, 9, 20, 22, 38–39, 40, 42, 56, 63, 68, 83–84, 87, 90, 121, 125, 178, 181, 193, 196; "Physics of the Not-Self," 60–61, 210n.7; *Rude Assignment,* 5, 23, 54, 62, 194; *Satire and Fiction,* 141; *Self-Condemned,* 19; *Tarr,* 7, 18–19, 70, 151, 189, 201n.5, 204n.20, 223n.45; *Time and Western Man,* xii, 15, 24, 65, 75, 87, 95, 114, 133–34, 165, 176 (*see also* other relevant headings); "What It Feels Like to Be an Enemy," 6–7.

McAlmon, Robert, 9–10, 201n.9
McLuhan, Marshall, 149
Marinetti, 11, 29, 31, 106, 214–15n.37
Materer, Timothy, 199nn.5,6, 201n.10, 208n.31, 209n.3, 212–13n.23, 216n.1
Meyers, Jeffrey, 199n.6, 208n.31, 214n.29
Michel, Walter, 199n.6
Moszkowski, Alexander, 165–72
Munton, Alan, 210n.7

Nietzsche, Friedrich, 17, 20, 46, 92, 116, 174, 175, 189, 196–97, 221n.31, 222–23n.42

Oppositions, xiii–xv, 125–28, 137, 173, 186–87, 190, 192, 200n.7; critical stance, *see* Enemy, stance; Domestic Adversary, xv, 117–129, 139, 169, 185, 188, 193–96, 206n.25, 222n.41; paradox, xiv, 22–23, 60, 68, 73, 87–89, 117, 119, 121, 124, 126, 137, 140, 186, 189, 193; polar pairs, xiii–xiv, 75, 89, 103, 114, 117, 120, 121, 127–28, 143, 192; relations with others hidden by, xiv, 24–33, 94–116, 117

Pound, Ezra, xi, 6, 9, 24–33, 64, 116, 136, 150–53, 178, 191, 204–5nn.20,21, 206n.24, 207n.26

Index

Principles, Critical and Philosophical, xiii, 73–74, 176, 188, 192; common sense, 65, 69–74, 76, 101, 191; mind, 61–64, 73–74, 77–78, 85, 88–90, 105, 108–11, 114, 118–20, 143, 144–46, 171, 173, 174, 183, 187, 188, 191; personality, 52–64, 73–74, 81–82, 85, 100–1, 105, 118–20, 122, 171, 185, 187, 188, 191, 194, 209n.3; space, 75–86, 98, 103, 107, 108–10, 120, 212n.18; stability, 80–83, 85, 90, 103, 107, 109–10, 188, 196; vision, 65–70, 73–74, 76–78, 85, 88–90, 95, 141, 212n.15; "most essential ME," 65, 74, 79, 91, 117, 119, 125
Pritchard, William H., 192, 199n.6, 216n.1

Read, Forrest, 153
Richards, I. A., 13, 200n.7
Ruskin, John, 174, 185
Russell, Bertrand, 80, 112, 213n.23, 215n.46

Schenker, Daniel, 208n.31, 210n.7, 213n.23
Sisson, C. H., 164, 199n.6
Sorel, Georges, 128
Space. *See* Principles, space
Spengler, Oswald, 35–36, 116, 165, 169, 180, 183, 193, 221n.31
Stein, Gertrude, 7–8, 11–13, 24, 136, 192, 201n.7
Stock, Noel, 207n.26

Time-cult, 24–25, 58, 63, 67–68, 71, 75–83, 87, 93, 154–55, 158–60, 163, 165–66, 168–69, 172, 174, 176, 179–80, 191, 193–94, 196. *See also* Bergson, Henri; Joyce, James
Time. *See* Time-cult
Tomlin, E. W. F., 214n.29

Vorticism, 11, 29, 31, 32, 206n.25

Wagner, Geoffrey, 133, 138, 147, 199nn.5,6, 201n.7, 209n.3, 210n.7, 213–14n.29, 214n.37, 216n.1, 221n.31

Walsh, Ernest, 9–10, 201n.9
West, Rebecca, 149, 218n.9
Whistler, James McNeill, 6, 8, 17, 200n.3
White, Hayden, 222–23n.42
Whitehead, Alfred North, 107, 165, 182
Williams, Raymond, 174, 175, 185, 189, 202n.11, 221–22nn.31,32
Wilson, Edmund, 159–61
World War I, 83–85, 96, 112

Zeitgeist, 22, 165, 166, 181, 185, 188, 206n25. *See also* Culture Model

A Note about the Author

SueEllen Campbell is associate professor of English at Bowling Green State University. Her articles on Wyndham Lewis and on modern literature have been published in the *Journal of Modern Literature, Twentieth Century Literature,* and *Modern Fiction Studies.* She is now working on a study of American non-fiction wilderness narratives.